THE UNDECIDED COLLEGE STUDENT

Third Edition

THE UNDECIDED COLLEGE STUDENT

An Academic and Career Advising Challenge

By

VIRGINIA N. GORDON, PH.D.

Assistant Dean Emeritus
Associate Professor
Ohio State University
Columbus, Ohio

CHARLES C THOMAS • PUBLISHER, LTD.
Springfield • Illinois • U.S.A.

Published and Distributed Throughout the World by

CHARLES C THOMAS • PUBLISHER, LTD.
2600 South First Street
Springfield, Illinois 62704

ISBN 978-0-398-07706-8 (hard)
ISBN 978-0-398-07707-5 (paper)

Library of Congress Catalog Card Number: 200650119

With THOMAS BOOKS *careful attention is given to all details of manufacturing and design. It is the Publisher's desire to present books that are satisfactory as to their physical qualities and artistic possibilities and appropriate for their particular use.* THOMAS BOOKS *will be true to those laws of quality that assure a good name and good will.*

Printed in the United States of America
MM-R-3

Library of Congress Cataloging-in-Publication Data

Gordon, Virginia N.
The undecided college student : an academic and career advising challenge / by Virginia N. Gordon.–3rd ed.
p. cm.
Includes bibliographical references and indexes.
ISBN 0-398-07706-1 – ISBN 0-398-07707-X (pbk.)
1. Counseling in higher education–United States. 2. Vocational guidance–United States. 3. College student orientation–United States. I. Title.

LB2343.G64 2007
378'.194250973–dc22

2006050119

To Sean, Andrew, Katelyn, Patrick, and Alyssa –
The Future

FOREWORD

When I wrote the foreword to this volume over two decades ago, I compared the scattered attempts to help and study undecided students as analogous in many ways to the development of orphan drugs in medicine. Up to then our knowledge of undecided students had proceeded slowly because there had been only sporadic interest in the necessary research and very little financial support for even that research. Up to then most research had been the by-product of some "more important" research, and most of the programs and professional practices devised to provide assistance were stimulated by individual practitioners and researchers rather than by institutions.

The revised version of this volume updates the vast literature that has proliferated in the last decade. This volume will continue to be the major resource for assembling the diverse speculation and theory, the research evidence, and the multiple organizational and professional practices for helping college students who have been characterized as "undecided, unwilling, or unable" to make appropriate educational and vocational decisions. Virginia Gordon has done an impressive job in updating this substantial literature in one volume. Academics, counselors, and researchers will no longer have to scrounge through a wide array of journals, books, and technical reports to obtain a comprehensive and systematic account of the research (old and new), the model programs for assisting students, and the diverse theory for understanding the undecided student.

This volume should continue to stimulate the creation and evaluation of more informed and systematic vocational assistance. Most people will find the use of developmental speculation and theory to integrate and organize the services and techniques of academic advising to be congenial and plausible. Hopefully, this particular orientation will lead to more explicit evaluation as well as more explicit theory. And, whatever orientation a person adopts, the reader has a useful summary of all theoretical orientations.

JOHN L. HOLLAND
March, 2006

INTRODUCTION

Academic and career undecided college students have been the focus of college administrators, faculty, counselors, academic advisors, student affairs professionals and researchers for eighty years. Many fascinating ideas about who they are, why they are undecided, and how to assist them with decision making have been generated, debated, and some even implemented.

When students enter college, many of them feel overwhelmed with the great number of academic major and career options open to them. Many admit they know very little about what is involved in some of the occupations they are considering. Many are unsure of how their personal strengths and limitations relate to coursework required in particular majors and/or the tasks required in specific occupations. They are often trying to make direct connections between their college major and the "jobs" they will be prepared to enter after college.

The students themselves have mixed feelings about being "undecided." Some are scared, anxious, apologetic, and very negative about their situation. Others are open, flexible, and curious. Many students succumb to societal and parental pressures and make initial choices based on very little if any solid information about academic programs or career fields. Other students deal with the "chicken and egg" question of not knowing which to select first–a career field or college major. Many students solve this dilemma by choosing an area in which the major and occupation are obviously and directly related. Many students change their majors because of changing interests, academic experiences, or becoming more vocationally mature. These students obviously need the same type of advising and career exploration assistance offered to undecided students.

Undecided students are such a heterogeneous group and the administrative variations on campuses are so different that it is difficult to comprehend generally the enormity and complexity of trying to identify and advise them. It is not only difficult to understand the diversity of this group as a whole, but the needs of individual students are sometimes just as diverse. Some advisors tend to work intuitively with undecided students and prescribe activities that may or may not be responsive to their individual needs.

Tracing the research about undecided students over the past decades is a fascinating endeavor. The progressive ideas of the theorists and researchers of the 1950s to current post-modern theorists and the new constructs about indecision with all of its implications for undecided individuals, offer a picture born of changing times and perspectives. This has not altered the need of undecided students, however, to learn the basic knowledge and skills necessary to make timely, realistic and satisfying academic major and career decisions.

This volume offers a comprehensive examination of this special population–from a review of the vast research about them to practical methods for advising and counseling them. Throughout this book, the term "undecided" is used as the descriptor for students unwilling, unable, or unready to make educational and/or vocational decisions. Many campuses use other more positive terms to describe these students. Examples are "exploratory," "open-majors," or "special majors," to name a few. The term "undecided" is used here because of its use in the research literature and the easy identification with its meaning.

If one of the purposes of our colleges and universities is to help students set and implement educational and career goals, then we must be cooperatively engaged in that venture. Creating an environment that encourages and supports undecided students while they are making important educational, career, and life decisions must be central to that purpose.

CONTENTS

THE UNDECIDED COLLEGE STUDENT

Chapter 1

WHO ARE UNDECIDED STUDENTS?

The fascination with college students who are not committed to an educational or career direction has been continuous for eighty years. The first recorded study (as cited by Crites, 1969), was published in the *Personnel Journal* in 1927 by R.B. Cunliffe who surveyed college freshmen in Detroit. He found that 9 percent of the students who responded to a survey indicated they were undecided. Other studies in the next two decades reported that from 9 percent to 61 percent of the high school and college students were undecided. A great many earlier investigations of indecision were parts of studies intended to research other problems. Achilles (1935) (scholastic study), Kilzer (1935) (college-bound versus noncollege-bound), Nelson and Nelson (1940) (religious attitudes), and Kohn (1947) (family influences) looked at correlates of indecision while investigating other topics (Crites, 1969).

Early researchers attempted to differentiate undecided from decided students dichotomously (Ashby, Wall, & Osipow, 1966; Baird, 1967; Holland & Holland, 1977). Other early studies concentrated on more psychological factors such as anxiety, locus of control, and identity (Appel, Haak, & Witzke, 1970; Goodstein, 1965; Kimes & Troth, 1974; Rose & Elton, 1971). Later studies classified students according to their level of undecidedness (Gordon & Steele, 2003; Savickas, 1989), while other researchers classified them by the interaction of cognitive and affective dimensions of career indecision (Chartrand et al., 1994; Feldman, 2003). A great deal of research has studied multiple types of decided and undecided students (Gordon, 1998).

Although not always using undecided students as subjects, a great many characteristics related directly or indirectly to indecision have been studied, such as career-related barriers (Holland, Daiger, &

Power, 1980; Swanson, Daniels, & Tokar, 1996), career decision problems or difficulties (Kelly & Lee, 2002; Lancaster et al., 1999; Osipow & Gati, 1998), career self-efficacy (Betz & Luzzo, 1996; Gianakos, 1999), and cross-cultural differences (Arbona, 1996; Sharf, 1997; Mau, 1999).

The results of all the years of research efforts have only confirmed the prevailing consensus that undecided students comprise a complex, heterogeneous group and their reasons for indecision are just as varied. Kelly and Pulver (2003) list several limitations to the various research studies that may account for the disparity in results. They suggest (1) the dearth of predictive evidence, (2) the failure to consider academic aptitudes, (3) the use of "convenience samples" that include decided as well as undecided subjects, (4) the way statistical analyses are interpreted, and (5) the variation in the personality variables included in the studies. All contribute to a complex and confusing picture of who they are.

Reasons for this complexity may lie also in the different ways writers and researchers define "indecision." Early approaches, according to Osipow (1999), were based simply on asking students to rate their degree of decidedness from survey questions. Today indecision is considered a developmental phase that is part of the decision-making process. As Osipow points out, indecision is no longer the purview of adolescence and early adulthood, but is now viewed from a broad life-span perspective. Career plans often need to be revised because of the challenge of a changing and complex workplace. Osipow suggests that broadening the term should be helpful in understanding the many shades of this stage of the decision making process.

In spite of this vast amount of research and the complexity it presents, understanding the origins of indecision and how undecided students differ from truly decided ones can provide helpful insights. Being cognizant of the research that has focused on treatments and interventions is also important in advising and counseling them effectively.

ORIGINS OF INDECISION

Attempts to determine the antecedents of career indecision have a long and varied history. Early studies concentrate on various correlates of decision rather than on undeciding persons or the levels of their indecision. In more recent years, researchers have viewed indecision as an important topic itself and have tried to identify characteristics common to indecision. One of the earliest studies is that undertaken by Holland and Nichols (1964). The purpose of their investigation is to validate an indecision scale, but in the process some of the personal characteristics of undecided individuals are identified. The subjects used in this research are National Merit finalists, who are asked to respond to activities in which they "frequently, occasionally, or never engaged." Items are identified that appear to describe a cluster of personal traits common to undecided students. Some of these include a socially oriented cluster, an artistic-creative cluster, and an aggressive cluster of activities. The researchers point out that, in the past, indecision was identified with confusion, illness, and the need for counseling. This study suggests that, for some people, indecision is an aspect of the rate of personal development and that intellectual curiosity and creativity are characteristics of students who cannot narrow their interests.

Antecedents of indecision have been examined in a variety of ways. Osipow (1983) suggests four reasons for "misdirected" career development as proposed by vocational theorists: (1) vocational choices that are inconsistent with the individual's self-information, (2) students' not keeping pace developmentally with their peers, (3) emotional instability, and (4) frozen behavior between two desirable choices. Osipow sees retarded rate of development as the reason that causes the most difficulty.

Tyler (1953) postulates a number of antecedents for vocational indecision. She suggests that opinions and attitudes of family and friends can act as deterring factors. For example, a parent's expectations may create a situation that prevents a student from deciding. A cluster of reasons for indecision may emanate from not accepting or not being satisfied with the role that the occupation represents, even though the skills and activities within the occupation are appealing. Sex-role stereotyping of occupations may be a factor, too. Tyler also discusses the multipotential individual who is interested and talented in many directions and finds it difficult, if not impossible, to narrow down the alternatives. Another cause of indecision, according to Tyler, might be not accepting realistic limitations or obstacles that stand in the way. After accepting the fact that a particular decision is impossible, the person may be more open to considering other options.

Ginzberg et al. (1951) discuss deviant and variant choice patterns. The deviant pattern indicates general indecisiveness rather than a specific state of indecision. The variant pattern indicates delayed crystallization of vocational choice, which can be considered a normal process.

LoCascio (1964) uses the terms *impaired* and *delayed* to denote the same two patterns of vocational choice. Delayed development describes an individual who is unaware of, or not ready to learn, the developmental tasks associated with making a choice. Impaired development is similar to Ginzberg's deviant pattern in that the individual has not mastered the vocationally relevant tasks necessary to make a choice, and little learning occurs.

Holland and Nichols (1973) are very explicit about indecision in career choice. If two career choices are of equal strength, or if the first is blocked and no second choice is present, indecision will result. An over- or underestimation of an individual's abilities for the vocational choice could also lead to conflict in vocational decision making.

In a widely quoted study dealing with indecision in college freshmen, Ashby, Wall, and Osipow (1966) categorize their subjects into three types: decided, tentatively decided, and undecided. The study's objective is to compare personality traits and background characteristics among these three kinds of students. Variables included in the study are interest patterns, personality traits, self-ratings on Holland's personality types, academic abilities, high school information, and family background data such as parents' income and education.

The three groups demonstrate no differences on the personality, school, and family background variables; however, they are differentiated by academic ability and achievement. The decided and undecided students are academically superior to the tentatively decided ones.

Ashby, Wall, and Osipow conclude that the antecedents for being undecided and tentatively decided are important considerations in understanding a student entering college. The reservations that the tentatively decided students have about their choices are rooted in knowledge of their academic deficiencies. The undecided, on the other hand, are considered academically capable but need help with formulating a choice. Ashby, Wall, and Osipow find them more dependent than the other two groups. These results have ramifications for counseling approaches and treatments for different types of students.

Using a large national sample of over 12,000 college freshmen, Baird 91967) studies the characteristics of undecided students as they compare to those of students who have made a vocational choice. The students are tested with a wide variety of measures including the *Vocational Preference Inventory,* extracurricular achievements, competency scales, range of experiences, indecision, dogmatism, life goals, and aspirations. Undecided male students are found to be slightly less interested in science. Both undecided men and women are not "vocationally oriented." Other than these two factors, the overwhelming conclusion of the study is that no real differences exist between students who have decided on a vocation and students who have not.

Baird (1967) not only examines the personality differences between decided and undecided college freshmen but also investigates differences in academic aptitude and educational goals. The students' American College Test (ACT) scores and high school grade point averages are used, as well as statements concerning students' goals in attending college. No differences are indicated on the mean of the composite ACT score. However, the undecided students emphasize the college goal of developing their minds and intellectual abilities more often than that of choosing a vocational or professional goal. Thus, undecided students seem more intellectually and less vocationally oriented.

Contrary to former beliefs (Williamson, 1939), these studies point out that the undecided student is not necessarily more emotionally immature or less intellectually able. No differentiation appears in interest patterns or background variables between the decided and the undecided college freshman.

Appel, Haak, and Witzke (1970) identify the factors associated with indecision concerning an academic major or career choice. Their *Career Decision Readiness Inventory* samples dimensions of decision-making behavior. They propose six meaningful factors describing undecided students: (1) situation-specific choice anxiety, (2) data-seeking orientation, (3) concern with self-identity, (4) generalized indecision, (5) multiplicity of interests, and (6) humanitarian orientation. This study serves as an example of the direction that many early researchers took to confirm that multiple causes of indecision exist.

Zytowski (1965) submits that some indecision might be explained by avoidance behavior. Some individuals avoid committing themselves to a career direction because the idea of working repels them or they have a fear of commitment. Serling and Betz (1990) found that fear of commitment was higher in undecided than decided students. It was also positively related to other antecedents of indecision such as anxiety and negatively related to self-esteem.

Later research by Leong and Chervinko (1996) also found that fear of commitment influenced indecision. They examined career indecision and its relationship to the selected negative personality traits of perfectionism, self-consciousness, and fear of commitment. Although they found fear of commitment to be a strong predictor of career indecision, certain dimensions of perfectionism and self-consciousness predicted it as well.

Past research on gender differences in undecided students has been conflicting. In early research, for example, undecided females have been found to experience role conflict and fear of success (Orlofsky, 1978), anxiety, and lowered self-confidence (Slaney, Stafford, & Russell, 1981). Male undecided students were found to be nonconforming (Rose & Elton, 1971) and less academically able (Elton & Rose, 1971). Other studies, however, have found no gender differences between decided and undecided students (Harren, Kass, Tinsley, & Moreland, 1978).

Graef, Wells, Hyland, and Muchinsky (1985) used systematic life history information to predict antecedents of vocational indecision. They were able to suggest typologies or biographical profiles based on vocational maturity and identity, in addition to decidedness. They found unexpected differences between males and females. The nature of the biodata predicted differences in vocational identity, maturity, and decidedness for males and females. The best predictors for decidedness in females are generally academic in nature, while the best predictors for males tend to be those of a more social-interpersonal nature.

Gianakos and Subich (1988) found a relationship of sex and sex-role orientation in the way both men and women choose a college major. In their study, women over-selected the traditionally feminine-type areas of study. When men selected majors in Holland's conventional work environment, they tended to select higher-status ones whereas the women selected majors in the low status/low education end of the spectrum. They concluded that occupational stereotyping, in the guise of major choice, continues in college populations.

In another study, Gianakos and Subich (1986) suggest that sex-role orientation is a more reliable approach than gender in understanding undecided students. They found that sex-role orientation is strongly related to students' level of vocational undecidedness. Androgynous persons were more undecided than those with a traditional sex-role orientation. No gender-related effects were found.

Although there have been no recent studies specifically focused upon the gender of undecided students, there is a great deal of continuing research on the career development needs of women. For example, Fassinger and O'Brien (2000) identify two central themes that are apparent in the differences between female and male vocational patterns and issues. They are (1) the underutilization of women's abilities and talents characterized by low status, pay, and opportunities for advancement, and (2) problems of role overload and compromised career aspirations as a result of family roles and responsibilities. Fassinger and O'Brien conclude that "although the *extent* of women's participation in the labor force is increasingly similar to men, the *nature* of that participation differs markedly because of the difficulty for women of accessing desirable careers and balancing the responsibilities of work and personal lives" (p. 254).

With the majority of students in higher education now women, academic and career choice and implementation for women is an important issue for advisors and counselors. Since more recent research has focused on critical issues for diverse subgroups of women (e.g., women of color, White women, lesbians, women with disabilities), to find information related to decision status, one must search within this literature.

Another important area that has not been studied extensively is cross-cultural differences. Two theoretical perspectives on career indecision are offered from researchers from Canada and Belgium, respectively. Guay et al. (2003) proposed a model of career indecision based on self-determination theory. They found support for the model that posits peer and parental styles as a predictor of career indecision through perceived self-efficacy and autonomy. Germeijs and De Boeck (2003) used three factors of indecision derived from decision theory to examine the factors most important in career decision-making. They suggest that not knowing possible alternatives, not understanding the values implicit in decision making, and being uncertain about making educational choices can lead to indecision. They found that only the valuing factor and the outcomes factor seemed to be associated with career indecision.

Creed, Patton, and Bartrum (2004), researchers from Australia, studied career indecision in terms of internal and external barriers, cognitive style, and choice. These barriers predicted career indecision in males only. Internal and external barriers, along with optimistic/pessimistic cognitive style, however, predicted career decidedness. Arce (1995) compared American and Peruvian students in the levels and types of career indecision they were experiencing. She found no differences in age and sex, but the American students showed a higher level of indecision.

Using a broad set of personality dimensions, Newman, Gray, and Fuqua (1999) studied how personality factors might relate to high and low career indecision groups. The high indecision group scored significantly lower than the low indecision group on 12 of the *California Psychological Inventory* factors. Consensuality played the most substantial role in distinguishing high and low indecision groups. Students with high levels of career indecision appeared less socially developed. They scored lower on several interpersonal dimensions related to social ascendancy and leadership potential. There was also a tendency toward nonconformity or resistance to prescribed rules and expectations with the high career indecision group. These results suggest that select interpersonal qualities, maturity, and social conformity are related to indecision.

The domain of career decision problems to examine career indecision has not been adequately explored (Osipow, 1999). Kelly and Lee (2002) found six reliable factors associated with career indecision: lack of and need for information, trait indecision, disappointment with others, identity diffusion, and choice anxiety. They concluded that career indecision is a result of (1) predecision problems of information deficits and identity diffusion; (2) trait indecision and choice anxiety, and (3) conflicts or disagreements with others that inhibit the implementation of a career choice.

Feldman (2003) discusses the nature of early career indecision. He defines career indecision as "the inability to formulate initial career goals and experience commitment to initial vocational choices" (p. 500). He points out that the resolution of early career decision does not mean changes will not occur throughout one's work life. Early career indecision has both cognitive and affective elements and may be viewed from either a negative or positive perspective depending on the level of involvement and when it occurs.

Feldman also discusses the antecedents of early career indecision in terms of personality, demographic status, vocational interests and abilities, early work experiences, and family environments. He then relates these early indecision factors to how they affect job search behavior and short-term consequences for students, as well as for the organizations that will employ them.

Career indecision as a multidimensional concept is reinforced by Osipow (1999). Methods for assessing career indecision have proliferated over the last twenty-five years and offer useful and sophisticated means to determine the types of decidedness students are experiencing.

Indecisive Students

An important distinction about the severity of indecision was made by Tyler in 1953. Tyler distinguishes between indecision and indecisiveness, the etiology of the two being totally different. Indecisiveness is a result of unsatisfactory habits or thinking that permeates the individual's total life. Until these personal problems or uncertainties can be resolved, a career or educational decision cannot be reached. Tyler also comments upon the place of immaturity in indecisiveness and how choices are a part of developmental sequences. A person will not be able to make later decisions if earlier ones are not resolved.

Crites (1969) defines an indecisive individual as "one who cannot make a vocational choice even after all the conditions for doing so, such as a choice supply, incentive to make a choice, and the freedom to choose are provided" (p. 306). Crites recognized, however, that "work must be done before indecision and indecisiveness can be differentiated empirically as they have been conceptually" (p. 306). Since Crites pointed this out in 1969, there has been little progress in the ability to distinguish between undecided versus indecisive individuals, and in differentiating them empirically for assessment and counseling purposes.

Goodstein (1965) describes an indecisive student as the extreme case of one who is not able to make a career (or any other type of) decision. A few students need in-depth counseling for a more generalized problem when they cannot make a choice (Fuqua, Newman, & Seaworth, 1988; Salamone, 1982; Van Matre & Cooper, 1984). Indecisive students often have trouble making decisions in many areas of life. High levels of anxiety associated with personal or social conflicts are debilitating. Even though all information is known about possible, realistic alternatives, the indecisive student is still unable to make a commitment.

Hartman and Fuqua (1983) describe students who are chronically undecided due to serious psychological problems. Some students not only find that anxiety associated with indecision impairs their progress but also are too externally controlled or experience identity confusion. Hartman and Fuqua stress the multidimensional nature of indecision and discuss the need for more research to determine other psychological antecedents associated with it. Appropriate interventions need to be developed to help students who are undecided due to these psychological dysfunctions.

It is important to recognize that these few students need counseling help beyond the expertise of most academic advisors. Crites (1981) suggests that even though the surface problem may be career related, a few clients need personal counseling and may find a personality change a desirable counseling outcome. Career decision problems may be resolved once the psychological problems are dealt with.

Guay et al. (2006) attempted to distinguish developmental from chronic indecision over time on the dimensions of self-efficacy and autonomy. One half of the students in the study were decided, while the undecided students fell into two groups–the developmentally undecided (27%) and the chronically undecided (25%). The researchers found a need to carry multiple assessments of career indecision over time to more accurately determine the two types. At the first of three time periods, those who were chronically undecided had lower levels of autonomy than the developmentally undecided.

Unlike the chronically undecided students, the developmentally undecided students showed increased self-efficacy over time. Guay et al. suggest that this is the result of higher levels of autonomy for the developmentally undecided and contributed to the initiation of behaviors such as information-seeking about themselves and the work world. Low levels of autonomy may have impeded the development of self-efficacy beliefs among the chronically undecided group. Guay et al. conclude that "perceived autonomy is an important motivational resource to help students develop their self-efficacy beliefs and thus to reduce their levels of career indecision" (p. 249). They suggest that chronically undecided students need to be identified early so that interventions can be initiated.

Haraburda (1998) found that subjects who scored high in decisiveness had few psychological symptoms and were less neurotic than those who were indecisive. Subjects who were low in decisiveness scored lower in extraversion, agreeability, openness to new experiences, and conscientiousness.

Germeijs and DeBoeck (2002) constructed a scale for indecisiveness. They posited that indecisiveness does not refer to any specific kind of decision, but to all kinds of decisions. They sought to demonstrate that career indecision and indecisiveness are two separate constructs. Their "indecisiveness scale" was constructed on eleven features: difficulty, don't know how, feeling uncertain, takes a long time, delaying, avoidance, leaving to others, reconsideration, worrying, regretting, and calling oneself indecisive. They found two different factors: an indecisiveness factor, referring to problems students encounter with decision-making in general, and a career indecision factor referring to educational decision problems. Low self-esteem is associated more with indecisiveness than with career indecision. The researchers concluded that persons who are indecisive require a different type of counseling than persons who are only undecided about a particular decision. After designing a study to distinguish the effects of counseling on undecided and indecisive students, Heppner and Hendricks (1995) came to the same conclusion, that is, different approaches are required for clients with different career problems.

As Osipow (1999) suggests, new research raises the question about the personality attributes of indecisive and undecided persons and whether they even share the same characteristics. He contends that measuring indecisiveness as a separate entity from indecision has been difficult since on the surface they often look the same.

More research on indecisiveness is provided in the following section on *Career Indecision Types.* Figure 1 summarizes some of the descriptors of indecisiveness from various research studies.

Career Indecision Types

An important shift in approaches used to define the characteristics

Figure 1.
SOME DESCRIPTORS FOR INDECISIVENESS FROM RESEARCH STUDIES*

High anxiety
Immaturity
Unable to make a commitment to a decision
Poor self-efficacy
Identity confusion
Externally controlled
Low self-esteem
Lack of autonomy
Problems with general decision-making
Dependent decision makers
Lack of goal clarity
Avoidant behavior
Helplessness
High perceived need for resolution

*Individual indecisive students may display only some of these characteristics.

of undecided students has taken place in recent years. Multiple variables that had previously been identified (e.g., vocational identity, anxiety, locus of control, career salience) were used to identify clusters of characteristics that could be attributed to undecided students. As a result, different subtypes of undecided students emerged. By tying types of indecision to a group of variables, it was hoped that the ensuing typologies of vocationally undecided students would lead to a better understanding of this phenomenon and perhaps suggest more focused, effective advising or counseling interventions. Figure 1 summarizes eighteen attempts at defining groups of undecided students by clustering the characteristics that have emerged from research.

Holland and Holland (1977) examined many characteristics attributed to decided and undecided students. Using a large sample of high school and college juniors, they found decided and undecided students were alike on most measures, but substantial differences were found in identity and vocational attitudes among undecided students. They were one of the first to suggest the importance of identifying multiple subtypes of undecided students. Later efforts by Holland, Daiger, and Power (1980) led to an instrument for identifying the concerns of undecided students, *My Vocational Situation* (MVS). The MVS measures "the clarity of a person's vocational goals and self-perceptions" (p. 28). A low score implies a person with poorly defined goals and coping behaviors.

Another historical effort to identify subtypes was done by Osipow, Carney, Winer, Yanico, and Koschier (1976). Over the past thirty years the instrument they developed, the *Career Decision Scale* (CDS), has become a standard in research for identifying causes of indecision. Although Osipow (1994) discourages its use in using "sub-factor" scales in identifying multiple subtypes of undecided students, research studies continue to use it for this purpose (Barak & Friedkes, 1982; Hartman, Fuqua, & Blum, 1985; Martin, Sabourin, Laplante, & Coallier, 1991; Savicas & Jarjoura, 1991; Shimizu, Vondracek, & Schulenberg, 1994; Winer, 1992). Vondracek, Hostetler, Schulenberg, and Shimizu (1990) used the CDS's factor-based subscales to create a typology of career indecision. They found that significant differences on the various indecision scales were due to gender and career decision status.

Another early study on subtypes was reported by Jones and Chenery (1980). They developed a model of vocational decision status using an instrument, the *Vocational Decision Scale* (VDS), that was constructed for use in this study. Decision status was determined by using undecided students' level of indecision, comfort level, and reasons for being undecided. The authors found that most undecided students had an unclear sense of identity, low career salience, low comfort level with their situation, lacked self-confidence, experienced high anomy, and were in the process of breaking away from significant others (which the authors called a "transitional self"). Jones and Chenery concluded that viewing vocational indecision from a multiple subtype perspective appears to provide a clearer picture of indecision as opposed to the one-dimensional approach of the past.

Wanberg and Muchinsky (1992) used Jones and Chenery's vocational decision status model to form a typology of decision status from vocational indecision and personality constructs. In addition to measuring the degree of career indecision, the other variables used were anxiety, locus of control, self-esteem, and self-consciousness. Four subtypes were identified through cluster analysis: Confident Decided, Concerned Decided, Indifferent Undecided, and Anxious Undecided. These authors indicate that it is useful to include both undecided and *decided* students in a typology since they contend that decided students may also need career counseling. They also believe that many of the Concerned Decided students may be those who change their majors later. While they did not duplicate Jones and Chenery's findings completely, they did find support for the existence of two of their subgroups.

Van Matre and Cooper (1984) also used decided students in their attempt to group students. They reconceptualized indecision as a complex, multidimensional problem composed of an undecided state and an indecisive trait. They identify a "Decided-Undecided State" and a "Decisive-Indecisive Trait.) While not substantiated through research, they contend that an orthogonal approach is useful as a way to develop practical assessment tools for the four indecision-indecisiveness configurations that they identify.

Fuqua, Blum, and Hartman (1988) identified four groups of students through a cluster analysis using five related variables that have consistently been found in studies of career indecision (i.e., state anxiety, trait anxiety, locus of control, identity, and career indecision). Group 1 students were career decided, showed little anxiety, and had good identity formation. The second group of students were moderately undecided, had increased levels of anxiety, had less identity formation, but had an internal locus of control. Group 3 students, however, indicated serious indecision, moderate levels of anxiety, poor identity formation, and an external locus of control. The fourth group of students indicated serious indecision, excessive anxiety, poor identity formation, and an external locus of control. The authors concluded that "singular therapeutic approaches and programs will provide an adequate response for all individuals in such a heterogeneous group" (p. 372).

Savickas and Jarjoura (1991) used career development theory to classify clusters of students. They used the Career Decision Scale (CDS) (Osipow, Carney, Winer, Yanico, & Koschierl, 1976) to group students based on their response to the scales items. Although constructed as a "typological approach" to understanding different types of decisional problems, the CDS was used in this study to identify possible subgroups. Five subtypes of students emerged with three of them reflecting the problems associated with the vocational development tasks of the exploration stage. Type A students indicated problems with the task of implementing a tentative choice. Type B included problems with the task of specifying a choice through advanced exploration, and Type C included problems with crystallizing a field-and-level preference through unrealistic and had difficulty in compromising their situation with idealistic or naive expectations. Type E seemed to be indecisive and could not make decisions about anything, not just career choices. These researchers suggest that the first three types of students were "on task," or able to identify what was needed to make career choices. The students in the last two groups were having problems that thwart task coping.

Lucas and Epperson (1988, 1990) also identified subgroups of vocationally undecided students through personality variables. Their 1990 study attempted to refine their earlier findings but included many more variables; identity, informational needs, occupational aspirations, lifestyle, career salience, self-esteem, anxiety, locus of control, and decision-making style. Five clusters emerged. Students in the first cluster exhibited high anxiety, low self-esteem, external locus of control, dependent decision-making style, and low identity. Cluster 2 students showed some anxiety, lower self-esteem, and external locus of control, and needed vocational information. Cluster 3 students indicated low anxiety, high self-esteem, internal locus of control, and a need for vocational information. Cluster 4 students showed some anxiety, lower self-esteem, and an internal locus of control. The last cluster of students indicated little or no anxiety, external locus of control, no interest in work activities, and no need for information. Lucas and Epperson also conclude that it is useful to identify subgroups of undecided students so that appropriate and efficient treatment strategies might be developed.

The other studies cited in Figure 1 offer interesting approaches for subgrouping undecided students. Haag-Mutter (1986) hypothesized three types from the literature: developmentally indecisive, acute situational-reaction indecisive, and chronically indecisive. Newman, Fuqua, and Minger (1990) found that decided students had as much anxiety as undecided students.

Larson, Heppner, Ham, & Dugan (1988) identified four distinguishable types based on variables that had not been used in previous studies, including career problem-solving, career myths, support systems, self-knowledge, perceived pressure, academic self-efficacy, occupational knowledge, career obstacles, decision status, and career planning behavior. Cluster analysis revealed four distinct subtypes of undecided students: planless avoiders, informed indecisives, confident but uninformed, and uninformed. These researchers used more stringent criteria in selecting undecided students for their study and found this made a difference in their results. Using many characteristics attributed to undecided students in a cluster approach offers great promise in identifying more focused and effective interventions to assist them in the academic and career planning process.

More recent studies have examined the effect of counseling interventions (Kelly & Pulver, 2003; Lucas, 1993), testing new instruments (Chartrand et al., 1994; Larson & Majors, 1998); ego-identity development (Cohen et al., 1995), and goal instability (Multon et al., 1995). Lucas (1993) performed a validation study on the cluster types in her earlier research and applied that research to counseling interventions. Lucas states that "The ultimate purpose of clustering undecided students is to hypothesize differential interventions for students who show unique indecision patterns" (p. 444). She found that Cluster 1 students dealt with a large range of personal problems in relatively few counseling session. Cluster 3 students, conversely, tended to present fewer concerns and dealt with those concerns in a larger number of counseling sessions. Clusters 2 and 4 students were not clearly predicted and may require a more thorough assessment of how relationships with parents, significant others, or peers affect their view of themselves and future aspirations. Lucas concludes that different types of undecidedness can be recognized and measured, and can be tested on differential intervention strategies.

Rojewski (1994) used the *Career Decision Scale* (Osipow et al, 1976) to measure indecision in adolescents from rural areas and found three types of career indecision: tentatively decided, transitional indecision, and chronic indecision. The three types reflect the intensity of tasks and situations typically encountered by adolescents in general. Chartrand et al. (1994) found a four-cluster configuration which revealed interactions between cognitive and affective dimensions of career indecision. Their findings argue against a single continuum conceptualization of undecided types. One group had predominantly information concerns while another had affective concerns. Although the other two groups had similar levels of career indecision, the second group reported high anxiety levels. This may help to confirm past research that indicated cognitive and affective barriers may be similar at the very extreme ends of career undecidedness.

Multon, Heppner, and Lapan (1995) found that high school students who were classified into subtypes and by goal instability had significantly different dispositional characteristics. The chronic undecided type had a disposition toward pervasive indecisiveness. Although students in the second group indicated they had a clear career direction, they were high in goal instability. A third "developmentally normal" subtype reported that they knew themselves and their values and goals, but were less clear about their career decision. The fourth subtype had a clear sense of self- and occupational identity. They were also comfortable in their career decision-making ability and knowledge of careers. The researchers conclude that more studies are needed to identify the important cognitive and affective variables that can discriminate subtypes of career undecidedness at the high school level.

Cohen et al. (1995) compared four clusters of career undecided students across five of Erikson's stages of ego-identity development. Their "ready-to-decide" group was the highest functioning and had resolved the first five psychosocial stages most successfully. Cohen and colleagues described chronically indecisive students as having difficulty in resolving psychosocial crises and suggested that therapy should address the earlier psychosocial stage tasks of trust, autonomy, initiative, and industry.

Larson and Majors (1998) used the *Coping with Career Indecision* (CCI) instrument that identifies career indecision subtypes of adolescents to examine general and career affective distress and career-specific personal agency. These factors involve the extent to which a person is proactive and engaged with the environment as they make a tentative choice of career or educational major. Discriminating between those students who were coping well and those who were experiencing distress, four groups were identified: Low Agency/Low Distress, High Agency/Low Distress, High Agency/High Distress, and Low Agency/High Distress. Issues concerning each group were identified and counseling suggestions were made for each type. The researchers concluded that the CCI is a useful part of a career assessment battery to differentiate meaningful subtypes of students involved in career planning. Career-specific and general affective distress and personal agency proved to be beneficial dimensions in understanding career planning at one point in time.

The purpose of Kelly and Pulver's study (2003) was to identify career indecision types and to evaluate the validity of the types by studying their response to a career exploration course, the outcome being a reduction in career indecision. In addition to measuring indecision, personality variables and ability measures were used to derive four indecision types. The four types identified were: (Type 1) well-adjusted information seekers; (Type 2) neurotic indecisive information seekers; (Type 3) low ability information seekers; and (Type 4) uncommitted extraverts. The well-adjusted information seekers may require only a brief, information-oriented career intervention. Type 2 needs more tools for gaining career information and instruction in decision-making, needs to initiate a program of exploring their career interests, and needs to stabilize their anxiety and distress while engaged in the career exploration and decision-making process. Type 3 needs to identify viable academic and career options that are realistic. Uncommitted extraverts, Type 4, are closed to new information and need counseling that helps them identify the steps necessary to turn their decisions into commitments. Three variables were important in differentiating the four career indecision types: neuroticism, extraversion and academic ability. The authors indicate that different indecision types need different combinations of the components to providing information, acquiring decision-making strategies, learning to manage negative affect, and finding appropriate person-environment matches for students with limited options.

Gordon (1998) summarized fifteen of the studies on career decidedness types cited above to determine if there are any patterns or similarities among the types identified. She postulated seven categories of students on a continuum of decided to indecisive. The seven categories that emerged were very decided, somewhat decided, unstable decided, developmentally undecided, seriously undecided, and chronically indecisive. She suggested advice and counseling approaches for each type. Gordon concluded the effectiveness of an intervention will be mediated by the subtype of vocational problem the student is experiencing.

Kelly and Lee (2002) contend that the quality of research and practice related to counseling interventions for career indecision has been undeveloped. There is little research to specify the type of treatment most appropriate for different career decision problems. Kelly and Lee claim this is because of the failure to adequately describe the domain of career decision problems and the absence of theoretical postulates relating indecision to other career development constructs. Figure 2 describes some of the studies that explore different types of undecided students.

Figure 2.
RESEARCHED SUBTYPES OF UNDECIDED STUDENTS*

Researchers	*Variables Studied*	*Subtypes*	*Characteristics*
Kelly & Pulver (2003)	anxiety, general indecisiveness, need for career and self-knowledge information, aptitudes, indecision, five personality aspects, neuroticism, extraversion, openness, agreeableness, conscientiousness	Well-adjusted information seekers	High need for self-knowledge and career information, low neuroticism, strong math and verbal abilities
		Neurotic indecisive information seekers	High career choice anxiety, general indecisiveness, need for information, high neuroticism, low extraversion
		Low ability information seekers	High information need, high extraversion, low openness score, low verbal/math ability
		Uncommitted extraverts	Low need for self knowledge, high extraversion and agreeableness scores, low neuroticism
Larson & Majors (1998)	career indecision, problem-solving behaviors and attitudes, career self-efficacy, college major decidedness, career barriers, environment engagement and emotional distress	Low agency/High distress	Distressed over choice of major, uses avoidance, perceives career barriers
		High agency/High distress	Uncomfortable with major choice, experiencing moderate distress, confident in ability to make choice, reports a few barriers, perceives self as effective problem-solver
		High agency/Low distress	Comfortable with college major choice, minimal distress, confidence in ability to make choice, perceives few barriers, effective problem-solver
		Low agency/Low distress	Some comfort in making major choice, minimal distress, little

continued

Figure 2–*Continued*
RESEARCHED SUBTYPES OF UNDECIDED STUDENTS*

Researchers	*Variables Studied*	*Subtypes*	*Characteristics*
			confidence in decision-making, perceives self as poor problem-solver, and many career obstacles
Cohen, Chartrand, & Jowdy (1995)	ego development, career choice anxiety, general indecisiveness, need for self-knowledge and career information	Ready to Decide	Most successful resolution across all identity stages, fewest career difficulties
		Developmentally Undecided	Moderate resolution of identity stages, decision difficulties centered around anxiety
		Choice Anxious	Moderate resolution of identity stages, decision difficulties centered around need for career information
		Chronically Indecisive	Least successful resolution of identity stages, most career difficulties
Multon, Heppner, & Lapan (1995)	goal instability, career decidedness, self-efficacy, goal attainment, viewing self in relation to others, general affective disposition	High Goal Instability/ Career Undecided	Career choice discomfort, lack of career knowledge, negative affectivity, pervasive aimlessness and uncertainty, high goal instability, lack strong motivation
		High Goal Instability/ Career Decided	Clear career direction, high goal instability, general anxiety, low self-efficacy
		Low Goal Instability/ Career Undecided	Unclear about career direction, developmentally normal, need for information
		Low Goal Instability/ Career Decided	Clear sense of self and occupational identity, confident, knowl-

continued

Figure 2–*Continued*
RESEARCHED SUBTYPES OF UNDECIDED STUDENTS*

Researchers	*Variables Studied*	*Subtypes*	*Characteristics*
			edgable, clear in decision-making
Chartrand et al. (1994)	career confidence, personal, emotional, and informational needs, goal instability, self-esteem, vocational identity	Developmentally Undecided	High need for career information, goal-directed and confident, emotionally stable
		Ready to Decide	Low cognitive and affective scores, more vocationally mature, low levels of anxiety, high self-esteem and vocational identity
		Indecisive	High levels of anxiety, needs information, poorly developed vocational identity, low goal-directedness, low self-esteem
		Choice Anxious	High levels career choice anxiety, moderate levels of general indecisiveness and self-knowledge, low need for career information, lack confidence and goal-directedness
Rojewski (1994)	career maturity, career indecision	Tentatively Decided–Crystallizing Preferences	Formalizing plans, confident, some expressed career concerns
		Transitionally Undecided	Cognitively immature, greater indecision, strong need for occupational information, reinforcement and support
		Chronic Indecision/ Impaired Development	Unable to identify career interests and viable career options, lacks information, difficulty with decision-

continued

Figure 2–*Continued*
RESEARCHED SUBTYPES OF UNDECIDED STUDENTS*

Researchers	*Variables Studied*	*Subtypes*	*Characteristics*
			making, immature career attitudes
Wanberg & Muchinsky (1992)	career indecision, anxiety, locus of control, self-esteem, self-consciousness	Confident Decided Concerned Decided Indifferent Undecided Anxious Undecided	External descriptors: comfort, certainty, indecision, occupational information, public and private self-consciousness, social anxiety
Savickas & Jarjoura (1991)	indecision, time perspective (developmental stages)	Implementing a choice or making plans	Decided
		Specifying a choice through advanced exploration	
		–crystallized preference	Need support
		–multipotentialed	Many alternatives
		–opposed	Need support in dealing with significant others
		Crystallizing a preference –exploring self and occupations –having trouble choosing	Need self-knowledge, and occupational information, need support
		Unrealistic or learning to compromise	
		–perfectionistic	Idealistically
		–frustrated	blocked
		Indecisive or	Blocked
		learning to make decisions	Overwhelmed, highly anxious

continued

Figure 2–*Continued*
RESEARCHED SUBTYPES OF UNDECIDED STUDENTS*

Researchers	*Variables Studied*	*Subtypes*	*Characteristics*
Vondracek, Hostetler, Schulenberg, & Shimizu (1990)	Career Decision Scale: (Osipow et al. Diffusion Support Approach-Approach External Barriers Indecision	Decided-decided Decided undecided Undecided-decided Undecided-undecided	Low approach-approach and External barriers High on diffusion (Results differed over time–6 month periods and 3 years)
Lucas & Epperson (1990)	identity, informational needs, occupational aspirations, lifestyle, career salience, self-esteem anxiety, locus of control, decision-making style	5 Clusters:	
		Cluster 1	High anxiety, low self-esteem, external locus of control, dependent decision-making style, low identity
		Cluster 2	Some anxiety, lower self-esteem, external locus of control, need vocational information
		Cluster 3	Low anxiety, high self-esteem, internal locus of control, need information
		Cluster 4	Some anxiety, lower self-esteem, internal locus of control
		Cluster 5	Little/no anxiety, external locus of control, no interest in work activities, no need for information
Newman, Fuqua, & Minger (1990)	decision status, career maturity, anxiety	Undecided serious Undecided not serious Decided uncomfortable	Decided students had as much anxiety as undecided students; Undecided and lower comfort decided groups had lower

continued

Figure 2–*Continued*
RESEARCHED SUBTYPES OF UNDECIDED STUDENTS*

Researchers	*Variables Studied*	*Subtypes*	*Characteristics*
		Decided somewhat comfortable Decided moderately comfortable Decided very comfortable	identity and maturity scores
Lucas & Epperson (1988)	lifestyle career salience, self-esteem, anxiety, identity, locus of control	Happy & Work Oriented	Well-adjusted, somewhat undecided, actively exploring
		Caught in a Dilemma	Lower on career salience, low on problem-solving
		Undecided and Limited Interests	Scored low on all variables, lack motivation
		Anxious and Unclear Goals	High anxiety, low self-esteem, need occupational information, lack of clarity
Larson, Heppner, Ham & Dugan (1988)	career problem-solving, career myths, support systems, self-knowledge, perceived pressure, academic self-efficacy, occupational knowledge, career obstacles, decision status, career planning behavior	Planless Avoiders	Very undecided, lack information, poor problem-solvers, lack of confidence, avoidant behavior
		Informed Indecisives	Poor problem-solving skills, no need for information, lack of confidence, negative self-appraisal
		Confident but Uninformed	Lack information about career-planning process, good problem-solving abilities
		Uninformed	Average problem-solving skills, lack career-planning information, lack

continued

Figure 2–*Continued*
RESEARCHED SUBTYPES OF UNDECIDED STUDENTS*

Researchers	*Variables Studied*	*Subtypes*	*Characteristics*
			occupational information
Fuqua, Blum, & Hartman (1988)	anxiety, identity, locus of control, decision status	Group 1	Career decided, little anxiety, good identity formation
		Group 2	Moderate indecision, increased anxiety, less identity formation, internal locus of control
		Group 3	Serious indecision, moderate levels of anxiety, poor identity formation, external locus of control
		Group 4	Serious indecision, excessive anxiety, poor identity formation, external locus of control
Haag-Mutter (1986)	Hypothesized from literature	Developmentally indecisive	Vocationally immature, lack of self-knowledge and occupational information
		Acute situational-reaction indecisive	Situational or environmental barriers
		Chronically indecisive	Paralyzed, anxious procrastination, dependency, manipulation, lack of confidence, helpless-ness, external locus of control
Van Matre	Hypothesized literature: state of decidedness	Decided-Decisive	Functional, needs confirmation, limited symptomology

continued

Figure 2–*Continued*
RESEARCHED SUBTYPES OF UNDECIDED STUDENTS*

Researchers	*Variables Studied*	*Subtypes*	*Characteristics*
	and undecidedness idedness/trait of decisiveness and indecisiveness	Undecided-Decided	Needs information about self and/or vocational opportunities
		Decided-Indecisive	Chronic anxiety, externally control-led, low satisfaction with decision
		Undecided-decisive	Chronic anxiety, confused, reactive, high perceived need for resolution
Jones & Chenery (1980)	decision-making stages, anxiety, identity, career salience, anomy	Model of vocational decision status using: –level of indecision –comfort level –reasons for indecision	Most undecided had unclear sense of identity, low career salience, low comfort level, lacked self-confidence, high anomy, and was breaking away from significant others (transitional self)
Holland & Holland (1977)	Extensive list of variables including those from the Career Maturity Inventory Anomy Scale, Identity Scale, Self-Directed Search, Interpersonal Competency Scale, and Preconscious Activity Scale	Group 1	Delays a decision until reality dictates
		Group 2	Slightly: vocationally immature, inter-personally incom-petent, anxious, and alienated
		Group 3	Moderate to severe case of variables in Group 2

*This chart does not contain all the studies on undecided students concerned with defining subtypes, but it is a representative sample of the research on the topic.

CHARACTERISTICS OF UNDECIDED STUDENTS

Other research concerned with indecision describes the characteristics of the undecided student. Some variables, such as identity and anxiety, were studied early and extensively. Others, such as self-efficacy and the identification of career indecision types, while more recent, have contributed additional insights into the characteristics of undecided students. Being aware of the vast array of student characteristics can also help target advising and counseling approaches, as well as develop programs and other interventions to assist them. The following describes research that has been performed on some of the most relevant characteristics.

Choice Anxiety

A concept proposed by Goodstein (1965) has received much consideration. Goodstein identifies two groups of undecided individuals. The first type is undecided for a number of reasons, such as vocational immaturity or lack of readiness for the developmental tasks necessary to form a decision. For this person, the inability to reach a decision provokes a feeling of anxiety. Societal or educational pressures to make a choice intensify his or her anxiety. This person simply needs occupational information or help in learning decision-making skills. According to Goodstein, such an individual is experiencing indecision, and a variety of experiences or information should provide the needed help. The anxiety associated with the choice process would consequently by alleviated.

The second type of undecided person described by Goodstein is the indecisive one. This individual finds the anxiety associated with the choice process debilitating and has difficulty reaching a decision about anything. Contrasted to the person who is undecided and anxious about this lack of decision, the indecisive individual finds the decision-making process and commitment itself anxiety arousing.

Goodstein describes anxiety associated with vocational choice as free-floating anxiety that is delimited in this specific area. Anxiety cues are difficult to identify in this process, and the individual is hard pressed to identify the exact circumstances of anxiety arousal. Nonadaptive behavior regarding the lack of vocational plans is often seen by counselors as stemming from a void of prior experience that could have provided the opportunity to learn responses. As Goodstein points out, however, before an indecisive individual can make a choice, factors contributing to existing personal-social conflicts must be dealt with.

Kimes and Troth (1974) investigate the relationship between career decisiveness and trait anxiety. They find that students who have a career in mind but are not moving toward a decision and those who have not made a career decision have a significantly higher mean trait anxiety score than those who have definitely decided. Students who are completely undecided have the highest mean trait anxiety score. As the level of anxiety proneness increases, the level of decidedness decreases. Kimes and Troth conclude that high anxiety-prone individuals may have more difficulty in making occupational choices than individuals who are less anxiety prone. One of the factors associated with indecision by Appel, Haak, and Witzke (1970) is situation-specific anxiety. Much of the research on anxiety and occupational choice has focused on how an individual's anxious state deters or inhibits the decision-making process.

This relationship between anxiety and indecision is substantiated by other studies (Fuqua, Seaworth, & Newman, 1987; Fuqua, Newman, & Seaworth, 1988). Cooper, Fuqua, and Hartman (1984) suggest that some undecided students may have high anxiety related to *indecisiveness* and may be experiencing interpersonal discomfort in the form of "submissive tendencies, passivity, and an acute need for social acceptance" (p. 356). Hawkins, Bradley, and White (1977) found that state anxiety was related to lack of occupational commitment, but trait anxiety was not. Kaplan and Brown (1987) support Goodstein's (1965) contention that there are two types of undecided students: those whose anxiety is an important antecedent of indecision and those who feel some anxiety as a result of being undecided.

Hartman and Fuqua (1983) suggest that in addition to anxiety, other correlates of indecision should be taken into consideration when working with students who are experiencing indecision. An individual's locus of control may be a factor in precipitating career indecision (Rotter, 1966). Students with an internal locus of control assume more control and responsibility for making career choices while those with an external locus of control may look to significant others to make decisions for them or may believe that academic and career choices are largely influenced by chance or luck. Some studies have indicated that indecision is related to external locus of control (Cellini, 1978;

Kazin, 1977). Undecided students with an external locus of control may need a more structured approach to exploration from an external source.

O'Hare and Tamburri (1986) indicate that anxiety is the outcome of the inability to cope with a stressful situation. They suggest that coping strategies are important mediators on anxiety in the career decision process. They used four types of coping behaviors to demonstrate their effect on undecided students' career decision making: support, efficacy, reactive, and avoidant. They found that trait anxiety was the primary discriminator among state-anxious groups. Students who experienced high trait anxiety did not use self-efficacy coping behavior. These students also attempted to escape anxiety-provoking situations by avoiding them. The researchers suggest that counselors should be aware of trait anxious students who use symptom-altering and escape-avoidance behaviors. One approach might be to help them extinguish fear responses and develop a sense of self-efficacy.

Career Identity

Lack of career identity is considered an important antecedent of indecision. Erikson (1968) signifies that identity formation is a critical task in adolescence. Individuals who are exploring their identity also tend to be in the planning phase of career decision making.

Super (1957) suggests that self-concept and occupational choice are closely related. Holland (1997) defines identity as "the possession of a clear and stable picture of one's goals, interests, and talents" (p. 5). When one's vocational identity is not formed or solidified, career decision-making is difficult.

In a large sample of both high school and college youth, Holland and Holland (1977) found a significant positive correlation between identity and vocational choice. They submit that students who consider themselves undecided do not differ in any group of personal characteristics, except in terms of their own sense of identity and vocational maturity. Holland and Holland were among the first to suggest that researchers should be looking at broad patterns of variables that indicate multiple subtypes instead of spending their energies looking for specific variables that describe undecided students as a single type.

Gordon and Kline (1989) examined the relationship between ego-identity and career decidedness. When Marcia (1966) operationalized

Erikson's construct of ego-identity statuses, he categorized four developmental identity statuses:

1. Diffusion–individuals who have not made a commitment, but have experienced an exploration or crisis period;
2. Foreclosure–refers to individuals who have made a commitment without an exploration or crisis period;
3. Moratorium–indicates an individual has been involved in a period of crisis;
4. Identity achievement–refers to individuals who have experienced exploration or a crisis before making a commitment.

Gordon and Kline (1989) found three of the four ego-identity statuses were significant with both career decidedness and major decidedness. Students who were more career decided reported a significantly higher mean score on achievement than those who were more career undecided. Students who were more decided about a career choice were less diffused and had a lower mean score for moratorium than those who were undecided about a career. Significant differences were also found in ego-identity statuses and major decidedness. The results reinforce the notion that decided as well as undecided students are at varying levels of ego-identity development and that students at different levels of exploration and commitment require a sensitivity to how and when information and personal support are offered.

Savickas (1985) found that when the identity crises have been successfully resolved, higher levels of career maturity and clear career goals were achieved. Blustein and Phillips (1990) found that those who have achieved a stable identity tend to use rational and systematic decision-making strategies. Brisbin and Savickas (1994) examined how career indecision scales measured self-chosen goal-setting and goals that were set for students by their significant others. Although individuals have high scores on decidedness, their choice may not be actually crystallized. The decided student may actually be foreclosed rather than "achieved-crystallized." The authors suggest that high scores on career decision scales, while good screeners, should also be interpreted carefully.

Cohen et al. (1995) compared four clusters of career undecided students across five of Erikson's stages of ego-identity development. Their ready-to-decide group was the highest functioning and had resolved the first five psychosocial stages most successfully. Cohen and colleagues described the chronically indecisive students as having difficulty in resolving psychosocial crises and suggested that counselors should address the early psychosocial stage tasks of trust, autonomy, initiative, and industry.

Vondracek et al. (1995) also addressed identity by using Erikson's psychosocial stages. They examined the relationship between identity statuses and career indecision that is based on career decision-making barriers. They found a relationship between indecision and the Diffusion and Moratorium identity statuses. Identity Achievement students had significant lower career indecision scores than those in the other three identity status groups. They also found the Foreclosure students were no different from the other noncommitted identity status groups in the amount or type of indecision experienced. The researchers suggest that career indecision might be placed in a more positive framework if there is more consideration given to identity exploration and formation. They emphasize that "meaningful exploration" may be a better objective for most adolescents who are not ready to make a decision.

Career Self-Efficacy

Self-efficacy is the confidence that individuals have in their ability to master specific tasks. Taylor and Betz (1983) studied career self-efficacy in relation to indecision and found that students who have less confidence in their ability to complete decision-making tasks were more undecided than those reporting higher levels of confidence.

Betz (1992) used Bandura's original model to show how self-efficacy expectations develop through performance accomplishments, vicarious learning, emotional arousal, and verbal persuasion. Betz indicates that "career self-efficacy" is a general term that summarizes the possibility that "low expectations of efficacy with respect to some aspect of career behavior may serve as a detriment to optimal career choice and development in the individual" (p. 24).

Betz and Luzzo (1996) indicate that the most consistent correlate of career decision-making self-efficacy is career indecision. Stronger perceptions of career decision-making are related to lower levels of career indecision as measured by the *Career Decision-Making Self-Efficacy Scale* (CDMSE) (Taylor & Betz, 1983). Taylor and Popma (1990) found that the CDMSE differentiated between three groups of students categorized on the basis of college major status–declared majors, tentative major choice and undecided students. They suggest that an individual's "attribution of control over events and consequences in life, . . . may determine the amount of confidence in successfully completing career decision making tasks" (p. 28).

Gianakos (1999) found that differences in self-efficacy is associated with Super's (1957), career choice patterns (i.e., stable, conventional, multiple-trial, and unstable patterns). Individuals with stable and multiple-trial patterns reported greater confidence in their abilities to successfully undertake the career-related tasks of goal selection, gathering occupational information, problem-solving, realistic planning and self-appraisal. Individuals with unstable patterns reflect a lack of clarity and their chronic indecision may be symptomatic of identity diffusion. Gianakos concludes that counseling for persons with conventional or unstable career choice patterns should include personal as well as career counseling.

Since Taylor and Betz (1983) published their early research on career self-efficacy, this construct has gained in importance. The great amount of research on this topic over the last two decades in particular, attests to its relevance for indecision as well as its importance for many aspects of career decision making.

Career Maturity

Another important concept that has implications for advising the undecided student is career maturation. Career maturity can be defined as the readiness of an individual to make informed, age-appropriate career decisions and to cope with appropriate career development tasks (Savickas, 1984). The earliest studies on vocational maturity were initiated by Donald Super (Super & Bohn, 1970). Super (1983) identified five dimensions of career maturity: planfulness, exploration, information gathering, decision making, and reality orientation. Super's work stimulated other theorists (Crites, 1969; Ginsberg et al., 1951; Gribbons & Lohnes, 1964) to examine other dimensions of vocational maturity or readiness for vocational planning. Other correlates include realistic occupational aspirations and expectations, higher career decision-making, self-efficacy, an internal locus of control, and higher levels of career salience (Crites, 1996). Research also has established a strong relationship between career maturity and career decidedness.

John Crites (1981) lists five stages of career maturation. Undecided students must accomplish these five tasks before they are vocationally mature enough to make a decision:

1. *Orientation to vocational choice:* This implies an awareness of the need to choose and an awareness of the factors involved in choosing a major or occupation.
2. *Information and planning:* This refers to the amount of reliable information an individual possesses with which to make a decision. Students must also learn to plan logically and chronologically for the future.
3. *Crystallization of traits:* This refers to the psychological attributes a person brings to decision-making, such as interest patterns, explicit values, and increasing independence. Crystallization requires the ability to bring all the relevant factors together into a coherent whole.
4. *Wisdom of vocational preferences:* This refers to how closely individuals' career decisions agree with various aspects of reality. For example, do they have the prerequisite ability for their preferred occupation, appropriate interests for the chosen field, available financial resources for relevant training, etc.? Is the choice realistic in every way?

Students are often forced by institutions to make decisions at a time when they are not developmentally ready. Developing career maturity is a critical task that needs to be acknowledged and dealt with in individualizing advising approaches for undecided students. The developmental advisor can be extremely helpful in making certain that students are aware of the tasks associated with career decision-making and helping them develop the skills necessary to accomplish this process.

Naidoo (1998) reviewed four decades of research on career maturity. He found various correlates of the career maturity construct. More recent research focuses on age and grade level differences; race, ethnic, and cultural differences; locus of control and socioeconomic differences; sex and gender differences; and work salience. Career maturity is better differentiated by educational level than age, and career maturity development differs by gender. Indirect and direct relationships exist between locus of control and many career-related variables, such as career decision, career commitment, career exploration and occupation-seeking behaviors.

The relationship between career maturity and career decision-making attributional style was examined by Powell and Luzzo (1998). They found significant relationships between students' career maturity and their attributional style for career decision-making. Their results reinforce the claim that individuals' attributional style is related to their attitude toward the career decision-making process. When students believe they have control over and responsibility for their own career development, they will have a more positive attitude toward career decision-making.

Levinson et al. (1998) reviewed six measures that assess career maturity. They suggest that measures of career maturity may be used to identify a student's readiness to make career decisions and to identify the knowledge and skills they need for realistic and informed decision-making. Being sensitive to students' readiness to make career decisions is important for designing exploratory activities to determine interests, aptitudes, work values and personality factors. Readiness is an especially important consideration for advising or counseling students who are undecided.

Other Characteristics

Many other factors associated with undecided students have been researched, either in conjunction with other variables or independently. Many early studies explored a plethora of characteristics that were thought to explain indecision or attempted to describe undecided students. Attitudes, values, and self-defeating behaviors are just a few that were explored. In addition to interest in undecided high school and first-year college students, other studies examined undecided upperclass and graduating seniors.

Nelson and Nelson (1940) find a relationship between social, moral, and religious attitudes and vocational choice. Students choosing certain occupations such as banking, dentistry, music, and government service prove more conservative than students who choose journalism, social work, law, and agriculture. Undecided students place near the middle of this distribution. Miller (1956) compares the choice of work values among students who are undecided and those who are tentatively or definitely decided. The "no-choice" group tends to emphasize security and prestige, while those who have formulated a choice place higher value on career satisfaction.

Hornak and Gillingham (1980) treat career indecision as self-defeating behavior. Students rationalize their lack of responsibility for not deciding by citing lack of concentration, labeling, blaming others, comparing and distorting feedback, and relying on external evidence or forces. Habitual use of these negative techniques, according to Hornak and Gillingham, reinforces indecisive behavior. A more positive approach is for the students to become involved in the decision-making process so that they may learn responsibility for their own behavior.

The role of depression and dysfunctional career thinking in career indecision was researched by Saunders, Peterson, Sampson, and Reardon (2000). As expected, they found vocational identity, state and trait anxiety, locus of control, depression and dysfunctional career thoughts all significantly associated with the state of career indecision and with each other. The researchers suggest that confused or disabling thought processes inhibit individuals from thinking through a career problem and render them unable to make a decision in a logical and systematic way. A strong vocational identity with the absence of dysfunctional career thoughts provides the foundation for a high state of career decidedness. Saunders et al. suggest that depression, like extreme anxiety, may lead to an inability to effectively consider educational and career options.

Lounsbury et al. (1999) investigated career decidedness in relation to personality constructs (using a Big Five personality measure) and life satisfaction. They found career decidedness is related to three core personality constructs, measured both in terms of general personality dispositions and work-based personality traits. Their finding that decidedness is negatively related to neuroticism was not surprising. The researchers suggest that college students who are having difficulty choosing a career and subsequent vocational path would be more likely to experience worry, distress, tension, anxiety and other personality factors. They pose an unanswered question: Does neuroticism cause career indecision, or vice-versa?

Lounsbury et. al, also found that career decidedness was related to conscientiousness which emphasizes such pro-social attributes as orderliness, self-discipline, deliberation, dependability and competence. Higher levels of career decidedness are also associated with higher levels of life satisfaction. They suggest that career planning and development interventions include a Big Five personality measure given to students prior to a career program or service to help inform and allow a more differentiated approach to be initiated.

Emotional Intelligence

The role of emotional intelligence in career decision-making is a recent area of interest. Some researchers assert that the emotional aspect of career decision-making plays an important role (Goleman, 1995; Kidd, 1998). Brown, George-Curran, and Smith (2003) found that the career activities of career decision-making self-efficacy and vocational exploration and commitment are both significantly related to aspects of emotional intelligence. That is, students who indicated higher ability to perceive, access, and generate emotions were more likely to report greater confidence in their career decision-making tasks. Conversely, students who were less attuned to understanding, analyzing and regulating emotions experience difficulty in committing because they were less aware of how to use their emotions to guide their thoughts and actions.

Emmerling and Cherniss (2003) used the *Mayer-Salovey-Caruso Emotional Intelligence Test* (MSCEIT) to measure risk, the kind and amount of self-exploration, and how information is processed. They concluded that individuals who have difficulty experiencing, perceiving, and identifying feelings have greatly diminished ability to use emotions to facilitate the career decision-making process. Advisors and counselors of undecided students might want to pay attention to the emotional interplay between judgments, feelings, and actions, since these play an important role in educational and career commitment and decision-making.

Most of the research cited above deals with students who are undecided before entering college or during their freshman year. Looking at another subgroup, Lunnelborg (1975) compares undecided college graduates three months after graduation with those who have chosen a vocation. The undecided graduates seem to be students who did not do as well in college, are less satisfied with their college experience, and were not as motivated by vocational goals while in college. No differences emerge between the decided and undecided graduates as to when they choose a major, or the amount of paid employment they experience prior to graduation. The undecided graduates are not motivated to seek out career-related activities for their future.

Another study involving graduating seniors is that completed by Elton and Rose (1970). Undecided students are identified as freshmen and followed up as they approach graduation. Three groups of graduating seniors are discussed: those who are undecided as freshmen, those whose senior choice changes from an earlier one, and those whose choice remains constant. No differences are found on personality or ability measures, and those who are undecided eventually make a choice consistent with their ability, according to the study.

Vocationally undecided graduating seniors were studied by Puchkoff and Lewin (1987) to determine their responsiveness to an offer of vocational assistance. They compared students who sought vocational counseling and those who did not. Both groups appeared to be experiencing anxiety in relation to their vocational future, but no significant differences were found between the groups on levels of expressed anxiety or locus of control. Although those taking part in the counseling viewed it relevant and helpful, the differences between the two groups were not significant.

The vast amount of research on undecided students during the 1970's and 1980's provides an impressive body of knowledge about them, as well as the related, complex factors involved in career development and career decision-making. Newer studies continue to illuminate who undecided individuals are, and why they are undecided. The characteristics of undecided students summarized above touch only a small part of this expansive literature. The early researchers contributed a wealth of knowledge that built a foundation on which continuing research efforts are continually being refined and expanded.

CAREER DECISION-MAKING INFLUENCES

Family Influences

Family factors have been viewed as antecedent influences on career choice (Holland, 1997; Roe, 1957). Lopez and Andrews (1987) believe that indecision can be conceptualized as the outcome of a larger set of transactions between the person and the family. They use a family systems perspective to explain indecision within the context of family interrelationships. They suggest that career decision-making can catalyze a transformation in family functioning. Indecision is indicative of inadequate parent-child separation and the family's failure to achieve an appropriate structural change. Parent-young adult overinvolvement and other dysfunctional family patterns may inhibit the individuation process and contribute to the student's indecisiveness (Lopez, 1983).

Other studies discuss the effects of family interaction on indecision (Kinnier, Brigman, & Noble, 1990; Schumrum & Hartman, 1988; Zingaro, 1983). While Eigen, Hartman, and Hartman (1987) found no evidence that career indecision is related to family interaction patterns, they do suggest that students may develop an ability to make career decisions in two different kinds of family systems: (1) early family interactions that foster stable decision-making and (2) those associated with developmentally delayed decision-making. The latter may come from too tight or too loose family patterns, and thus prevent individuation or lack of emotional attachment, which leads to premature separation without enough guidance to enable effective decision-making.

Pearson and Dellman-Jenkins (1997) examined parental influences on decisions about college major. They questioned whether a larger portion of first-generation college students would be undecided about a college major when compared with students whose parents who graduated from college. They explored the influence of family structure, gender of student, and parental encouragement on student's undecidedness about a major. The hypothesis that first-generation college students would be more undecided than students whose parents graduated from college was not supported. Students indicated that factors other than their parents also influenced their decision about a major. These included individual work experiences, academic course work, and personal experiences. "Teacher" was ranked over parents as the most influential source.

Gender was found by Pearson and Dellman-Jenkins to be the only variable that produced differences in college major decidedness. Significantly more females than males were decided about a major. Causes of this may be that the greater percentage of females was enrolled in education and nursing, both traditionally female dominated, while the greater percentage of males was enrolled in business, a more traditionally male dominated field. Significant group differences were also found with gender and mothers who graduated from college. Fewer women than men reported mothers who graduated from college. Pearson and Dellman-Jenkins suggest that the media, which was ranked third among influences, might be perpetuating career stereotypes and might affect the self-efficacy or a nonbelief that women can master certain tasks when considering an occupation.

The researchers also found that parents' encouragement can have an impact on students' decision to attend college. The majority of students who reported lack of parental encouragement indicated they had fathers or mothers who did not graduate from college. While most fathers encouraged their children to attend college, more than twice as many who did not live with their children offered no encouragement. Pearson and Dellman-Jenkins emphasize that it is important to study parental influences on students' success in college and the "internal workings" of the college major selection decision process.

Guerra and Braungart-Rieker (1999) found that students' views of their parental relationship are related to career decision-making. There was also support for ego-identity status being predictive of career decision-making. Career indecision was predicted by a greater degree of identity moratorium and diffusion. Commitment to a career choice is more likely for students who are seeking independence from their parents but are also securely attached to them. Students who perceived their mothers as being more encouraging of independence had less career indecision than those whose mothers were overprotective. Although students viewed their fathers as more encouraging of independence than their mothers, support by mothers may be more important, according to the researchers.

Guerra and Braungart-Rieker also found the existence of career indecision within various majors. Students in different majors had varying views of paternal acceptance. Students majoring in business or engineering reported more acceptance from their fathers while those in the humanities indicated their fathers were not accepting. These researchers suggest that advisors and counselors may want to focus on major choice and the subspecialties where greater indecision is found.

Schultheiss and Blustein (1994) tested family relationships in predicting ego-identity status. Earlier research had found that career development tasks evoke direct support from parents, who may be able to offer different kinds of support to their adolescents while they are exploring and developing career plans. In contrast, in this study they found that the broader, more encompassing, and often emotionally laden identity formation process evoked differential responses between adolescents and parents. They also found that parental attachment plays a considerably more important role in the identity formation process for women than it does for men.

The differences in parental involvement in their children's career decision-making between three countries was studied by Downing and D'Andrea (1994). English and American parents exhibited a strong bias in favor of university attendance and related careers. Those parents were negatively inclined toward their children pursuing working-class careers. Swiss parents were more inclined to leave these decisions to their children. The researchers found that in the United States the majority of children are given little systematic assistance in planning their education and career development.

English and American children's parents seem to reflect the uncertainty of opportunities and assistance available to their children. Downing and D'Andrea emphasize the need to help parents become informed of the opportunities and training plans for their children.

Erickson's construct of ego-identity status was used by Berrios-Allison (2005) to examine family influences on students' occupational identity. She used a family systems perspective to examine the attachment and separation-individuation process in traditional college students' identity and career development. A family system involves patterns of emotional connectedness and separation. She defines occupational identity status as "an identity outcome based on the amount of exploration and commitment that adolescents have experienced in relation to their occupational choices" (p. 235).

Berrios-Allison found that tolerance for connectedness and separateness explained variances in the Achievement, Foreclosure, Moratorium, and Diffusion of occupational identity status among students. Families that were connected or supportive encouraged occupational exploration and commitment. Students who were decided on a major were more likely to be Achieved, while students who were undecided tended to be less Achieved. Students from higher income families were more likely to achieve than those from lower income families. Latinos and Caucasians tended to achieve more compared to Asian, Native, and African Americans.

In Moratorium occupational identity status, Berrios-Allison found that open and problem communication with the mother figure was significant. Students who lived in residence halls were less likely to be in Moratorium. As expected, students in foreclosure had decided on a major prematurely and had not experienced the exploration process. Families that are controlling may cause their students to be dependent on them to make decisions.

Diffused students came from families that were more intrusive and controlling. Students who experienced an early separation from one of their parents were more likely to be Diffused. Berrios-Allison emphasizes that students struggling with occupational issues may benefit not only from career advising and counseling but from interventions that focus on the family dynamics that can affect the decision-making process.

In an unrelated but interesting study, Hill, Ferris, and Martinson (2003) examined the effect that newer work venues have on family life. They looked at how working traditional, virtual, and home offices influenced work and family life. The virtual office is described as having the flexibility to work whenever it makes sense to telecommunicate from home. The influence of the virtual office was mostly positive on work aspects but had a negative influence on family life. The influence of the home office appeared to be mostly positive while the influence of the traditional office was most negative on aspects of both work and personal/family life.

Advisors and counselors need to be aware of the influence that families, especially parents, have on the educational and career choices of their students. This is especially important for students who come from cultural backgrounds that involve close family ties and expectations.

Career Barriers

The concept of perceived career barriers is receiving renewed attention (Swanson, Daniels, & Tokar, 1996; Creed, Patton, & Bartrum, 2004). Early references to career barriers were made in connection with gender and ethnic discrimination, perceived lack of ability, and lack of educational opportunities (Crites, 1969; Farmer, 1976; Fitzgerald, Fassinger, & Betz, 1995; O'Leary, 1974). Recent studies have also looked at career-related barriers in ethnicity and gender. McWhirter (1997), for example, compared the differences in perceived education and career-related barriers between Mexican Americans and Euro-American high school students. Female participants anticipated more barriers than male students and Mexican Americans anticipated more barriers than Euro-American students.

Swanson, Daniels, and Tokar (1996) indicate that the type and number of barriers that students perceive can be a limiting factor in the career choice process. They conceptualize barriers as external conditions or internal states that make career progress difficult. They hold the view that barriers are not impenetrable but can be overcome. Examples of barriers on the *Career Barriers Inventory* (CBI) include: Sex Discrimination, Lack of Confidence, Multiple-Role Conflict, Racial Discrimination, Disapproval by Significant Others, Decision-Making Difficulties, and Disability/Health Concerns. Advisors and counselors may want to determine how students perceive barriers that might hinder their career progress and how to devise ways to overcome them.

Luzzo and McWhirter (2001) compared sex and ethnic differences in the perception of education and career-related barriers and levels of coping efficacy. The majority of students reported they were of European descent; Native and African Americans, Asian and Hispanic students were represented in smaller numbers. As expected, women perceived significantly greater career-related barriers than men. Women were more likely to perceive barriers of experiencing negative comments about their sex (e.g., insults or rude jokes), experiencing sex discrimination, and to have a harder time getting hired than men.

Ethnic minority students perceived significant greater education and career-related barriers than the European American students. The barriers they perceived were the expectation that they would experience negative comments about their ethnicity and discrimination. They also perceived more barriers associated with financial and childcare concerns. Ethnic minority students reported significant lower coping efficacy for perceived career-related barriers than Euro-American students. They also possess lower self-efficacy for coping with and managing those barriers.

Lindley (2005) examines barriers within the framework of social cognitive career theory (Lent, Brown, & Hackett, 2000). Students' perceptions of barriers are important because they may limit career choice even when all other factors are positive. Lindley uses Holland's theory of career choice because it spans the wide range of vocational interests and offers a vehicle for measuring self-efficacy within specific domains. An unexpected finding is the extent to which women perceived barriers as having an impact on their career-related outcome expectations. Lindley suggests the results may reflect a tendency to idealize outcomes that are unattainable.

Women who chose investigative or conventional careers perceived more barriers than women who chose social careers. Conventional and realistic self-efficacy emerged as a significant predictor of coping efficacy for men. Men have confidence for occupations in the realistic and conventional domains and have more confidence in their ability to overcome educational and career barriers. Lindley concluded that high self-efficacy and outcome expectations for career choice support aspects of Social Cognitive Career Theory constructs. She also concluded that more specific distinctions need to be made among the variables associated with career barriers.

Retention

The retention issue for undecided students has been of interest to researchers for almost thirty years (Beal & Noel, 1980; Foote, 1980; Daubman & Johnson, 1982; Titley & Titley, 1985). Most of these studies suggest that undecided students are attrition-prone. Lewallen (1993), however, found no significant differences in predictors of persistence between college students who were decided and undecided.

Habley and McClanahan (2004) state that in spite of many years of retention data, only 47% of campuses in their ACT retention survey established a goal for the retention of students from their first to second year. The programs with the greatest impact on retention that respondents to the ACT survey indicated were (1) freshman seminar courses for credit, (2) tutoring programs, and (3) academic advising interventions with selected student populations. Seventy-five percent of the respondents reported that "advising interventions with selected student populations" was a common practice and 12% reported that these advising interventions have the *greatest* impact on the retention of special students.

One of the most important student characteristics that contributed to attrition, according to the respondents to the ACT survey, is "lack of educational aspirations and goals" (p. 11). Eighty-three percent of the colleges responding indicated that career development workshops or courses were among the most common retention practices used.

Leppel (2001) suggests that college persistence may be related to choice of major. She explored two persistence effects related to major field of study: goal commitment and interest in subject matter. The undecided students in her study had low academic performance and low persistence rates. She suggests that these students need to receive immediate advising and counseling, since both interest in subject matter and committing to a goal involve choosing a field of study. Cuseo (2003) also emphasizes the importance of comprehensive academic support services for first year students. He advocates "front loading" as a way to ensure the greatest long-term impact on students (p. 300). Programming for first-year undecided students is especially important, since if not acknowledged and supported upon entry, many flounder and drift if no commitment to an academic direction is made within a reasonable amount of time.

Steele, Kennedy, and Gordon (1993) demonstrated the value of special advising for students who were in transition from one major to another. When provided with a comprehensive academic and career advising program to help them select an alternative major, those involved in the program exhibited higher retention and graduation rates than matched or randomly selected groups of major-changers who did not receive the special treatment.

Cuseo (2003) emphasizes that academic advisors are a critical influence in the retention of students. He lists five reasons why the advising connection has such a significant impact on retention: (1) student satisfaction with the college experience, (2) effective educational and career planning and decision-making, (3) student utilization of campus support services, (4) student-faculty contact outside the classroom, and (5) student mentoring (p. 1). All of these services and activities are especially important for the retention of undecided students. Training advisors to understand the characteristics of undecided students and how to approach students who are in different phases of academic and career decision-making is a critical aspect of advising programs designed for this student population.

Tinto (1997) found that integrating students intellectually and socially into the life of the institution are important determinants of retention. Programs for undecided students must encompass a wide array of advising, counseling, and services if they are to ensure that students are involved at every level of campus life.

SUMMARY

This chapter reviewed the extensive research on the origins of career indecision; some of the characteristics of undecided students (i.e., choice anxiety, career identity, career self-efficacy, career maturity), and career decision-making influences such as family and career barriers. Some of this research has been contradictory over the years. Some studies conclude that undecided students are no different than decided ones, while others demonstrate differences in personality traits and demographic variables. A helpful body of knowledge has been gleaned from concentrating on identifying multiple indecision types within the decided and undecided populations, and the manner in which decision-making skills mediate the influences that have import on the process at a given time.

One striking impression from this longitudinal review is the amount of research generated about undecided students from the 1950s through the 1980s. There has been a decline in indecision research, however, in the 1990s and into the new century. Kelly and Lee (2001) attribute this decline to "an inadequate description of the career indecision domain and . . . to the absence of theoretical postulates relating indecision to other career development constructs" (p. 303). Another problem is that few counseling interventions have been empirically studied. Future efforts, according to Kelly and Lee, should be directed toward a complete description of the domain of decision problems. Some theoretical frameworks dealing with many of the constructs discussed above will be reviewed in the next chapter.

REFERENCES

Achilles, P. (1935). Vocational motives in college career decisions among undergraduates. *Occupations, 13,* 624–628.

Appel, V., Haak, R., & Witzke, D. (1970). Factors associated with indecision about collegiate major and career choice. *Proceedings, American Psychological Association, 5,* 667–668.

Arce, E.M. (1995). The effects of social support and self esteem on career indecision: Cross cultural differences in a cluster analysis among two groups of undergraduate students. (Eric Document Service No. ED415355).

Arbona, C. (1996). Career theory and practice in a multicultural context. In M.L. Savickas & W.B. Walsh (Eds.), *Handbook of career counseling theory and practice,* (pp. 45–54). Palo Alto, CA: Davies-Black.

Ashby, J., Wall, H., & Osipow, S. (1966). Vocational uncertainty and indecision in college freshmen. *Personnel and Guidance Journal, 44,* 1037–1041.

Baird, L. (1967). *The undecided student–How different is he?* ACT Research Report No. 2. Iowa City: American College Testing Program.

Barak, A., & Friedkes, R. (1982). The mediating effects of career indecision subtypes on career-counseling effectiveness. *Journal of Vocational Behavior, 20,* 1–3.

Beal, P.E., & Noel, L. (1980). *What works in student retention.* Iowa City: American College Testing Program and National Center for Higher Education Management Systems.

Berrios-Allison, A.C. (2005). Family influences on college students' occupational identity. *Journal of Career Assessment, 13*(2), 233–247.

Betz, N.E. (1992). Counseling uses of career self-efficacy theory. *Career Development Quarterly, 41,* 22–26.

Betz, N.E., & Luzzo, D.A. (1996). Career assessment and the career decision-making self-efficacy scale. *Journal of Career Assessment, 4*(4), 413–428.

Blustein, D.L., & Phillips, S.D. (1990). Relation between ego-identity statuses and decision-making styles. *Journal of Counseling Psychology, 37,* 160–168.

Brisbin, L.A., & M.L. Savickas, M.L., (1994). Career indecision scales do not measure foreclosure. *Journal of Career Assessment, 2,* 352–363.

Brown, C., George-Curran, R., & Smith, M. (2003). The role of emotional intelligence in the career commitment and decision-making process. *Journal of Career Assessment, 11*(4), 379–392.

Cellini, J.V. (1978). *Locus of control as an organizing construct for vocational indecision and vocational differentiation.* Unpublished doctoral dissertation, The Ohio State University.

Chartrand, J.M., Martin, W., Robbins, S., McAuliffe, G., Pickering, J., & Calliotte, J. (1994). Testing a level versus an interactional view of career indecision. *Journal of Career Assessment, 2*(1), 55–69.

Cohen, C.R., Chartrand, J.M., & Jowdy, D.P. (1995). Relationships between career indecision subtypes and ego-identity development. *Journal of Counseling Psychology, 42*(4), 440–447.

Cooper, S.E., Fuqua, D.R., & Hartman, B.W. (1984). The relationship of trait indecisiveness to vocational uncertainty, career indecision, and interpersonal characteristics. *Journal of College Student Personnel, 25,* 353–356.

Creed, P.A., Patton, W., & Bartrum, D. (2004). Internal and external barriers, cognitive style, and the career development variables of focus and indecision. *Journal of Career Development, 30*(4), 277–294.

Crites, J.O. (1969). *Vocational psychology.* New York: McGraw Hill.

Crites, J.O. (1981). *Career counseling models, methods and materials.* New York: McGraw Hill.

Crites, J.O. (1996). Revision of the Career Maturity Inventory. *Journal of Career Assessment, 4,* 131–138.

Cunliffe, R.B. (1927). Whither away and why: Trends in the choice of vocation in Detroit. *Personnel Journal, 6,* 25–28.

Cuseo, J. (2003). Academic advisement and student retention: Empirical connections and systematic interventions. Retrieved April 6, 2006, http://www.brevard.edu/fyc/listserv/remarks/cuseorentation.htm

Daubman, K., & Johnson, D.H. (1982). *Comparisons among continuing, withdrawing and nonreturning students.* Academic Leave and Withdrawal Office Research Report, Student Affairs Research Report #7, University of Maryland. (ERIC Document Reproduction Service No. ED233628)

Downing, J., & D'Andrea, L.M. (1994). Parental involvement in children's career decision-making. *Journal of Employment Counseling, 31*(3), 115–126.

Eigen, C.A., Hartman, B.W., & Hartman, P.T. (1987). Relations between family interaction patterns and career indecision. *Psychological Reports 60,* 87–94.

Elton, C., & Rose, H. (1970). Male occupational constancy and change: Its prediction according to Holland's theory. *Journal of Counseling Psychology, 17,* 6.

Elton, C., & Rose, H. (1971). A longitudinal study of the vocationally undecided male student. *Journal of Vocational Behavior, 1,* 85.

Emmerling, R.J., & Cherniss, C. (2003). Emotional intelligence and the career choice process. *Journal of Assessment, 11*(2), 153–167.

Erikson, E. (1968). *Identity: Youth and crises.* New York: Norton.

Farmer, H.S. (1976). What inhibits achievement and career motivation in women? *Counseling Psychology, 6,* 12–14.

Fassinger, R.E., & O'Brien, K.M. (2000). Career counseling with college women: A scientist-practitioner-advocate model of intervention. In D.A. Luzzo (Ed.), *Career counseling of college students,* (pp. 253–265). Washington, D.C.: American Psychological Association.

Feldman, D.C. (2003). The antecedents and consequences of early career indecision among young adults. *Human Resource Management Review, 13,* 499–531.

Fitzgerald, L.F., Fassinger, R.E., & Betz, N.E. (1995). Theoretical advances in the study of women's career development. In W.B. Walsh & S.H. Osipow (Eds.), *Handbook of vocational psychology: Theory, research and practice* (2nd Ed.), (pp. 67–109). Mahway, NJ: Lawrence Erlbaum.

Foote, B. (1980). Determined and undetermined major students: How different are they? *Journal of College Student Personnel, 20,* 29–34.

Fuqua, D.R., Blum, C.R., & Hartman, B.W. (1988). Empirical support for the differential diagnosis of career indecision. *Journal of Counseling Psychology, 36,* 364–373.

Fuqua, D.R., Newman, J.L., & Seaworth, T.B. (1988). Relation of state and trait anxiety to different components of career indecision. *Journal of Counseling Psychology, 35,* 154–158.

Fuqua, D.R., Seaworth, T.B., & Newman, J.L. (1987). The relationship of career indecision and anxiety: A multivariate examination. *Journal of Vocational Behavior, 30,* 175–186.

Germeijs, V., & De Boeck, P. (2002). A measurement scale for indecisiveness and its relationship to career indecision and other types of indecision. *European Journal of Psychological Assessment, 18*(2), 113–122.

Germeijs, V., & De Boeck, P. (2003). Career indecision: Three factors from decision theory. *Journal of Vocational Behavior, 62*(1), 11–25.

Gianakos, I. (1999). Patterns of career choice and career decision-making efficacy. *Journal of Vocational Behavior, 54,* 244–258.

Gianakos, I., & Subich, L.M. (1986). The relationship of gender and sex-role orientation to vocational undecidedness. *Journal of Vocational Behavior, 29,* 42–50.

Gianakos, I., & Subich, L.M. (1988). Student sex and sex role in relation to college major choice. *Career Development Quarterly, 36,* 259–268.

Ginzberg, E., Ginsburg, S.W., Axelrod, S., & Herma, I.L. (1951). *Occupational choice.* New York: Columbia University Press.

Goleman, D. (1995). *Emotional intelligence.* New York: Bantam Books.

Goodstein, L. (1965). Behavior theoretical views of counseling. In B. Steffre (Ed.), *Theories of counseling.* New York: McGraw Hill, pp. 140–192).

Gordon, V.N. (1998). Career decidedness types: A literature review. *Career Development Quarterly, 46*(4), 386–403.

Gordon, V.N., & Kline, D. (1989). Ego-identity statuses of undecided and decided students and their perceived advising needs. *NACADA Journal, 9,* 5–15.

Gordon, V.N., & Steele, G.E. (2003). Undecided first-year students: A 25-year longitudinal study. *Journal of the First-Year Experience, 15*(1), 19–38.

Graef, M.I., Wells, D.L., Hyland, A.M., & Muchinsky, P.M. (1985). Life history antecedents of vocational indecision. *Journal of Vocational Behavior, 27,* 276–297.

Gribbons, W.D., & Lohnes, P.R. (1964). Relationships among measures of readiness for vocational planning. *Journal of Counseling Psychology, 11,* 13–15.

Guay, F., Ratelle, C., Senecal, C., Larose, S., & Deschenes, A. (2006). Distinguishing developmental from chronic career indecision: Self-efficacy, autonomy, and social support. *Journal of Career Assessment, 14*(2), 235–251.

Guay, F., Senecal, C., Gauthier, L., & Fernet, C. (2003). Predicting career indecision: A self-determination theory perspective. *Journal of Counseling Psychology, 50*(2), 165–177.

Guerra, A.L., & Braungart-Rieker, J. (1999). Predicting career indecision in college students: The roles of identity formation and parental relationship factors. *Career Development Quarterly, 47*(3), 255–266.

Haag-Mutter, P. (1986). *Career indecision.* (ERIC Document Reproduction Service No. ED 286143).

Habley, W., & McClanahan, R. (2004). *What works in student retention?* Iowa City, IA: ACT, Inc.

Haraburda, E.M. (1998). *The relationship of indecisiveness to the five factor personality model and psychological symptomology.* Unpublished Doctoral dissertation. Columbus, OH: Ohio State University.

Harren, V.A., Kass, R., Tinsley, H., & Moreland, J.R. (1978). Influence of sex-role attitudes and cognitive styles on career decision making. *Journal of Counseling Psychology, 25,* 390–398.

Hartman, B.W. & Fuqua, D.R. (1983). Career indecision from a multidimensional perspective: A reply to Grites. *The School Counselor, 30,* 340–349.

Hartman, B.W., Fuqua, D.R., & Blum, C.R. (1985). A pathanalytic model of career indecision. *Vocational Guidance Quarterly, 33,* 231–240.

Hawkins, J.G., Bradley, R.W., & White, G.W. (1977). Anxiety and the process of deciding about a major and vocation. *Journal of Counseling Psychology, 24,* 398–403.

Heppner, M.J., & Hendricks, F. (1995). A process and outcome study examining career indecision and indecisiveness. *Journal of Counseling & Development, 73,* 426–437.

Hill, E.J., Ferris, M., & Martinson, V. (2003). Does it matter where you work? A comparison of how three work venues (traditional office, virtual office, and home office) influence aspects of work and person/family life. *Journal of Vocational Behavior, 63*(2), 220–241.

Holland, J.L. (1997). *Making vocational choices–A theory of vocational personalities and work environments* (3rd Ed.). Odessa, FL: Psychological Assessment Resources.

Holland, J.L., & Nichols, R. (1964). The development and validation of an indecision scale: The natural history of a problem in basic research. *Journal of Counseling Psychology, 11,* 27–34.

Holland, J.L., & Nichols, R. (1973). Vocational guidance for everyone. *Educational Researcher, 3,* 9–15.

Holland, J.L., & Holland, J.E. (1977). Vocational indecision: More evidence and speculation. *Journal of Counseling Psychology, 24,* 404–414.

Holland, J.L., Daiger, D., & Power, P. (1980). Some diagnostic scales for research in decision-making and personality: Identity, information and barriers. *Journal of Personality and Social Psychology, 39,* 1191–1200.

Hornak, J., & Gillingham, B. (1980). Career indecision: A self-defeating behavior. *Personnel and Guidance Journal, 59,* 252–253.

Jones, L., & Chenery, M.F. (1980). Multiple subtypes among vocational undecided college students. A model and assessment instrument. *Journal of Counseling Psychology, 27,* 469–477.

Kaplan, D.M., & Brown, D. (1987). The role of anxiety in career indecisiveness. *Career Development Quarterly, 36,* 148–162.

Kazin, R.I. (1977). *The relationship between types of indecision and interest test patterns.* Unpublished doctoral dissertation, The Ohio State University.

Kelly, K.R., & Lee, W. (2002). Mapping the domain of career decision problems. *Journal of Vocational Behavior, 61*(2), 302–326.

Kelly, K.R., & Pulver, C.S. (2003). Refining measurement of career indecision types: A validity study. *Journal of Counseling & Development, 81*(4), 445–455.

Kidd, J.M. (1998). Emotion: an absent presence in career theory. *Journal of Vocational Behavior, 52*(3), 275–288.

Kilzer, L. (1935). Vocational choices of high school seniors. *Educational Administration and Supervisors, 21,* 576–581.

Kimes, H., & Troth, W. (1974). Relationship of trait anxiety to career decisiveness. *Journal of Counseling Psychology, 21,* 277–280.

Kinnier, R.T., Brigman, S., and Noble, F. (1990). Career indecision and family enmeshment. *Journal of Counseling and Development, 68,* 309–312.

Kohn, N. (1947). Trends and development of the vocational and other interests of veterans at Washington University. *Educational and Psychological Measurement, 7,* 631–637.

Lancaster, P., Rudolph, C., Perkins, S, & Patten, T. (1999). Difficulties in career decision making: A study of the reliability and validity of the career decision difficulties questionnaire. *Journal of Career Assessment, 7,* 393–413.

Larson, L.M. & Heppner, P.P. (1985). The relationship of problem-solving appraisal to career decision and indecision. *Journal of Vocational Behavior, 26,* 55–65.

Larson, L.M., & Majors, M.S. (1998). Applications of the coping with career indecision instrument with adolescents. *Journal of Career Assessment, 6*(2), 163–179.

Larson, L.M., Heppner, P.P., Ham, T., & Dugan, K. (1988). Investigating multiple subtypes of career indecision through cluster analysis. *Journal of Counseling Psychology, 35,* 439–446.

Lent, R., Brown, S., & Hackett, G. (2000). Contextual supports and barriers to career choice: A social cognitive analysis. *Journal of Counseling Psychology, 47,* 36–49.

Leong, T.L., & Chervinko, S. (1996). Construct validity of career indecision: Negative personality traits as predictors of career indecision. *Journal of Career Assessment, 4*(3), 315–329.

Leppel, K. (2001). The impact of major on college persistence among freshmen. *Higher Education, 41,* 327–342.

Levinson, E., Ohier, D., Caswell, S., & Kiewra, K. (1998). Six approaches to the assessment of career maturity. *Journal of Counseling & Development, 76*(4), 475–483.

Lewallen, W.C. (1993). The impact of being "undecided" on college-student persistence. *Journal of College Student Development, 34,* 103–112.

Lindley, L.D. (2005). Perceive barriers to career development in the context of social cognitive career theory. *Journal of Career Assessment, 13*(3), 271–287.

LoCascio, R. (1964). Delayed and impaired vocational development: A neglected aspect of vocational development theory. *Personnel and Guidance Journal, 42,* 885–887.

Lopez, F.G. (1983). A paradoxical approach to vocational indecision. *Personnel and Guidance Journal, 61,* 410–412.

Lopez, F.G., & Andrews, S. (1987). Career indecision: A family systems perspective. *Journal of Counseling and Development, 65,* 304–307.

Lounsbury, J., Tatum, H., Chambers, W., Owens, K., & Gibson, L. (1999). An investigation of career decidedness in relation to "Big Five" personality constructs and life satisfaction. *College Student Journal, 33*(4), 646–652.

Lucas, M.S. (1993). A validation of types of career indecision at a counseling center. *Journal of*

Counseling Psychology, 40(4), 440–446.
Lucas, M.S., & Epperson, D.L. (1988). Personality types in vocationally undecided students. *Journal of College Student Development, 29,* 460–466.
Lucas, M.S., & Epperson, D.L. (1990). Types of vocational undecidedness: A replication and refinement. *Journal of Counseling Psychology, 37,* 382–388.
Lunneborg, P. (1975). Interest differentiation in high school and vocational indecision in college. *Journal of Vocational Behavior, 7,* 299–303.
Luzzo, D.A., & McWhirter, E.H. (2001). Sex and ethnic differences in the perception of educational and career-related barriers and levels of coping efficacy. *Journal of Counseling & Development, 79*(1), 61–67.
Marcia, J.E. (1966). Development and validation of ego identity status. *Journal of Personality & Social Psychology, 3,* 551–558.
Martin, F., Sabourin, S., Laplante, B., & Coallier, J.C. (1991). Diffusion, support, approach, and external barriers as distinct theoretical dimensions of the Career Decision Scale: Disconfirming evidence. *Journal of Vocational Behavior, 38,* 187–197.
Mau, W. (1999). Cultural differences in career decision-making styles and self-efficacy. *Journal of Vocational Behavior, 57,* 365–378.
McWhirter, E.H. (1997). Perceived barriers to education and career: Ethnic and gender differences. *Journal of Vocational Behavior, 50*(1), 124–140.
Miller, C.H. (1956). Occupational choice and values. *Personnel and Guidance Journal, 35,* 244–246.
Multon, K., Heppner, M.J., & Lapan, R. (1995). An empirical derivation of career decision subtypes in a high school sample. *Journal of Vocational Behavior, 47,* 76–92.
Naidoo, A.V. (1998). *Career maturity: A review of four decades of research.* (ERIC Document Service ED419145)
Nelson, E., & Nelson, N. (1940). Student attitudes and vocational choices. *Journal of Abnormal and Social Psychology, 35,* 279–282.
Newman, J., Fuqua, R., & Minger, C. (1990). Further evidence for the use of career subtypes in defining career status. *Career Development Quarterly, 39,* 178–188.
Newman, J., Gray, E., & Fuqua, R. (1999). The relation of career indecision to personality Dimensions of the California Psychological Inventory. *Journal of Vocational Behavior, 54,* 174–187.
O'Hare, M.M., & Tamburri, E. (1986). Coping as a moderator of the relation between anxiety and career decision-making. *Journal of Counseling Psychology, 33*(3), 255–264.
O'Leary, N.E. (1974). Some attitudinal barriers to education and career: Ethnic and gender differences. *Journal of Vocational Behavior, 50,* 124–140.
Orlofsky, J.L. (1978). Identity formation, achievement, and fear of success in college men and women. *Journal of Youth and Adolescence, 7,* 49–62.
Osipow, S.H. (1983). *Theories of Career Development* (3rd Ed.). Englewood Cliffs, NJ: Prentice Hall.
Osipow, S.H. (1994). The career decision scale: How good does it have to be? *Journal of Career Assessment, 2,* 15–18.
Osipow, S.H. (1999). Assessing career indecision. *Journal of Vocational Behavior, 55,* 147–154.
Osipow, S.H., & Gati, I. (1998). Construct and concurrent validity of the career decision-making difficulties questionnaire. *Journal of Career Assessment, 6*(3), 347–364.
Osipow, S.H., & Reed, R. (1985). Decision-making style and career indecision in college students. *Journal of Vocational Behavior, 27,* 368–373.
Osipow, S.H., Carney, C., Winer, J., Yanico, B., & Koschier, M. (1976). *Career Decision Scale* (3rd revision). Columbus, OH: Marathon Consulting and Press.

Pearson, C., & Dellman-Jenkins, M. (1997). Parental influence on a student's selection of a college major. *College Student Journal, 31*(3), 301–314.

Powell, D.F., & Luzzo, D.A. (1998). Evaluating factors associated with the career maturity of high school students. *Career Development Quarterly, 47,* 145–159.

Puchkoff, S.C., & Lewin, P.G. (1987). Student responsiveness to specialized college services: Contribution of personality variables and perceptions of services. *Journal of Counseling Psychology, 34,* 330–332.

Roe, A. (1957). Early determinants of vocational choice. *Journal of Counseling Psychology, 4,* 212–217.

Rose, H.A., & Elton, C.F. (1971). Attrition and the vocationally undecided student. *Journal of Vocational Behavior, 1,* 99–103.

Rojewski, J.W. (1994). Career indecision types for rural adolescents from disadvantaged and nondisadvantaged backgrounds. *Journal of Counseling Psychology, 41*(3), 356–363.

Salomone, P.R. (1982). Difficult cases in career counseling: II The indecisive client. *Personnel and Guidance Journal, 60,* 496–500.

Saunders, D., Peterson, G., Sampson, J.P., Jr., & Reardon, R. (2000). Relation of depression and dysfunctional career thinking to career indecision. *Journal of Vocational Behavior, 56,* 288–298.

Savickas, M.L. (1984). Measuring career maturity: The construct and its measurement. *Vocational Guidance Quarterly, 32,* 222–231.

Savickas, M.L. (1985). Identity in vocational development. *Journal of Vocational Behavior, 27,* 329–337.

Savickas, M.L. (1989). Annual review: Practice and research in career counseling and development, 1988. *Career Development Quarterly,* 100–134.

Savickas, M.L., & Jarjoura, D. (1991). The career decision scale as a type indicator. *Journal of Counseling Psychology, 38*(1), 85–90.

Schumrum, T., & Hartman, B.W. (1988). Adult children of alcoholics and chronic career indecision. *Career Development Quarterly, 37,* 118–126.

Schultheiss, D.P., & Blustein, D.L. (1994). Contributions of family relationship factors to the identity formation process. *Journal of Counseling & Development, 73,* 159–166.

Serling, D.A., & Betz, N.E. (1990). Development and evaluation of a measure of fear of commitment. *Journal of Counseling Psychology, 37,* 91–97.

Sharf, R.S. (1997). *Applying career development theory to counseling* (2nd Ed.). Pacific Grove, CA: Brooks/Cole.

Shimizu, K., Vondracek, F.W., & Schulenberg, J. (1994). Unidimensionality versus multidimensionality of the Career Decision Scale. *Journal of Career Assessment, 2,* 1–14.

Slaney, R., Stafford, M., & Russell, J. (1981). Career indecision in adult women: A comparative and descriptive study. *Journal of Vocational Behavior, 19,* 335–345.

Steele, G., Kennedy, G., & Gordon, V. (1993). The retention of major changers: A longitudinal study. *Journal of College Student Development, 34,* 58–62.

Super, D.E. (1957). *The psychology of careers.* New York: Harper & Row.

Super, D.E. (1983). Assessment in career guidance: Toward truly developmental counseling. *Personnel & Guidance Journal, 61,* 555–562.

Super, D.E., & Bohn, M.J. (1970). *Occupational psychology.* Belmont, CA: Wadsworth.

Swanson, J.L., Daniels, K.K., & Tokar, D.M. (1996). Assessing perceptions of career-related barriers: The career barriers inventory. *Journal of Career Assessment, 4*(2), 219–244.

Taylor, K.M., & Betz, N.E. (1983). Applications of self-efficacy theory to the understanding and treatment of career indecision. *Journal of Vocational Behavior, 22,* 63–81.

Taylor, K.M., & Popma, J. (1990). An examination of the relationships among career decision-making self-efficacy, career salience, locus of control, and vocational indecision. *Journal of Vocational Behavior, 37,* 17–31.

Tinto, V. (1997). Classrooms as communities: Exploring the educational character of student persistence. *Journal of Higher Education, 68,* 6, 599–622.

Titley, R.M., & Titley, B.S. (1985). Initial choice of college major and attrition: the "decided" and "undecided" after 6 years. *Journal of College Student Personnel, 26,* 465–466.

Tyler, L. (1953). *The works of the counselor.* New York: Appleton-Century-Crofts.

Van Matre, G., & Cooper, S. (1984). Concurrent evaluation of career indecision and indecisiveness. *Personnel and Guidance Journal, 62,* 637–639.

Vondracek, F., Hostetler, M. Schulenburg, J.E., & Shimizu, K. (1990). Dimensions of career indecision. *Journal of Counseling Psychology, 37,* 98–106.

Vondracek, F., Schulenberg, J., Skorikov, V., Gillespie, L., & Wahlheim, C. (1995). The relationship of identity status to career indecision during adolescence. *Journal of Adolescence, 18,* 17–29.

Wanberg, C.R., & Muchinsky, P.M. (1992). A typology of career decision status: Validity extension of the vocational decision status model. *Journal of Counseling Psychology, 39*(1), 71–80.

Williamson, E.G. (1939). *How to counsel students.* New York: McGraw Hill.

Winer, J.L. (1992). The early history of the Career Decision Scale. *Career Development Quarterly, 40,* 369–375.

Zingaro, J.C. (1983). A family systems approach for the career counselor. *Personnel and Guidance Journal,* 62, 24–27.

Zytowski, D.G. (1965). Avoidance behavior in vocational motivation. *Personnel and Guidance Journal, 43,* 746–750.

Chapter 2

THEORETICAL FRAMEWORKS RELEVANT TO UNDECIDED STUDENTS

In addition to research studies, many theoretical concepts can enlighten our understanding of undecided college students. As Schunk (2000) indicates, "Theories provide frameworks for interpreting environmental observations and serve as bridges between research and education" (p. 3). The wide array of theoretical frameworks available from many disciplines (e.g., psychology, sociology, business) offers a feast of ideas and concepts that can enhance our understanding of the characteristics of undecided students, as well as how their needs are different from many "decided" ones.

As Creamer (2000) reminds us, "given the scope of the academic advising phenomenon, advisors may be required to understand many theories–not only one or two–in order to grasp sufficient knowledge to be useful in advising students" (p. 18). The insights these theoretical constructs provide can be applied in many practical approaches to help undecided students through their transition to decidedness.

This chapter will consider how different theoretical orientations can not only help us understand how undecided students engage in the academic and career decision-making process, but how other social, cultural, and psychological factors influence how they think, learn, and make decisions. The sample theoretical frameworks offered here include developmental theory, career choice theory, and learning theory.

A DEVELOPMENTAL APPROACH

Although vocational psychologists have considered indecision a problem in the past, the developmental approach acknowledges the differing characteristics, needs, and rate of maturation unique to each student. If entering college students are thought of as developing, maturing adults with specific psychosocial and cognitive tasks to accomplish, the programs and services offered to undecided students take on specific content, sequence, and timing. From this perspective, many so-called "vocational problems" emerge as normal developmental tasks that are resolved at varying times and rates among students during the college years.

The developmental approach views undecided students *not* as persons searching for an academic or career niche but as individuals continually engaged in a series of developmental tasks that ultimately enable them to adapt and change in a pluralistic world. Thus the scope, variety, and timing of program elements and services for undecided student must incorporate both student and career development concepts and principles (Gordon, 1981; Laff, 1994; McCalla-Wriggins, 2000). Some of these tenets and how they relate to undecided students follow:

1. **All human beings develop through a life cycle that has continuity and form.**

Historical as well as recent research in this area provides an increased awareness and respect for the continuous psychological, social, and physical development of individuals of all ages (Buehler, 1962; Erikson, 1968; Havighurst, 1972).

Implications for Undecided Students–Since individuals develop at their own unique pace and level, undecided students cannot be easily grouped as a whole, or have sweeping generalizations made about them. While past research has identified characteristics they seemingly have in common, some of the evidence may be questioned on the basis of limited samples, uncontrolled external variables, and the inconsistencies of the populations being examined. However, a few generalizations about the stages and tasks that undecided students confront are possible. This means that the services offered should be based on the students' needs and not institutional requirements or traditional methods for doing things.

2. Development is stage and task related.

Super et al. (1963) describe life/career development stages and the developmental tasks associated with each stage. Chickering and Reisser (1993) describe seven psychosocial tasks or vectors that students need to resolve during the college years.They consider these tasks sequential and cumulative. Perry (1999) views the cognitive and moral development of college students in stages; they move from a closed, dualistic perspective to a more open, relativistic one.

Implications for Undecided Students–Thinking of development as stage and task related is particularly relevant to understanding undecided students. The issue of career maturity, including a readiness to commit to an academic or career choice, is crucial to understanding this population. Many undecided students (and indeed many decided ones) are not ready developmentally to make important career and life decisions at eighteen years of age. According to Chickering, students at this age are more concerned with developing physical and social competencies, establishing interpersonal relationships, and finding emotional independence. Career choice implies that issues of identity have been resolved and that a sense of purpose and integrity has been developed to a certain level. Identifying and personalizing values are integral parts of career selection and satisfaction. Perry (1999) describes many freshmen as dualistic, unable to analyze cognitively and synthesize the personal and occupational information necessary to career decision-making. Yet, freshmen are expected to commit themselves to a career field with superficial information and limited experience in the real work world.

3. Certain developmental tasks are more dominant at certain stages in the life cycle than others.

College students must accomplish certain tasks if they are to be well adjusted in later life. Learning the career choice *process,* for example, is more important for a freshman than making the choice of major or career itself. Confronting identity issues in college is better than trying to resolve problems of social competency and autonomy in midlife.

Implications for Undecided Students–Traditional-aged college students deal with developmental tasks unique to the eighteen- to twenty-three-year-old. According to Chickering, a few of these tasks are establishing independence, developing intellectual competence, learning to manage their body more effectively, learning to manage emotions relating to sex and aggression, and becoming more self-directed and interdependent. College personnel working with older adult students recognize in these students other developmental issues, as well as a reexamination of some of the old ones. Adults returning to college are often searching for new meaning in their lives, prioritizing their values in new and different ways, or looking for new career challenges. Career development tasks are often age related. An undecided student at eighteen is approaching the career decision-making process from a very different perspective than an undecided homemaker returning to college after a twenty-year hiatus.

4. Developmental tasks progress from the simple to the increasing complex.

Chickering identifies cycles of differentiation and integration of developmental tasks. As students assimilate new knowledge and learn new behaviors, they must integrate them with existing knowledge and patterns, so that they may function successfully at more complex and appropriate levels of thought and behavior.

Baxter-Magolda's (1992, 2001) research indicates that students' ways of knowing and reasoning move from being an "absolute knower" who depends more on authorities' views to a "transitional knower" who is capable of a more complex way of thinking. This is especially important when gathering and interpreting information. Transitional or independent thinkers are able to collect and interpret more complex amounts of academic and career information than the absolute or dualistic thinker. Baxter-Magolda also theorizes that college students need to develop "self-authorship," that is, composing one's own reality in the reality of others. Self-authorship "requires complexity in defining one's belief system, a coherent identity, and mutual relations" (Baxter-Magolda & King, 2004, p. xxii).

Implications for Undecided Students–The programs and services offered undecided students must reflect many levels of ability to differentiate and integrate aspects of the decision-making process. When students are gathering information, for example, the advisor often makes assumptions about their research and interviewing skills. Before sending students out to collect information about major alternatives, the advisor must make sure they have the ability to accomplish such a task. An "absolute knower," for example, may be searching for the "right" major and be unable to compare and contrast a variety of academic fields. This may lead to discouragement and frustration. The advisor must be sensitive to the level of complexity that particular students are able to tolerate, to recognize where they are in the process, and begin the intervention at that level (Baxter-Magolda, 1992).

5. Many developmental tasks are interrelated and are dealt with simultaneously.

When students enter college they are concerned with being accepted by a new peer group, coping with new academic demands, and with pressures related to educational decisions. Developing social competence and succeeding academically have great impact on the career options that are open and realistic for a given student. Personal, social, and career concerns are interrelated at different times during the college years. The levels of intensity concerning these issues vary as well.

Newer research on Chickering and Reisser's vectors suggests that there is a need to reconsider their sequential nature (Foubert et al., 2005). Rather than conceptualize them as building blocks or steps, Foubert et al. found a horizontal movement, triggered by environmental factors.

Implications for Undecided Students–Some undecided students feel pressured to make a choice of major when they arrive on campus. They are so occupied with other adjustment concerns and personal or academic issues, however, that major exploration often becomes a lower priority. Some students drift during their freshman year and do not explore majors in an orderly way because they are so preoccupied with the other tasks at hand. A developmental program geared to the undecided student should acknowledge their involvement with other tasks and help them integrate these tasks into major and career exploration.

A developmental advising program recognizes that an environment must be created both to challenge and to support students as they risk each forward movement in their personal, academic, and vocational development (Perry, 1999; Baxter-Magolda, 1992; Knefelkamp, Widick, & Parker, 1978). Environmental management is increasingly recognized as an essential vehicle that ensures that conditions and resources are available to help students grow outside the classroom as well as in it (Baxter-Magolda & King, 2004; Crookston, 1972).

Creating special programs for undecided students is essential if their developmental needs are to be served. The developmental tasks in which students are deeply involved in academic and career decision-making are achieving a personal identity, developing a purpose or direction for their life, and learning to identify and personalize their values into a lifestyle. Although career decisions are made throughout a lifetime, the patterns established during the college years have great impact on how future decisions are approached and resolved.

CAREER DECISION THEORY

The relationship between vocational psychology and decision-making theory has a long and varied past. Many years ago, one of the prevailing thoughts was that people make decisions that fit their ideas of (1) what they are like, (2) what they can be like, (3) what they want to be like, (4) what their situation is like, (5) what their situation might become, and (6) the way they see these aspects of self and situation as being related. Choice is therefore guided by individuals' self-concept and the context of their decision situation.

Also, in 1963, David Tiedeman and R. O'Hara describe the decision-making process as comprising a series of tasks that need to be resolved. When people experience discomfort or discontinuities, they initiate purposeful action in the form of decision-making behavior. Tiedeman and O'Hara divide the decision-making process into two phases–planning and action. Students attempting to choose a major or occupation, for example, move through a series of tasks associated with the planning stage. The four planning stages are particularly relevant to understanding the undecided student.

Exploration Stage

Students at this stage have a vague anxiety about the future. Often they are not aware that there is an orderly process for exploration and choice; thus, they do not have a plan of action. At this point they have no negative choices. Undecided students in the exploration stage need help identifying their strengths and interests and how these relate to academic programs. They need to be made aware that a process for exploration does exist before they can move on to the crystallization stage.

Crystallization Stage

At this stage, students are progressing toward a choice and are beginning to identify some alternatives. They are now able to weigh the advantages and disadvantages of certain alternatives. They may even have made a tentative choice. They are able to recognize earlier decisions as inappropriate. These students are making normal progress through the planning phase.

Many undecided students are in the crystallization stage. It is important at this point to provide support while they are testing each alternative. Information resources and opportunities to experience certain academic courses or work environments are crucial at this stage. Firsthand experiences help students crystallize or focus on the elements involved in specific alternative choices.

Choice Stage

Students at the choice stage have made a definite commitment to a particular goal. They feel satisfied with and relieved about their decision. If their choice appears to be realistic, they move on to the clarification stage. If, however, they have not made a choice based on relevant information about the area or their abilities to perform in it, they may find the choice is not viable. Many students enter college at the choice stage without having negotiated the first two stages. Tiedeman and O'Hara view these stages as progressive, but they may also be regressive. Many individuals recycle through these stages at different points in their lives when different career choices need to be resolved.

Clarification Stage

The last stage in the planning cycle is clarification, in which the consequences of choice are internalized. Since a definite commitment has been made, a plan of action can be initiated and implemented. The advisor's obligation to undecided students is to support them through the clarification stage.

The action stages of induction, reformation, and integration occur as the choice is successfully synthesized with the student's image and the decision is integrated into his or her life.

Vincent Harren (1979) provides a career decision-making model based on Tiedeman and O'Hara's assumptions. He identifies four interrelated parameters that specify how the characteristics of the decision-maker, the type of decision, and the milieu in which the decision is made are integrated into the process itself.

Harren postulates a four-stage sequential process for decision-making. He begins with an awareness stage, in which individuals become attentive to their situation. If dissatisfaction results, they move into the planning stage. This incorporates the exploration and crystallization stages of Tiedeman and O'Hara's paradigm. Here information is gathered, and alternatives are identified and narrowed. When a specific alternative is settled upon, a transition is made into the commitment stage, in which the decision is integrated into the individual's self-concept system. If the fit is confirmed, there is a transition into the final or implementation stage. At this time, the decision is assimilated into the new context, unless the individual's needs and values change or external factors affect the decision adversely. If that happens, the individual turns away from implementation and recycles through the process so that other alternatives may be identified and explored.

Harren also incorporates student development concepts into his model. Within the career decision-making process, certain developmental tasks must be resolved. These include autonomy, interpersonal maturity, and development of a sense of purpose. This explains why undecided persons vary in their level of ability to perform the decision-making tasks. The timing of the decision and the maturity of the individual affect his or her readiness and ability to accomplish specific tasks.

Harren's model not only provides an explanation of the progression that students experience in making decisions but also offers a rationale for providing specific advising and career-counseling activities at specific periods in the process of exploration and choosing a major.

Levels of Indecision

Another practical application of Tiedeman and O'Hara's concept is understanding the various levels of indecision among individual undecided students. Advising approaches for students who are tentatively decided, for example, can be very different from those for the totally undecided. When undecided students are placed within Tiedeman and O'Hara's planning stages, certain antecedents of indecision may be apparent, and possible advising interventions may be suggested. Students who are completely undecided may be in Tiedeman and O'Hara's exploration stage, in which seemingly no progress is being made. This level is similar to Harren's awareness stage, in which students begin to realize that they need to pay some attention to their situation.

Students who have identified two or more alternatives are making progress and need to gather and organize information about each option. These tentatively decided students are ready to explore and crystallize their alternatives, according to Tiedeman and O'Hara.

Tiedeman and O'Hara's choice stage implies that a decision has been reached, but if the students still has doubts, a real commitment is not made. Students who verbalize their indecision but have internally made a choice often need to reality-test the idea before publically committing to it. While this is a small group, advising approaches to them can be very different. Figure 3 outlines these levels of indecision, and possible causes and interventions for each level are suggested.

When all doubts are satisfied, the students move on to the clarification stage. Here they need help formalizing an action plan so that they may actually perform in the major or career field they have chosen. Harren calls this the implementation stage.

While these stages or levels are theoretical, they facilitate understanding of an orderly progression of becoming decided. There are many levels and types of approaches that may be initiated with a particular student. Some students are ready for information gathering, while others are ready to process the information they already have. Some are developmentally ready to move on to the next set of tasks, while others are not. This is why an individual advising approach to undecided students needs to be in tune with the particular student's stage of readiness and development.

Gati (1996) describes the following features of career decision-making:

> (a) there is an individual who has to make a decision, (b) there are a number of alternatives to select from, and (c) the decision-maker has certain aspects or criteria that can be used to compare and evaluate the various alternatives in order to locate the most preferred one. (p. 170)

He further states that there are other unique features of career decision-making, that is, the number of potential alternatives, the vast amount of information available, and the large number of criteria and attributes that are required to adequately characterize occupations and the individual's preferences. He indicates that

Figure 3.
LEVELS, ANTECEDENTS, AND INTERVENTIONS FOR INDECISION*

Levels of Indecision	*Possible Causes or Antecedents*	*Possible Approaches or Interventions*
COMPLETELY UNDECIDED (considering no choice)	Search for one "right" choice Lack of value identity Failure to identify or use known interest patterns Uncertainty about abilities Inability to organize thoughts Narrowing of options due to gender stereotyping No feeling of pressure to move toward decision Resistance of parental/societal pressures to choose Lack of hobbies or extra-curricular experiences Void of information about occupations Lack of work experience	Help explore cause of indecision Teach decision-making process Help begin to identify values and interests Provide sex-role identity counseling Provide anxiety counseling Help organize information search through Internet and other sources Help generate alternatives Dispel myths about career choice Help identify and test abilities and skills Enroll in career course Provide Internet sources for information exploration Provide personal/social counseling when indicated Explore possible career goals

continued

Figure 3–*Continued*
LEVELS, ANTECEDENTS, AND INTERVENTIONS FOR INDECISION*

Levels of Indecision	*Possible Causes or Antecedents*	*Possible Approaches or Interventions*
TENTATIVELY DECIDED (considering two or more choices)	Multiplicity of interests Value conflict/confusion Inadequate information about alternatives General inability to make decisions Uncertainty about abilities Reluctance to give up any one choice Attempt to please other people	Help clarify values Help explore and organize information on self, majors, and occupations on Internet or other sources Confirm choice through information on Internet Help combine best elements of alternatives into one Provide anxiety counseling Teach decision-making process Enroll in career course Force field analysis to compare alternatives Compare how each choice fits goals
UNCOMMITTED DECIDED (choice has been made)	Resistance to outside pressure to declare choice Inadequate information about choice Uncertainty about ability for choice Lack of direct occupational relationship to educational choice High competition in choice Gender opportunities of those in occupation (e.g., males in nursing) Job market known to be poor Inadequate rewards Attempt to please others Fear of being "locked in" to choice	Review decision-making process Allow time Help acquire more information about choice Use Internet to check information Help check accuracy of academic and occupational information Help clarify values implicit in choice Provide anxiety counseling Help confirm accuracy of self-information Provide reassurance counseling Help determine how choice fits life goals

*These are not intended to be inclusive or exclusive. One student's indecision may incorporate a combination of several causes, and many approaches may be used simultaneously or over a period of time.

when applied in a counseling situation, decision theory must be adapted to these unique features. Gati describes how computerized systems can facilitate the decision-making process by leading them through the process step by step.

Walsh and Osipow (1988) made a distinction between descriptive models of decision-making and prescriptive ones. Descriptive models ask "How *are* decisions made?" while prescriptive models address the question, "How are decisions *best* made?" (p.13). Walsh and Osipow (1988) point out that in addition to the descriptive and prescriptive models, there are other general constructs that have been considered when used to develop assessments of decisional processes. Some of these constructs are incorporated in the theories outlined below.

HOLLAND'S THEORY OF PERSONALITIES AND WORK ENVIRONMENTS

One of the most cited career choice theories, and one that is extremely adaptable to practical application, is that of John Holland (1997). As Holland states, his "theory consists of several simple ideas and their more complex elaborations" (p. 1). Some of his theoretical assumptions and how they might be used in advising undecided students follow.

1. *Holland categorizes people as one of six personality types: Realistic, Investigative, Artistic, Social, Enterprising, or Conventional (Holland, 1997, p. 2). He also categorizes work environment into six model types (given the same names) that have certain physical and social characteristics in common (p. 41).*

   Each personality type exhibits certain characteristics such as interests and competencies that "create a special disposition that leads to the way (students) think, perceive, and act in special ways" (p. 2). As a result, each personality type seeks out environments that are compatible with its attitudes, skills, and values. Holland (1997) indicates that by comparing individuals' attitudes with each environmental type, a dominant personality type can be determined. Since there are certain elements of each type in most people, a "pattern of similarity and dissimilarity" or a personality pattern can be determined (p. 3). Each environment contains physical settings to which personality types are attracted. Individuals who are a Social type, for example, will dominate Social environments because they have many characteristics in common (e.g, beliefs, preferences, competencies, self-perceptions and values) (p. 25).

2. *People prefer environments that are compatible with their interests, abilities, attitudes, and values.*

   Although people search for environments where they feel comfortable, environments also search for people "through friendships and recruiting practices." The environment reflects the nature and typical characteristics of personality types attracted to it.

3. *How individuals behave will be influenced by their personality type and how they interact with their environment.*

   Holland states that if we know individuals' personality pattern or profile and their environmental pattern, we can forecast some outcomes, such as choice of vocation, personal interests and competence, and educational and social behavior.

4. *Some secondary theoretical tenets may be made based on the above named assumptions:*

   Consistency–Consistency is the degree of relatedness between personality types or between environmental models. Holland uses a hexagon to demonstrate these relationships. For example, Realistic and Investigative types have more in common than Realistic and Social types.

   Identity–Holland defines identity as the "possession of a clear and stable picture of one's goals, interests, and talents" (p. 5). Identity reflects the clarity of people's vocational goals and self-perceptions and reflects their idea of who they are.

   Congruence–As Holland states, different personality types require different environments. A certain personality type will flourish in an environment that provides the opportunities and rewards that personality type needs. When the opportunities and rewards are not compatible with the person's needs, that environment is said to be incongruent.

Holland also emphasizes the importance of vocational stereotypes and how they can influence perceptions of what an occupation entails. Although some may doubt the accuracy of these stereotypes, research has shown they often reflect accurate assumptions.

Implications for Undecided Students–The possibilities for the use of Holland's theory with undecided students are unlimited. Holland details very specific applications of his theory (1997, pp. 193–217). Although he emphasizes assessment using many "devices" (e.g., *Self Directed Search* [SDS], *My Vocational Situation* [MVS], *Vocational Preference Inventory* [VPI]), he outlines other interventions as well. These include organizing information by his system, career courses, workshops, and self-help activities. He also discusses the need to help students define their own personal career theories (PCT) that include their personal characteristics, interests, and experiences that are not included in his typologies. (The descriptions of some of these practical applications are provided in more detail in Chapter 5.)

Gottfredson (2002) concluded that Holland's theory of vocational personalities provides an organizing typology that is compatible with ideas derived from social-cognitive theory and goal theory.

Eagan and Walsh (1995) use Holland's concept of person-environment congruence to determine if there are differences between congruent, incongruent, and undecided students, and their coping styles. They found that female undecided students used the coping strategy of social support more often than the male groups who were in congruent majors.

Smart, Feldman, and Ethington (2000) found they could identify distinct academic disciplines by their Holland code and found that faculty in these disciplines create an academic environment that emphasizes many of the characteristics of that type, including teaching approaches and goals, and how they interact with their students. This identification had a strong socializing influence on students' congruence with their academic environment. Artistic and Investigative environments were the most successful in socializing students to their respective patterns of abilities and interests. Social and Enterprising environments were less successful. When they studied major changers, one-third of the students who were Investigative or Enterprising types (including undecided) moved to Social-related majors.

Reardon and Bullock (2004) suggest that Holland's theory could provide a conceptual basis for undecided students to examine how different academic departments socialize or affect student in majors they are considering. If students decide to major in a department different from their personality type, they should be made aware that it might involve various personal adjustments and compromises. The authors suggest that research examining the congruence of students' personal types and their academic environments might lead to a better understanding of major persistence or poor academic performance.

SOCIAL LEARNING THEORY OF CAREER DECISION-MAKING

John Krumboltz (1996) has developed a learning theory approach to career decision making that "assumes people's personality and behavior repertoires can be explained most usefully on the basis of their unique learning experiences, while still acknowledging the role played by innate and developmental processes" (Mitchell & Krumboltz, 1996, p. 234). His theory views indecision as necessary and desirable to motivate learning activities. He uses the term "open-mindedness" in place of indecision.

Krumboltz indicates that students make educational and career decisions from the cumulative effects of learning experiences that are affected by various environmental circumstances and their cognitive and emotional reactions to these learning experiences and circumstances. Learning also occurs from self-observation and from observing others (Feller, Honaker, & Zagzcbski, 2001). Krumboltz suggests the advisor's or counselor's job is to stimulate new learning. That includes facilitating the learning of skills, interests, beliefs, values, work habits and personal qualities.

Implications for Undecided Students–Krumboltz outlines two kinds of action-oriented activities that should emphasize learning: (1) developmental or preventive activities that might include job shadowing, worksite observation, internships and externships; and (2) targeted or remedial activities that might include goal clarification, role playing, desensitization, or cognitive restructuring. He emphasizes that students need to be taught decision-making skills.

Krumboltz suggests four ways for advisors or counselors to help students who have problems with indecision, unrealism, or multipotentiality:

- Correct faulty assumptions
- Learn new skills and interests

- Identify effective strategies for coping with issues involving school, work or life
- Learn skills for coping with changing work tasks

Krumboltz foresees self-development as the new work ethic for the twenty-first century.

Okocha (2002) suggests that based on Krumboltz' theory, undecided students should be challenged to examine how their learning experiences and related assumptions may have impacted their thinking about careers. They would also benefit from information about occupational fields that are in decline and those that are on the rise.

Planned Happenstance Theory

Planned happenstance theory is an extension of Krumbolz's social learning theory of career decision-making. Chance plays an important role in career decision-making. Many students (and advisors and counselors) perceive that one of the tasks of decision-making is to eliminate chance. Today's workplace is undergoing constant changes that are often unpredictable (Casio, 2000). Careers do not follow a simple, logical progression.

In a study by Bright, Pryor, and Harpham (2005), 69 percent of the students reported that chance events influenced their career decisions. The role of locus of control was found to be moderately associated with chance events and more externally controlled individuals tend to report more chance events than their internally controlled counterparts.

Mitchell, Levin, and Krumboltz (1999) recommend that counselors teach students to "engage in exploratory activities to increase the probability that (they) will discover unexpected career opportunities. Unplanned events can become opportunities for learning" (p. 115). Krumboltz (1996) extends his theory to include creating and transforming unplanned events into opportunities for learning. Happenstance interventions when practiced by counselors assist individuals to generate, recognize, and incorporate chance events into their career development. Krumboltz replaces the concept of indecision with open-mindedness. He argues that indecision about long-term plans is sensible in a future that is uncertain. This is counter, however, to our culture's quest for definitive, incisive answers.

Implications for Undecided Students–There are some dangers in discussing chance with students who are undecided, since they may interpret this as an excuse for not taking responsibility for their own career decisions. An undecided student who relies on luck to solve problems is not as effective as one who is actively exploring and open to new ideas and experiences. Mitchell et al. (1999) urge counselors to teach students to engage in exploratory activities that increase the probability of exposing new opportunities. Students need to approach these new opportunities with an open, questioning mind and not be afraid to experiment. Mitchell et al. emphasize that "People who have adopted the planned happenstance model are willing to change plans, take risks, work hard to overcome obstacles, and be actively engaged in pursing their interests" (p. 123).

COGNITIVE INFORMATION PROCESSING THEORY (CIP)

Cognitive Information Processing (CIP) (Peterson, Sampson & Reardon, 1991) emphasizes the cognitive domain in career decision-making. Peterson, Sampson and Reardon indicate that career choice is a problem-solving activity that is based on how we think and feel. They use an information-processing pyramid to describe how cognitive and affective processes interact in career choice. What we know about ourselves (our values, interests, and skills) and occupations (knowledge of the college majors and occupations in which we have an interest) forms the first layer or foundation of the pyramid. The second layer is composed of the information processing skills that are essential in the decision-making process. Information processing focuses on how we locate, store, and use information. A sequential procedure known as the CASVE cycle illustrates the information processing skills of communication, analysis, synthesis, valuing, and execution. The quality of our decisions depends on how well we learn to use and process information. The authors suggest that students often get stuck here because they don't understand how career decisions are made.

The top layer of the pyramid, the "executive processing domain," is how we think about our decision-making. It is here that we initiate, coordinate, and monitor the storage and retrieval of information. Metacognitions (i.e., self-talk, self-awareness, monitoring, and control) govern when and how we solve career problems. If these thoughts are positive, good problem-solving results; if they are negative, indecisiveness can be the result. Self-awareness is necessary in monitoring and controlling internal and external influences in decision-making. Effective problem-solvers are aware of their values, beliefs, biases, and feelings. Control and monitoring are essential for deciphering the information needed to resolve a career problem.

Implications for Undecided Students–The CIP approach describes the factors that influence a student's readiness or capability to make appropriate career choices. Readiness takes into account the complexity of the various factors that influence an individual's career development (i.e., family, social, economic, and organizations factors) (Sampson & Peterson, 2000). Undecided students may not understand how they are making academic major or career decisions. The pyramid model can be used to help clarify the very complex factors involved in career decision-making by helping them visualize the various elements involved.

The CASVE cycle can demonstrate how information is processed and the questions that need to be asked. For example, advisors might ask students to describe how they are thinking and feeling about their career choices (Peterson, Sampson, Reardon, & Lent, 1996, p. 436). Using the CASVE process of communication (identifying thoughts and feelings about being undecided), analyzing (what it will take to resolve this career problem), synthesizing (identifying realistic alternatives from what is known), valuing (examining and prioritizing each alternative as it relates to one's value system), and execution (developing a plan of action to implement an alternative) can teach undecided students decision-making skills (Peterson, Sampson, Reardon, & Lent, 1996, p. 436). It can also be used to explore and challenge any dysfunctional metacognitions that might be hindering the decision-making process. For example, an irrational belief such as "I need to know what I want to do the rest of my life before I can decide" needs to be addressed before progress can be made. As undecided students progress through each phase of the cycle, advisors and counselors need to help them determine their perceptions of where they are stuck and how they might move to the next phase in order to move from indecision to decidedness.

OTHER USEFUL THEORIES

Gestalt Theory

Another example of an information processing approach is Gestalt theory, which involves perception. Information processing assumes that all cognitive processes are involved in learning: perceiving, rehearsing, thinking, problem-solving, remembering, forgetting, and imagining (Schunk, 2000).

Hartung (1995) advocates the use of Gestalt theory in career decision-making. He suggests that Gestalt theory can help to reframe the problem of career indecision. He describes it as a way to "emphasize the 'personal-emotional' and process elements which might inhibit individuals from bringing closure to their vocational situations" (p. 300).

The Gestalt model provides a view of career decision-making as a need or demand to make an educational or occupational choice. When homeostasis is not met (i.e., needs are thwarted and fail to meet the demands of the environment), a deficient capacity to use available resources exist. When Gestalt theory is applied to undecided students, it can make advising or counseling more personal by examining "*how* people stay more undecided (e.g., ignoring, avoiding, or minimizing the importance of the decisional process, blaming other for one's own inability to decide)" (Hartung, 1995, p. 311). By using the Gestalt approach, students can learn to take charge of their own career decision making practices.

Values-based Theory

Values have long been recognized as an important factor in goal-setting and career decision-making. Super and Bohn (1970) developed a work values inventory to determine how individuals viewed the importance of work or work salience. In a more occupationally-targeted approach, Katz (1993) identified ten work values and their relationships to general occupational areas. Identifying and prioritizing what one values in work is still considered an important factor in the career decision-making process.

Brown and Crace (1996), in their value-laden approach, offer a conceptual model of values in life-role choices. Brown and Crace speculate that the total number of human values probably lies between ten and sixteen (p. 213). They suggest that highly-rated values are especially important in making choices when alternatives are present. If values are not fully crystallized, indecision may result.

Implications for Undecided Students–One factor that might be useful in advising or counseling undecided students is to assist them in clarifying their personal and work values. To facilitate the crystallization of values, Brown and Crace (1996) suggest several strategies including comparing themselves to others, describing activities that produce emotions, describing their daydreams, or using imagery to describe a desired future. Once values are identified, the authors emphasize that they must be prioritized so the most important ones can be incorporated in goal setting.

Although the value-based approach that Brown and Crace (1996) advocate is targeted to individuals in an occupational transition, their strategies can be applied to major-changers or other academic situations in which students may be involved.

Expectancy-Value Theory

Another "value" approach is the Expectancy-Value theory that describes how much individuals value a particular outcome or goal and their expectation of attaining it. Achievement behaviors involve a conflict between approach (hope for success) and avoidance (fear of failure). The best way to promote a favorable outcome is to combine a strong hope for success with a low fear of failure. Strategies to promote this combination might include helping students to set realistic goals and proving feedback about their goal progress (Luzzo & Jenkins-Smith, 1998).

Students attribute their academic success and failures largely to ability, effort, task difficulty, and luck (Weiner, 1986). Attributions also affect one's expectations for successes, achievement behaviors, and emotional reactions. Students who believe they have low ability to succeed in the academic-career exploration process, for example, may put forth low effort. Perry and Penner (1990) found that attributional retraining improved the academic achievement of students with an external locus of control, but not those with an internal locus of control.

Implications for Undecided Students–Some undecided students may delay or avoid making an academic or career decision because they are afraid to fail in the majors or occupations they are considering. An attributional style that shows a strong sense of control over career development can predict career planning and exploration behavior, career decisiveness, and career commitment (Luzzo & Jenkins-Smith, 1998). A pessimistic attributional style may indicate that students feel a lack of control over the process or their beliefs, or that external forces are influencing their career decisions. Motivation to become involved in the career planning process can be enhanced when students have a high attribution for success.

Constructivist Theory

Constructivist theory is considered one of several "post-modern" approaches to career decision-making. Post-modern approaches refer to those "that emphasize the importance of understanding careers as they are lived . . . or our subjective experience of career development" (Niles & Bowlsbey-Harris, 2002, p. 87). According to constructivist theorists, people construct meaning through the process of organizing their own experiences. Constructivist career counseling is a general method of life planning (Peavy, 1995) and is centered through narrative approaches. The focus is on the individual's personal story that is grounded in life themes and meanings (Brott, 2004). Clients' stories, according to Brott, present an opportunity to gain insight into their self-awareness and develop a future orientation through action steps. From their life-themes students can look for academic and career-related themes and meanings that can help them make connections between different aspects of their lives. Brott's "storied approach" reflects a shift from finding a job to finding one's self. She describes many different assessment techniques that can assist in uncovering the themes and meanings in their personal stories (e.g., life-line, card sorts, life-role circles, goal map). Through personal narratives students can focus on a more integrative picture that helps them understand themselves and the directions they wish to move in the future.

Savickas (1995) describes how a constructivist approach views indecision as students' "subjective attempts to give meaning to crisis points in their lives" (p. 365). He offers a five step counseling model for career indecision using a "life-theme" approach. Students' stories can reveal their life-theme and "deal with the interaction between the linear incidents (life events) that make the plot (i.e., the plan of action) and the timeless, motionless, underlying themes that make the life" (p. 367). After the life-theme has been identified, the counselor narrates it back to the student and both edit it. The theme can then be used to understand and resolve the career indecision. Students learn to view their indecision not as a negative state, but "as a purposeful pause in their line of movement into the future" and to determine "what they want next in life" (p. 368). Savickas offers relevant questions that prompt students to understand their indecision within this context (p. 368):

- Under what circumstances was your indecision recognized?
- How does it feel to be undecided?
- Of what does the feeling remind you?
- Tell me an incident in which you had this same feeling.
- Do you have any idea of what haunts you?
- What part of your life story is most important to your current indecision?

From the constructivist perspective, advising and counseling outcomes should result in a changed outlook that can be accomplished through critical self-reflection, vicarious experiences and real world experiences (Peavy, 1992).

Chaos Theory

Chaos theory describes a set of methods used to study complicated and unpredictable behavior in systems. Advisors and "counselors are not dealing with simple static states but, instead, with complex adaptive systems" (Leong, 1996, p. 340). Many current approaches are based on models that are linear, univariate, and static. These no longer serve the diverse populations with whom we now work. Leong proposes that we need more complex systems that take into account the universal, group, and individual elements that make up career counseling relationships. Each individual is, in and of him or herself, a complex adaptive system. In spite of its name, chaos theory is a study of complicated and seemingly unpredictable behavior in systems that are capable of generating an order of their own.

When advising undecided students, chaos theory can be used "to examine comfort zones of uncertainty and create imaginative ways to address undecided students" (Beck, 1999, p. 45). Beck applies four concepts from chaos theory to advising undecided students: dependence on initial conditions, strange or unexpected attractors, emergent behavior in complex systems, and fractals. She suggests a critical initial condition is the trust level that advisors need to establish with their undecided advisees. A trusting relationship may alleviate some of the negative feelings of anxiety and frustration that some undecided students may be exhibiting. Students need to move from feelings of powerlessness and lack of control to freedom to explore, take risks, and change. Recognizing career decision-making as a complex system can help students view the process as a dynamic, moving one. Positive feedback, along with the disequilibrium they may be feeling, can motivate them to move forward. Fractals are "lessons of wholeness–their self-similarity property is characteristic of whole systems" (p. 48). Beck suggests that the key to working with undecided students is for advisors to look at the whole system within which they work and the whole student whom they advise. According to Beck, "advisors should advocate exploration, questioning, flexibility, and change to undecided students" (p. 47).

SUMMARY

The theoretical frameworks described above are only a few of the theories that can be applied from many disciplines and areas of thought to explain indecision and its ramifications for advising and counseling. No one theory is applicable to all situations, of course, but each can stimulate creative ways of understanding undecided students as they experience their journey to decidedness. Although a developmental theory perspective is extremely useful in our understanding of how undecided students (indeed, all students) progress through the academic and career choice process, there are many theoretical perspectives from which to examine their reasons for indecision, the personal characteristics that influence their decision status, and for suggesting ways of advising and counseling them.

REFERENCES

Baxter-Magolda, M.B. (1992). *Knowing and reasoning in college: Gender-related patterns in students' intellectual development.* San Francisco: Jossey-Bass.

Baxter-Magolda, M.B. (2001). *Making their own way–Narratives for transforming higher eduction to promote self-development.* Sterling, VA: Stylus.

Baxter-Magolda, M.B., & King, P. M. (2004). *Learning partnerships–Theory and models of practice to educate for self-authorship.* Sterling, VA: Stylus.

Beck, A. (1999). Advising undecided students: Lessons from chaos theory. *NACADA Journal, 19*(1), 45-49.

Bright, J.E.H., Pryor, R.G., & Harpham, L. (2005). The role of chance events in career decision-making. *Journal of Vocational Behavior, 66*(3), 561–576.

Brott, P.E. (2004). Constructivist assessment in career counseling. *Journal of Career Development, 30*(3), 189–200.

Brown. D., & Crace, R.K. (1996). Values in life role choices and outcomes: A conceptual model. *Career Development Quarterly, 44,* 211–223.

Buehler, C. (1962). Genetic aspects of the self. *Annals of the New York Academy of Sciences, 96,* 730–764.

Casio, W.F. (2000). The changing world of work: Preparing yourself for the road ahead. In J.M. Kummerow (Ed.), *New directions in career planning and the workplace,* (pp. 3–31). Palo Alto, CA: Davies-Black.

Chickering, A.W., & Reisser, L. (1993). *Education and identity* (2nd Ed.). San Francisco: Jossey Bass.

Christensen, T.K., & Johnson, J.A. (2003). Incorporating the narrative in career planning. *Journal of Career Development, 29*(3), 149–160.

Creamer, D.G. (2000). Use of theory in academic advising. In V. Gordon & W. Habley (Eds.), *Academic advising: A Comprehensive Handbook.* San Francisco, CA: Jossey-Bass.

Crookston, B.B. (1972). A developmental view of academic advising as teaching. *Journal of College Student Personnel, 13,* 12–17.

Eagan, A.E., & Walsh, W.B. (1995). Person-environment congruence and coping strategies. *Career Development Quarterly, 43,* 253–263.

Erikson, E. (1968). *Identity: Youth and crises.* New York: Norton.

Feller, R., Honaker, S., & Zagzcbski, L. (2001). Theoretical voices directing the career development journey: Holland, Harris-Bowlsbey and Krumboltz. *Career Development Quarterly, 49*(3), 212–224.

Foubert, J., Nixon, M., Sisson, V., Barnes, A. (2005). A longitudinal study of Chickering and Reisser's vectors: Exploring gender differences and implications for refining the theory. *Journal of College Student Development, 46*(5), 461–471.

Gati, I. (1996). Computer-assisted career counseling: Challenges and prospects. In M.L. Savickas & B.W. Walsh (Eds.), *Handbook of career counseling theory and practice,* (pp. 169–190). Palo Alto, CA: Davies-Black.

Gordon, V.N. (1981). The undecided college student: A developmental perspective. *Personnel and Guidance Journal, 59,* 433–439.

Gottfredson, G.D. (2002). John L. Holland's contributions to vocational psychology: A review and evaluation. *Journal of Vocational Behavior, 55,* 15–40.

Harren, V. (1979). A model of career decision-making for college students. *Journal of Vocational Behavior, 14,* 119–133.

Hartung, P.J. (1995). Developing a theory-based measure of career decision-making: The decisional process journey. *Journal of Career Assessment, 3*(3), 299–313.

Havighurst, R.F. (1972). *Developmental tasks and education* (3rd Ed.). New York: McKay

Holland, J.L. (1997). *Making vocational choices–A theory of vocational personalities and work environments* (3rd Ed.). Odessa, FL: Psychological Assessment Resources.

Katz, M.R. (1993). *A model for guidance for career decision-making: The guide in the machine.* Hillsdale, NJ: Erlbaum.

Knefelkamp, L., Widick, C., & Parker, C. (Eds). (1978). *New directions for student services: Applying new developmental findings, No. 4.* San Francisco, CA: Jossey-Bass.

Krumboltz, J.D. (1996). *A social learning theory of career counseling.* Stanford, CA: Stanford University Press.

Laff, N.L. (1994). Developmental advising for undecided students: Rethinking the relationships. In V.N. Gordon (Ed.), *Issues in advising the undecided college student,* (pp. 25–35). Columbia, SC: National Resource Center for The Freshman Year Experience.

Leong, F.T.L. (1996). Challenges to career counseling: Boundaries, cultures and complexity. In M. Savickas & W.B. Walsh (Eds.), *Handbook of career counseling theory and practice,* (pp. 333–360). Palo Alto, CA: Davies-Black.

Luzzo, D.A., & Jenkins-Smith, A. (1998). Development and initial validation of the assessment of attributions for career decision-making. *Journal of Vocational Behavior, 52*(2), 224–245.

McCalla-Wriggins, B. (2000). Integrating academic advising and career and life planning. In V. Gordon & W. Habley (Ed.), *Academic Advising: A comprehensive handbook,* pp. (162–176). San Francisco, CA: Jossey-Bass.

McCollum, V.J.C. (1998). Career advising: A developmental approach. *NACADA Journal, 18*(1), 15–19.

Mitchell, L.K., & Krumboltz, J.D. (1996). Krumboltz's theory of career choice and counseling. In D. Brown & L. Brooks (Eds.), *Career choice and development* (3rd Ed.), (pp. 233–276). San Francisco: Jossey-Bass.

Mitchell, K.E., Levin, A., & Krumboltz, J. (1999). Planned happenstance: Constructing unexpected career opportunities. *Journal of Counseling and Development, 77*(2), 115–125.

Niles, S.G., & Bowlsbey-Harris, J. (2002). *Career development interventions in the 21st century.* Upper Saddle River, NJ: Prentice Hall

Okocha, A.A. (2002). *Working with undecided college students.* ERIC Document Reproduction Service No. ED 465914.

Peavy, R.V. (1992). A constructivist model of training for career counselors. *Journal of Career Development, 18,* 215–228.

Peavy, R.V. (1995). *Constructivist career counseling.* ERIC Document Reproduction Service No. ED 401504).

Perry, W.G., Jr. (1999). Forms of intellectual and ethical development in the college years. San Francisco: Jossey-Bass.

Perry, R.P., & Penner, K.S. (1990). Enhancing academic achievement in college student through attributional retraining and instruction. *Journal of Educational Psychology, 82*(2), 262–271.

Peterson, G.W., Sampson, J.P., & Reardon, R. (1991). *Career development and services: A cognitive approach.* Pacific Grove, CA: Brooks/Cole.

Peterson, G.W., Sampson, J.P., Reardon, R., & Lent, J. (1996). A cognitive information processing approach. In D. Brown, L.Brooks, & Assoc. (Eds.), *Career choice and development* (3rd Ed.), (pp. 423–476). San Francisco: Jossey-Bass.

Reardon, R. & Bullock, E. (2004). Holland's theory and implications for academic advising and career counseling. *NACADA Journal, 24*(1&2), 111–122.

Sampson, J.P., & Peterson, G.W. (2000). Using readiness assessment to improve career services: A cognitive information-processing approach. *Career Development Quarterly, 49*(2),

146–174.

Savickas, M.L. (1995). Constructivist counseling for career indecision. *Career Development Quarterly, 43,* 363–373.

Schunk, D.H. (2000). *Learning theories: An educational perspective* (3rd Ed.). Upper Saddle River, NJ: Prentice Hall.

Smart, J.C, Feldman, K., & Ethington, C. (2000). *Academic disciplines–Holland's theory and the study of college students and faculty.* Nashville, TN: Vanderbilt University Press.

Super, D., Starishevsky, R., Matlin, N., & Jordaan, J. (1963). *Career development: Self-concept theory.* New York: College Entrance Examination Board.

Super, D., & Bohn, M.J. (1970). *Occupational psychology.* Belmont, CA: Wadsworth.

Tiedeman, D., & O'Hara, R. (1963). *Career development: Choice and adjustment.* New York: College Entrance Examination Board.

Walsh, W.B., & Osipow, S.H. (1988). *Career decision-making.* Hillsdale, NJ: Larence Erlbaum.

Weiner, B. (1986). *An attributional theory of motivation and emotion.* New York: Springer-Verlag.

Chapter 3

TYPES OF UNDECIDED STUDENTS

As determined in Chapter 1, undecided students comprise a diverse population. Each student may be considered unique, with special background, personal characteristics, and needs. This means that advising services must be as comprehensive and flexible as possible. One of the first steps in designing interventions is to obtain a profile of the students for whom services are being offered. Advisors and counselors on each campus must decide what characteristics are important to identify about their undecided students. This information is useful not only for immediate planning, but also for comparing data and determining trends over an extended period of time.

Important information to collect includes the number and type of new freshmen who are openly committed to exploration as well as other groups such as undecided upperclassmen and those in the process of changing majors. This chapter identifies multiple subgroups that can be found within the undecided population and describes some of their advising needs.

ENTERING FIRST-YEAR STUDENTS

Perhaps the largest and most obvious group is the traditional-aged freshmen who enter college unable, unready, or unwilling to commit themselves to a specific academic direction. This group can be easily identified through admissions information, SAT or ACT profile data, or surveys given during the orientation of new students. It is useful to determine their levels of indecision, reasons for enrolling in college, and reasons for being undecided, in order to develop advising and counseling services to help them. Figure 4, later in this chapter, provides an example of a brief orientation survey used for this purpose. Using this information longitudinally can be useful for long-term planning (Gordon & Steele, 2003).

Gordon (1998) reviewed fifteen studies that identified career decidedness types of students to determine if any similarities exist across the types the researchers described. She organized the results based on decision status (very decided to very undecided) and the characteristics or traits as described by the researchers. Seven categories of decided-undecided types were extrapolated from the fifteen studies. Many first-year students could fall into all undecided categories, but the most common are the *tentatively undecided* and the *developmentally undecided* students. *Tentatively undecided* students are described by the researchers as significantly closer to a decision than the other undecided types. They have been described as "ready to decide" by Chartrand et al. (1994), "undecided-decided" by Vondracek et al. (1990), and "tentatively decided" by Rojewski (1994). This group, although admitting to being undecided, feels comfortable with themselves and their situation. Cohen et al. (1995) found these ready-to-decide students had fewest career decision difficulties and the most successful resolution across all identity stages. Lucas and Epperson (1988) describe them as relatively well-adjusted, close to deciding, intuitive decision makers and confident that a decision will be made when it feels right.

The *developmentally undecided* students were identified by all of the researchers. Fuqua, Blum, and Hartman (1988) suggest that this type of student may resolve indecision through maturation. Multon et al. (1995) describe them as "developmentally normal" and suggest they need to gather information about themselves and the work world as well as develop decision-making skills. Although some students reported they were totally undecided, the developmentally undecided students in Rojewski's (1994) study could identify several tentative career possibilities, yet admitted they needed occupational information, reinforcement, and support before they could select one. Savickas and Jarjoura (1991) describe this group in developmental terms, that is, they were "crystallizing a preference through broad exploration of self and occupations" (p. 87).

Similar to tentatively undecided students, the developmentally undecided individuals are experiencing a normal transition during which they are building the competencies to perform the developmental tasks required to make a commitment to a choice. The other types of undecided students (i.e., seriously undecided and chronically undecided) are described in Chapter 1. Four of the types of *undecided* students suggested by Gordon (1998) are incorporated into the special groups of students described below.

Once a student has openly admitted a willingness to explore, specific interventions may be offered, for example, individual advising, freshman seminar or career exploration courses, workshops, Internet sites, and academic information sessions. Chapter 5 provides detailed descriptions of these program components.

Although first-year students comprise one of the largest subgroups, they are often the easiest to approach. The first step in advising individual freshmen involves determining specific areas of need. These needs may be classified as informational deficits, developmental skill deficits, or personal or social concerns.

Information Deficits

Undecided students may lack information in three general areas: (1) They may need to assess their own personal characteristics, such as values and goals, interests, abilities, energy levels, and needs. (2) They may lack information about the academic areas that are available for study on a given campus. Although students are provided catalogs, institutional websites, and other printed materials concerning majors, general requirements, scheduling, and other academically related tasks, they often need help interpreting or integrating this information. (3) A third informational deficit may be lack of knowledge about occupational areas. Understanding work tasks and being able to identify the rewards in certain occupations are only two types of occupational information needed to make a determination about its possibilities.

Developmental Skill Deficits

Although some undecided students have sufficient information upon which to base a decision, they lack appropriate decision-making skills and are therefore unable to formulate a choice. Former decision-making experiences may have proved counterproductive. For example, an impulsive style may have been used when more reflection and thought were needed. Implementing educational and vocational choices is a developmental task for which many students need advising help (Chickering & Reisser, 1993). Taking responsibility for a decision once it is made is an important part of the process as well.

Personal-Social Concerns

Some students may be experiencing self-conflict in several ways: (1) They may have a values-goal conflict. They may want a job that provides a great deal of money, but their interests are in areas in which salaries are not large, such as teaching and social work. (2) They may have an interest-ability conflict. Their interests may be in areas for which they have marginal ability, or their strengths may be in areas for which they have no interest. They may have a great deal of aptitude for mathematics, for example, but have no interest in the occupational or academic areas related to this subject. (3) They may have an interest-energy level conflict. Some students may not have the energy level required to obtain their goal. An individual may want to become a physician, for example, but his or her energy level to perform in such a demanding profession may be in question. (4) Some students may have a conflict with significant other people whom they admire or want to please. They may not be able to separate their own needs and wishes from the "shoulds" and "oughts" of others.

One or several of these deficits could be the cause of a student's indecision. Raising awareness and identifying specific areas in which deficits exist is an important component of individual or group advising. Sometimes a student's personal or social concerns indicate a need for referral to a professional counselor for indepth help. As indicated in earlier chapters, this is especially true of the student whom Goodstein (1965) identifies as *indecisive.* While the student experiencing indecision tends to have deficits in the informational and developmental skills areas, the indecisive student may need counseling for personal-social concerns or developmental problems.

While most advising is done with individual students, group advising can also be offered. The freshman orientation or seminar course is especially effective with entering students (Barefoot & Searcy, 1994). The course approach to self-assessment and major exploration and planning can be provided in a structured setting during students' first weeks on campus. Too often, undecided freshmen are not provided this type of supportive advisement immediately as they enter college.

Creating an open, supportive climate that encourages entering fresh-

Figure 4.
FIRST-YEAR ORIENTATION SURVEY

1. Male________________________ Female________________________

2. Age: 17–19________________ 23–25________________
   20–22 ________________ Over 25________________

3. Married________________ Not married____________

4. In which third of your high school class were you?
   Highest third_____ Lowest third_____
   Middle third_____ Not sure______

5. First-quarter freshman_____ Transfer_____

6. I will be living
   ______ in a residence hall
   ______ at home with parents or relatives
   ______ in own apartment or home

7. Why are you attending the university? (*Check one.*)
   a. ______ To prepare for an occupation
   b. ______ To become an educated person
   c. ______ Because my parents expect it
   d. ______ Because of the social opportunities
   e. ______ Because my friends are there
   f. ______ For personal growth
   g. ______ Other (please specify) ________________________

8. How undecided are you about a major? (*Check one.*)
   a. ______ I am completely decided on an academic major.
   b. ______ I have an idea of what I wish to major in but am not ready to commit myself.
   c. ______ I have several ideas but cannot decide on one.
   d. ______ I am completely undecided about an academic major.

9. How undecided are you about an occupation? (*Check one.*)
   a. ______ I am completely decided about an occupation.
   b. ______ I have an idea about an occupation I wish to pursue but am not ready to commit myself.
   c. ______ I have several ideas but cannot decide on one.
   d. ______ I am completely undecided about an occupation.

10. What kind of help would benefit you most in deciding on a major or occupation? (*Check one.*)
    a. ______ Information sessions with faculty about various majors
    b. ______ Information sessions with workers in various careers
    c. ______ Career-planning classes to help me explore various options

continued

Figure 4–*Continued*
FIRST-YEAR ORIENTATION SURVEY

d. _____ Tests to help me find out what I'm interested in
e. _____ Information sessions on employment opportunities
f. _____ Talking with a career counselor
g. _____ Actual field experience in a career area
h. _____ Working on the Internet taking various tests and gathering information
i. _____ Other (please specify) ____________________

11. For what major/career fields could you like specific information?
(Do not check more than three.)

a. _____	Business	i. _____	Government
b. _____	Health Professions	j. _____	Law
c. _____	Social Service	k. _____	Law Enforcement and Criminology
d. _____	Education	l. _____	Agriculture
e. _____	Science	m. _____	Engineering
f. _____	Math	n. _____	Environmental/ National Resources
g. _____	Computer Science	o. _____	Writing
h. _____	Art	p. _____	Other (please specify)__________

men to explore alleviates some of the anxiety and pressure they feel. A developmental advising approach offers the opportunity and provides the services this group of students needs to make reasoned, well-thought-out educational and vocational decisions (Gordon, 1981; Laff, 1994). Chapter 5 focuses on this type of advising.

MAJOR CHANGERS

Another important group of students beginning to receive long overdue attention is the students who enter college ostensibly decided about a major, but change their minds during the college years (Foote, 1980; Gordon & Steele, 1992; Kramer, Higley, & Olsen, 1994; Steele, 1994; Titley & Titley, 1980). Although it is estimated that these students comprise up to 75 percent of the college population, little has been written about who they are or how to advise or counsel them during this important period of transition.

Many students find that their ideas about an academic major or career field change as they progress through college. Students need to understand that initial decisions may be tentative and that changing their minds is not only acceptable, but often desirable behavior. For some students, this change could be logical and predictable.

Murphy (2000) and Micceri (2002) both found that each major change increased a student's graduation rate possibilities by 40 percent. Micceri found that those who change majors at least once show graduation rates between 70 percent and 85 percent, while those who retain their original major show rates between 45 percent and 50 percent. Micceri also found differences in major changers' graduation rates between majors. The greatest advantage occurs for major changers in fields ranging from Engineering (41 percent) to Education (53 percent), while the lowest advantage occurs in majors ranging from Music (25 percent) to Chemistry (24 percent).

It is often assume that students who declare a major need little career assistance. Many years ago, Goodson (1981) found, however, that decided students express the same need for help as undeclared students. In his survey of over two thousand students, Goodson discovered that declared majors express the need for occupational information, help in assessing their own personal strengths and limitations, and help with the decision-making process. Vocational developmental theorists view this phenomenon as normal behavior (Ginzberg, 1972, Super et al., 1963; Tiedeman & O'Hara, 1963). This has been substantiated in more recent research (Vondracek, 1990; Wanberg & Muchinsky, 1992). Many college students are in the midst of maturational and identity struggles; choosing an academic major from a myriad of choices is a developmental task for which they are not prepared.

Titley, Titley, and Wolf (1976) asked major changers to specify the occupations they can enter with their new major as well as their old one. Overall, they are more specific about occupations relating to their new major than those relating to the former one, which, again, is consistent with vocational developmental theory. Seniors, however, have a more difficult time specifying occupations than freshmen, which is interpreted as an example of developmental continuity and discontinuity in the choice of career among college students (Tiedeman & O'Hara, 1963). Seniors are more knowledgeable about a variety of options, however, and become less dualistic in their approach to the process.

Chase and Keene (1981) study the differences in academic motivation between students who declare a major by the fifth semester of enrollment and those who do not. They find that students who postpone a declaration of major achieve lower grades and take fewer credit hours. Chase and Keene conclude that the lack of clear academic goals is associated with lower levels of academic achievement. Selecting a stable and realistic major is an important variable in the satisfaction, success, and retention of college students (Pearson & Dellman-Jenkins, 1997; Wycoff, 1999).

Theophilides et al. (1984) studies entering freshmen at a large, selective public university and found that about 15 percent of the students changed their major by the end of their first year, and another 15 percent changed in their second year. However, they found that 45 percent of the students changed their major in both years. Elliott (1984) found no significant differences in academic success between those students who declared majors during their freshman year and those who changed their majors during the same period.

Orndorff and Herr (1996) examined differences and similarities in career uncertainty and in levels of involvement in the career development process between declared and undeclared college students. They found that decided students engage more in knowing their values, interests, and abilities than undeclared students, but have not engaged in exploring occupations more than undecided students. They speculate that this may help to explain why so many declared students change their major. Orndorff and Herr report that declared students as well as undeclared students function at a relatively low level in exploring occupations and declared students are in need of occupational exploration as much as undeclared students. Undeclared students appear to be in greater need of assistance in self-assessment and career planning than declared students.

Other studies (Plaud, Baker, & Groccia, 1990; Theophilides et al., 1984; Titley & Titley, 1980) point out that many entering freshmen express or experience uncertainty and anxiety in selecting an academic major and/or career direction. Many of these students, however, succumb to parental and societal pressures and declare a major upon entering college (Berrios-Allison, 2005; Pearson & Dellman, 1997). Since many of these decisions are based on little concrete information, it is inevitable that many of their ideas broaden and change during their college years.

The following descriptions are an attempt to speculate about some of the characteristics of these mind-changers. This is intended as a way of thinking about them theoretically, as well as practically. Overall, major changers can fit into many of the subtypes of both decided and undecided by the career indecision types summarized in Chapter 1. Since these students had chosen a major, or majors, earlier, they were ostensibly "decided" at one time. The hypothesized major changer types below may fit some of the types identified in the career indecision literature. Although it is dangerous to type students, the following descriptions are drawn from contacts with hundreds of students from diverse backgrounds.

Types of Major Changers

The Drifters

Some students sense very early that their initial choice of college major is wrong but are reluctant to seek help to explore other possibilities. Some are working students with very little time or energy to spend on exploration. Some do not feel pressures to seek out alternatives, while others simply do not know how. Some drifters procrastinate in other areas of life and put off making an alternative major choice until the system forces them to do so. From the literature of career indecision types, the Drifters may fall under the "anxious undecided" type identified by Wanberg and Muchinsky (1992), the "planless avoiders" of Larson et al. (1988), or Fuqua, Blum, and Hartman's (1988) "lack of structure" type.

Advisor Interaction: Academic advisors need to be more sensitive to the drifters' existence. If allowed to wander to long, they become frustrated and remain without goals. Since they have no sense of direction, they are more apt to drop out of college.

The drifters need information about other majors and a great deal of help in organizing an orderly search. They may need to learn basic decision-making skills. Some drifters graduate and become occupational drifters, but if they learn in college how to clarify values, make decisions, and set goals, they have learned skills necessary to life itself.

The Closet Changers

Some students change their major in their head but tell no one, least of all their academic advisor. Students enroll in their new major for several terms but seek no help in scheduling or other important advising tasks.

Some closet changers are afraid to admit a major change because it is against the wishes of a significant other person. Others are unsure of their ability to handle the academic requirements and disguise their new intentions until they can prove (or disprove) themselves. A strange selection of courses may be a clue to advisors that a certain student is a closet changer. Closet changers might resemble the "caught in a dilemma" type of Lucas and Epperson (1990), Multon et al.'s (1995) "anxious undecided" type, or the "undecided uncomfortable" career indecision type described by Jones and Chenery (1980).

Advisor Interaction: Closet changers often make choices internally without seeking help from external sources such as friends, academic advisors, or career counselors. Although they have decided on an alternative major in their heads, they do not publically commit themselves for many months. When closet changers are suspected, they need to be encouraged to confirm their new choice, to discuss scheduling with an advisor in their new area, and to take the appropriate action to change officially.

The Externals

The externals change major frequently. They consistently solicit advice from anyone who will offer it. They may hear about a new major from a roommate, family, a friend, or a student in one of their classes. They appear totally unorganized about their search and express the fear that they may miss a major that they should consider. Several career indecision types might resemble the Externals. Wanberg and Muchinsky (1992) used the term "concerned decided" while Kelly and Pulver (2003) call them "uncommitted extraverts."

Advisor Interaction: Sometimes the externals need to be confronted with their nonproductive approach to choosing a major and helped to organize a plan for exploration. They may need to prioritize their values or be taught rational decision-making techniques. They should be encouraged to choose a major within a reasonable but definite length of time and make a commitment to it. Once they make a commitment, they need to acknowledge responsibility for implementing it.

The Up-Tighters

Sometimes the major that students declare initially becomes unattainable or unrealistic. Their goals may be thwarted by rejection from a selective admissions area, or their abilities may not match their interests. This may be the only major they have ever considered, and they may feel depressed when they finally realize the futility of their situation. The up-tighters may resist examining alternatives at first, since it is difficult for them to accept reality. Some Up-Tighters might resemble the Lucas and Epperson's (1990) "anxious and unclear on goals" type or the "choice anxious" type of Chartrand et al. (1994).

Advisor Interaction: The up-tighters need a great deal of support and patience. Very often the emotional charge associated with changing majors needs to be acknowledged and dealt with before any other help is offered. The up-tighters may be helped to analyze what attracted them to their original choice and find the same values or similar to those tasks in alternative majors or occupations. A positive, structured approach to exploring alternatives with a great deal of encouragement and support is often the best way to help them.

The Experts

The experts know everything. They rarely request help of any type. Even though their choice of major may be totally unrealistic in view of their abilities or other factors, they continue to act as though they were in complete control of the situation. They may try to enroll in higher level courses for which they have no background. Like the up-tighters, the experts are students who *need* to change their major since their initial choice is not attainable, but they refuse to accept this–at least on the surface. Some of the Experts might fall into the "confident but uninformed" type of Larson et al. (1988) or the "developmentally undecided" identified by Chartrand et al. (1994).

Advisor Interaction: Working with the experts takes tact and sensitivity. Helping a student confront unrealistic aspirations is a difficult task. A nonjudgmental, encouraging attitude may help students realize that a change must be made and that there are alternatives that are just as viable and satisfying. Sometimes only a systems rule or regulation will force an expert to take action.

The Systematics

Systematics are students who acknowledge that their original major is wrong for them and take advantage of the academic and career advising services on campus. They realize the need for a coordinated approach for exploring alternative majors and go about it in an organized way. They gather information about possible alternatives, taking into consideration their own strengths and limitations. They discuss these alternatives with knowledgeable persons such as faculty or career advisors, but in the end the decision is theirs. They approach a decision with the right mixture of rational and intuitive thinking. They know the appropriate action to take once their decision is confirmed. The Systematics may fall into one of the "decided" categories identified in the career indecision literature, since they have made a realistic, although tentative choice. They might be called "decided-comfortable" by Jones and Chenery (1980), "well satisfied with their choice," by Holland and Holland (1977), or the "low goal instability/decided type" by Multon et al. (1995).

Advisor Interaction: Systematics are the kind of mind changer that advisors enjoy working with, since they are mature enough to take charge of the search for alternatives and accept responsibility for the decision once it is made. The ultimate goal of any advisor should be to help all mind changers become systematics.

Some colleges and universities need to examine their admissions procedures for requiring students to make choices prematurely. Rather than pressuring students to make a choice to meet bureaucratic requirements, colleges need to provide the climate and the services necessary to help students explore a wide variety of alternatives in an orderly way (Laff, 1994).

Students who are in the process of changing their major need the same type of help as those who prefer to be undeclared. They need information about the requirements in new majors and the career implications of these alternatives. They may need help in assessing their abilities for succeeding in a new major.

Academic advisors should have a clear procedure to follow when students decide to change major. They can help students think through the reasons for wanting to change. Referral to the proper resource for help is critical at this point. A combination of services is needed. A few students not only need academic information but may need to be referred to a career counselor as well.

Steele, Kennedy, and Gordon (1993) found that an advising program designed specifically for major changers produced students who were more likely to graduate and experience a more stable choice of their new major when compared to major changers who were not in the program. The program consisted of specially trained advisors, group counseling, major exploration workshops, and computerized career information systems. Most important was a three-credit hour course designed especially for the needs of these students in transition (Gordon & Sears, 2004). They concluded that a comprehensive, targeted advising program to assist major changers in exploring and deciding on alternative majors is the most effective vehicle for encouraging retention and graduation.

Helping Students in Transition

How can advisors help students who are in the process of changing their college major? There are several considerations that are important in advising or counseling this important group.

Timing of Help

To students in transition, timing of help is critical. Advising help may be offered too early for some (who are not ready to acknowledge that their choice is unrealistic or unattainable) or too late for others (who drop out). Students who feel pressured to make a change in a hurry do not spend the quality of time necessary to examine alternatives. Other students, who have been permitted to drift too long, become depressed or discouraged because they have no goal. Each student's timing is different. Help must be promptly available when students (and sometimes institutions) decide they are ready.

Advisor Accessibility

Advisor accessibility is related to timing but is important in itself. Students in the process of changing majors need to know where to go for help as soon as they decide to change. The academic and career resources and services on campus must be easily identified and available when the student needs them.

Intensity of Need

Students are often emotionally involved in the idea of changing majors. They may feel they are letting someone down, or perhaps a lifelong dream is being shattered. The intensity of this emotional reaction needs to be acknowledged as natural, and help provided to deal with it. Otherwise, emotional barriers may impede the progress of a student in transition.

Advisor Attitudes

Advisors working with students in transition need to possess positive attitudes about the change process. Advisors who view changing majors as a natural developmental phenomenon convey feelings of acceptance and support. Different advisors send very different messages (sometimes negative) in this regard. A few advisors may not possess the expertise necessary or else do not wish to deal with the problem. Help for those students is sometimes very random and unorganized across many campuses.

Advisors' Expertise

Not all advisors have the knowledge and skill to work with major changers. Students need an advisor who is a generalist in academic information, so that a wide variety of alternatives may be explored. Some students need a career advisor, since their exploration may need to include an evaluation of their own personal strengths, interests, values, needs, etc.

Other specific ways for helping students in transition are:

1. *Help students rethink their goals.* If the goals associated with students' original major are no longer viable, they need to reorder their priorities and establish new goals. Clarifying values is an important part of this process.
2. *Help them generate new alternatives.* Advisors and career counselors can help students identify many majors that might satisfy their interests and abilities. Some majors may satisfy the same intrinsic values as the original major, but students may need help in discovering these. If the student wants a totally new direction, alternatives need to be identified systematically and referrals made to faculty and other resources.
3. *Help them see how the credits they have already earned (if any) fit into other academic programs.* Students are often concerned about losing time or not graduating with their class. Since many general requirements may be used with many majors, students need to

know how to adapt their credits to alternative programs.

4. *Help them understand the occupational implications of alternative majors.* Many students today are job-oriented. They may have chosen their first major because of its direct connection to a specific occupation. This concern should be dealt with openly and realistically. Students are often unaware of the relationships between academic majors and career fields.
5. *Help them devise a plan of action.* This takes a great deal of help from many sources. In addition to academic information and faculty referral, students may need to talk to placement offices or workers in the community. They need help in identifying the specific action steps necessary to reach their new goals.

Research data suggest that unsuccessful attempts to settle on a major or to formulate clear career goals may be factors in attrition (Daubman & Johnson, 1982; Lewallen, 1993; Tinto, 1999). More research is needed to help identify who the major changers are, the type of assistance they need, and the effect of timing on their decisions. Rather than leaving these things to chance, organized, creative approaches need to be initiated for helping such a large and needy group.

UNDECIDED UPPERCLASS STUDENTS

A few students reach their junior year with no clear career or academic major decision. A study involving undecided upperclass students by Hagstrom, Skovholt, and Rivers (1997) found eight major themes that were expressed in interviews with these students. The themes were: fear of commitment, fear of judgment, self-doubt and low esteem, difficulty setting goals, family issues, reluctance to seek help, and desire for a personal, caring advising relationship. Beneath the search for majors were hidden barriers such as family issues, stress, fears, unrealistic beliefs, and goal-setting problems. The researchers conclude that efforts to advise these students often fail because the underlying concerns are not acknowledged or dealt with. Upperclass students may fall into several categories:

Multiplistic Students–Some students, even though they have been able to try out their ideas about a college major through course work and other experiences, still find it difficult to narrow down their choices. All their alternatives seem equally possible and realistic in regard to aptitudes and accessible careers. Most colleges or universities require a decision about a major by the junior year, and so the student is literally forced to make a choice.

When advising advanced undecided students with many areas of interest, a firmer, more confrontive approach is needed. Discussions center around what majors must be "given up" or how to combine several alternatives into one.

Most students, when faced with a forced choice, decide on one alternative with the knowledge that it can be changed later. This knowledge sometimes helps students to commit themselves, since the pressure of making a wrong decision is somewhat dissipated. In the end, many students find their tentative choice is a satisfying one and stay with it.

The Noncompetitive Undecided–Some students who enter college decided about a college major find, in time, that their original choices are thwarted (Steele, 1994). This may be due to poor academic performance in selective admissions areas, such as the health professions, or in popular, oversubscribed majors in which certain grade levels must be maintained. Some academic areas have, in recent years, seen such an influx of students that they are unable to handle the increased numbers because of limited faculty and other resources. Academic areas such as engineering, business administration, and nursing and other health areas have controlled their enrollments because of external circumstances and not by their own choosing. Many formerly decided students are in need of the same resources as undecided ones at this point, since they now need to generate new alternatives.

The noncompetitive undecided students, like the major changers described earlier, need special approaches. They may need help in resetting goals. They need to identify new options open to them based on their interests and academic record. Workshops offering information about academic majors similar to their original choice provide the information and counseling that is critical during this somewhat difficult transition.

Immature Students–A few upperclassmen still are not developmentally ready to make a choice. They have limited exposure to exploration courses, leisure time activities, or work experiences. They are not motivated to gather information. These students need to be encouraged continually to explore academic alternatives so as to prevent their arriving at their junior year without receiving any organized help or direction.

Crites (1981) suggests that the outcome of developmental counseling should be centered on the progression from orientation and readiness to decision making and reality testing. Chapter 2 discusses the developmental approach in working with undecided students. The immature upperclassman who has not reached a decision about a college major may need to be referred for career counseling.

The above categories are offered not as distinct types of undecided students but as possible reasons for their indecision. Some students reflect many of these characteristics. For example, a junior who has not reached a decision may be slower in personal development, be very anxious about a choice and procrastinate for this reason, and have trouble narrowing down because of many interests. Another group of students are those who are either too lazy or too busy to take the time to put into action a decision that they have already made.

SPECIAL CATEGORY UNDECIDED STUDENTS

In addition to freshmen who enter college undecided and students who change their major, other groups of undecided students require special advising approaches. Although, like the others, they are uncertain about an educational or career direction, these groups present an additional challenge because of their differing needs (Beatty, 1994).

Multicultural Undecided Students

According to the American Council on Education (1993), the number of ethnic minority students has increased significantly over the past three decades. Rapidly changing population demographics have provided an impetus for the development of multicultural career advising and counseling (Lee & Richardson, 1991). An important consideration when examining the effect of indecision on general career development is to acknowledge possible differences in racial and ethnic populations. While few studies have specifically examined indecision in these groups, one can assume that some students are undecided.

Cunningham (2003) cautions that the terms "multicultural" and "diversity" should not be equated with ethnic or racial minority status. Race and ethnicity are only two of the many identity factors that contribute to our world view. According to Cunningham, rather than concentrating on differences, advisors should learn about high context versus low context orientations such as time orientations, type of reasoning that is valued, types of verbal messages, societal role expectation, and interpersonal relationships. Advisors should continually look beyond their own cultural identity and offer thoughtful, responsive understanding and respect for others from different cultures.

While only one of the following studies deals with indecision in multicultural groups, some insights can be gleaned from the career counseling literature. DeVaney and Hughey (2000) write that "racial identity influences the vocational process in terms of career maturity, perceptions of racial climate, work adjustment, and work satisfaction, but has little impact on content variables such a needs, interests, or college major" (p. 234).

Hanna, Bemak, and Chung (1999) introduce wisdom as a fundamental quality of an effective multicultural counselor. They consider wisdom more important than counselor knowledge in working with multicultural individuals. Wisdom is a transcultural concept that is made up of a variety of characteristics that include listening skills, concern for others, the ability to take an overview of problems and the ability to reframe meanings. These characteristics transcend cultural boundaries.

Carlstrom (2005) offers some specific strategies for advising multicultural students in general. He cautions that when advisors are culturally different from a student, they may tend to ignore their cultural differences or approach the student from cultural assumptions that prevent them from seeing the student's individual identity. Competence in advising multicultural students includes listening empathetically and focusing on meaning. Advisors need to be sensitive to multicultural differences at both the cognitive and emotional levels.

Chung and Sedlacek (1999) surveyed Asian, Black, and White first year students to determine their perceptions, attitudes, and expectations. The two minority groups reported lower academic and social appraisals than the White students. Three factors causing the greatest concern among students were career, academic, and social issues.

Because of ethnic stereotypes, Asian Americans may feel pressured to enter mathematics-related and science-related majors and careers. Asian families, according to the authors, are more apt to participate in career counseling over personal counseling. Since children's career plans are largely a family decision among many Asian families, family involvement may be used to facilitate career planning.

A study by Arce (1996) compared two groups of college students from different cultural and social backgrounds. They assessed levels of indecision, social support, and self-esteem in American and Peruvian students. The intent of the study was to show that specific characteristics of Hispanics and Latinos are deeply rooted in their social and cultural traditions. While social support and self-esteem were not predictive of career indecision for American students, 29 percent of the indecision variance for Peruvian students is attributed to these two variables. Arce concludes that the lack of career choices available in the Peruvian education system may be related to how students approach the career decision-making process.

African American students report greater needs for career planning information, but are less likely to use the career services on campus. In an attempt to find out why this is so, Falconer and Hays (2006) conducted a study to determine what influential factors operated in the lives of Black students. Several categories and themes emerged from the data: (1) continuous connections with teachers, (2) positive influence of peer group, (3) struggles with family and community career expectations, and (4) a strong belief in the efficacy of mentors and networking. Mentoring was identified as the most desirable career intervention. There was some negative feeling about asking for help. The students indicated a mandatory career class for freshmen would be a way to acquire information without having to ask and risk feeling embarrassed for appearing uncertain. The researchers emphasized that advisors and counselors should be aware of the close association between African American students' academic development and career development and the amount of interpersonal support provided.

Black students may aspire to idealistic occupations, but may encounter the harsh reality of racism and racial discrimination when entering the world of work. Black students who have a stronger internal locus of control and a positive ethnic identity are more likely to perceive more occupational opportunities and to have higher career commitment.

Mau (2000) found cultural differences in the way American students reported preferences for decision-making style from Taiwanese students. The majority of both groups endorsed a rational style of career decision-making, while 16 percent of both groups scored highest in the intuitive decision-making style. Taiwanese students significantly endorsed the dependent decision-making style over the American students. Mau concludes the culture of Taiwanese students emphasizes social conformity and collective decisions. Unlike American students, who tend to make their own career decisions, Taiwanese students conform to familial and societal expectations (p. 374).

Mau (2000) also studied career self-efficacy between these two culturally different groups. He found that the Taiwanese students scored significantly lower on the decision-making self-efficacy measure than American students. Chinese students tend to attribute their success to their efforts while American students attribute their success to their abilities and talents. Mau concludes that the individually-oriented culture is more conducive to fostering self-efficacy, while the collective-oriented culture may inhibit the development of self-efficacy.

DeVaney and Hughey (2000) indicate that with the exception of Asian Americans, ethnic minorities are underrepresented in Holland's technical or scientific occupational categories that require a great deal of academic preparation. They found that 71 percent of Hispanic, 68 percent of Black, and 54 percent of White men work in realistic jobs. While 23 percent of White men worked in enterprising occupations, the type associated with greatest prestige and advancement, only 6% of Hispanic men and 10% of Black men did so. The percentages of ethnic minority women were similar to men who worked in prestiges occupations. Brown et al. (1991) found that Black women do better academically and are more likely to be employed in professional positions than either Black men or White women.

As indicated in Chapter 1, families often exert strong influences to follow culturally determined career myths, traditions, and rules. Educational and career decision-making is influenced by these cultural traditions and rules. Many minority students declare a major upon entering college because being undecided is not acceptable to many parents. The lack of research on racial and ethnic students who are undecided makes it difficult to understand who they are, their reasons for indecision, and specific ways to help them make educational and career decisions.

King and Raushi (1994) contend that when advisors develop a multicultural perspective it can be a deep, enriching step toward understanding persons culturally different from themselves. They suggest that "with such a perspective, the advisor can assist the undecided student in a way that empowers the student within his or her whole life context" (p. 97).

Undecided High-Ability Students

Although there is some research available about high-ability or "gifted" college students, there is little to characterize those who are undecided about an educational or career direction. Robinson (1997) points out that attention to the gifted learner at the college level represents uncharted territory and a new frontier.

Perrone, Malex, and Karshner (1977) identify some career development concerns unique to gifted students: (1) They are told at an early age that they are capable of succeeding in any career and may avoid testing their true competencies because of dear of failure or avoidance of success (Leong & Chervinko, 1996; Stroup & Jasnosk, 1977; Zaffrann & Colengelo, 1977). (2) Since they receive so much reinforcement they may find it more difficult to measure up to such high expectations. (3) They tend to foreclose too early on a career choice based solely on recognition and success in a particular academic field. (4) Their career interests and values need to be based on a wide range of experiences that are not usually part of the school curriculum. (5) Talented individuals often experience conflict between achieving excellence and being normal. (6) Talented people may become lifelong students because the role is comfortable. (7) Talented students may view a career as their principal means of self-expression and worth.

Hoyt and Hebeler (1974) identify many of the same career choice problems and needs. Multipotentiality presents a dilemma for gifted students since it carries beyond intellectual ability. Bright students often engage in a wide variety of social, athletic, and community activities. Since multipotentiality is a characteristic of most gifted students, selection of careers cannot be based on interests and abilities alone.

Gordon (1983) finds that undecided honors students are less decided about a college major than regular undecided students, less certain of their alternatives, and more uncomfortable during their first college term. They perform better academically, however, during their freshman year. Moderate levels of discontinuity between students and their college environment enhance personal growth more than either very high or low levels of discontinuity (Feldman & Newcomb, 1969; Pierce, 1970). It would seem that a certain amount of anxiety and uncomfortableness motivates these bright students to achieve at higher levels. While *very* undecided nonhonors student do not perform as well academically as *tentatively* decided nonhonors students, the degree of indecision has no effect on honors students.

Glennen, Martin, and Walden (2000) point out several myths associated with academically talented students. Like their peers they have problems adjusting to college and may have difficulties socially as well as academically. Also like their peers, they may have poor study habits and time management problems. The authors emphasize that academic advisors and counselors must have the knowledge, skills, and training necessary to provide advice and information these students need about opportunities available to them including information about postgraduate study.

Gerrity, Lawrence, and Sedlacek (1993) compared honors and nonhonors first-year students and found many similarities. There were, however, differences given by the two groups for reasons for coming to college. The most highly selected reason for honors students is to prepare for graduate school while nonhonors students come to college to get a better job. More honors students indicated an interest in careers within Holland's investigative and realistic types; nonhonor students report a greater interest in Holland's enterprising, artistic, and social career fields. Both groups indicated concern over career development issues and both groups reported interest in educational and career counseling.

Ender and Wilke (2000) discuss the issue of academic competence in high ability students. Honors students may enter college with high expectations for the academic achievement that they are used to. Ender and Wilke suggest that failure to excel in all subjects may be unsettling to these students and the pressure they put on themselves to perform, as well as the expectations of others, may lead to stress and anxiety. Advisors and counselors must help undecided honors students sort through many academic and career alternatives while being sensitive to the pressures students are feeling.

Multipotentiality is common among undecided honors students since many are interested and capable in a variety of academic and career fields. McDonald (2003) discusses this phenomenon as both a problem and a blessing. Ability in many areas offers a plethora of options. On the other hand, too many choices may be overwhelming to some, and make it difficult to settle on one major or career field. McDonald indicates, for example, that some high-ability business students have difficulty selecting a major within business, believing that multiple specializations will lead to more job offers. Some also have a tendency to double up on curricular requirements or overinvolved themselves in extracurricular activities. McDonald suggests that advisors teach high-ability students the steps involved in making decisions and discourage them from foreclosing too early before exploring the alternatives that are available.

Many undecided high ability students are interested in areas for which graduate or professional study is required (Friedman & Jenkins-Friedman, 1986; Gerrity et al., 1993; Hoyt & Hebeler, 1974). This means that advisors need to be familiar with these prerequisites, in addition to regular academic information. A generalist advisor with knowledge of related career opportunities can be very helpful as bright undecided students begin to explore many options.

Value clarification techniques are especially useful in advising undecided honors students since these individuals are capable of and have interests in many directions. Helping students clarify and prioritize their values is an important part of the sorting-out process that needs to be accomplished. Honors students often need help in "giving away" some of their alternatives rather than generating additional ones. They can also be helped to identify combinations of several interest areas. Often, combining several interests leads to an entirely new, more satisfying alternative that had not previously been considered. Creating their own major is another option that has appeal to many honors students.

Undecided honors students not only need time to explore but also need to learn to be flexible in making and implementing decisions, since in the future many tire of their vocation and want to change in order to be challenged anew. They also need to learn how to satisfy their other interests through nonvocational activities.

Undecided Student Athletes

Policies about selecting a major and progressing toward a degree by the National Collegiate Athletic Association (NCAA, 2005) make it difficult for a student athlete to enter college undecided about an academic direction. Policies toward progression toward a degree have an impact on the amount of time student athletes have to explore academic and career alternatives. Although many general education courses may be taken to meet the requirements for most majors and progression toward a degree, student athletes must complete a prescribed number of hours in their major by deadlines established by the NCAA to be eligible for participation in their sport. These policies also create problems for student athletes who want to change majors.

Parham (1993) suggests that college students in general, including student athletes, share common concerns. He addresses the additional challenges that student athletes face, however, including limited time for social and leisure activities, maintaining health and fitness, managing complex schedules and responsibilities, and terminating their involvement in sports because of injury or retirement. In a four-year study comparing student athletes with students who did not participate in athletics, Aires, McCarthy, Salovey, and Banaji (2004) found that athletes surpassed nonathletes on sociability/extraversion and self-reported well-being. The academic performance of athletes was not below what would be expected, based on their entering lower academic profiles and academic self-assessments.

Gruber (2003) identifies many of the issues that affect college athletes. She recommends that advisors determine the academic and athletic climate on their campuses including the philosophy and political and social climates surrounding the athletic department that affects the student athlete advising program. Faculty and student attitudes toward athletes are also an important factor in advising approaches. She reiterates the developmental advising issues that student athletes must deal with, such as balancing academics and athletics and meeting the expectations of coaches, parents, and the community.

Although the developmental tasks that student athletes face are similar to those of the students not engaged in sport, they may not have mastered some of the basic developmental tasks that Chickering and Reisser (1993) consider essential for college students to master if they are to successfully enter adulthood. Valentine and Taub (1999) use

Chickering's psychosocial theory of student development to present ways to build practical solutions for student athletes. Chickering's career and life planning vector of "developing purpose" is especially important when seeking ways to help undecided student athletes. Valentine and Taub point out that problems in this area may begin early in college for student athletes because of the restrictions in choice of academic degree program. Student athletes may be tempted to take an "easier" course of study because of inflexible training schedules and other time restrictions.

The time and energy needed for exploration is another problem, since, in addition to being a full-time student, the student athlete spends a significant amount of time in practice and participation in his or her sport. This means that exploration must be accomplished when athletic participation is at a lower level. Course work is an important vehicle for experimentation and exploration. Careful scheduling can help the student athlete experience a variety of academic options while fulfilling the general college requirements.

While a few students enroll in college initially to further their careers as professional athletes, many others view completing a college degree as important to their future outside of sports. Undecided student athletes with no clear-cut educational or career goals are at higher risk than those who have selected a major (Bland, 1985; Tutko, 1971).

Intercollegiate athletes who have unrealistic career goals and aspirations need academic and career counseling support throughout their college years (Ender, 1983; Gordon, 1986; Martinelli, 2000). Fletcher, Benshoff, and Richburg (2003) describe a systems approach to understanding college student athletes. When advisors and counselors understand the multilevel system under which student athletes must function, (including NCAA rules and regulations, university policies, athletic department standards, and team dynamics), they are better equipped to help students negotiate the challenges they face. Fletcher et al. also urge advisors and counselors to become more informed about the subculture of athletics on campus so they can confront their own gender and culture biases and address their own attitudes and assumptions about athletes.

After interviewing directors of academic support services in colleges with high athlete graduation rates, Gaston-Gayles (2003) found that these programs used intrusive advising and concentrated advising support during the freshman and sophomore years. Gaston-Gayles urges advisors to help student athletes focus on graduation and degree progress rather than so much emphasis on maintaining eligibility.

These and other findings carry important implications for advising and counseling undecided student athletes. Time management is an important skill for student athletes to acquire, since in addition to the hours needed for academic work, a great deal of time is spent participating in all phases of their sport. Unfortunately, this leaves little time to devote to exploring academic and career options. Martinelli (2000) indicates that the NCAA is recognizing the need for career development and guidance through its CHAMPS/Life Skills program. The career areas of the program focus on general career development, tasks for each year in school, work with agents, and the alumni career network that includes a seminar on life after sports (p. 209).

Helping undecided student athletes set realistic and personally satisfying educational goals is a critical advising function. Helping them select a major and monitoring the student's academic progress is important not only for maintaining athletic eligibility, but for the individual student's academic success and satisfaction throughout the college years.

Older Undecided Students

The number of nontraditional college students has grown to more than 6 million in 2000 (U.S. Census Bureau, 2001). This special population of older students enters college for many reasons. Some reenter for retraining for a specific career or to change their career directions. Older women in particular enroll in order to renew career efforts that were interrupted earlier, or to pursue a degree for the sake of receiving a broad education. Not all older students enroll in college with clear-cut educational or career goals.

As Luzzo (2000) point out, older adult students represent diverse backgrounds and motivations for returning to college. Some research indicates that age is positively correlated with students' attitudes toward career decision-making (Blustein, 1988; Luzzo, 1993). While younger students may be more concerned about making career decisions, older students report low levels of anxiety and fear. Luzzo also indicates that older students differ in career commitment, career decision making self-efficacy, and perceived decision-making needs. Many nontraditional students are likely to possess confidence in their ability to engage in career decision-making.

Chao and Good (2004) found that the nontraditional students in their study perceived that pursuing a college education gave them a sense of "hopefulness" that interacted with five other themes: motivation, financial investment, career development, life transition, and support systems. They actively integrated their college education into their career development and there was a closer connection between their educational and career goals than traditional age students. Many reported they viewed education as an opportunity to shift to a different occupation. The authors note that this close connection between educational and career aspirations underscores the importance of academic and career counseling with nontraditional students.

Undecided adult students present a different challenge than traditional-aged students. They offer a set of life experiences and circumstances that must be taken into account as they begin the exploration process. Most older students have a realistic view of their capabilities and their interests. They are often unsure, however, of the academic opportunities available to them (Champagne & Petitpas, 1989). They have had practice and experience with the decision-making process and are usually motivated to seek information actively in an organized way.

Many adults experience apprehension when returning to college. As Chao and Good (2004) suggest, "career transitions can be a source of stress, particularly if those transitions are motivated by adverse circumstances such as recent divorce, relocation, or changes in employment conditions" (p. 11). Some feel that being undecided is a temporary state that they must alleviate quickly. Others feel anxious about a decision as they test their abilities to perform college-level work. Adults returning to college may be viewed as developing individuals undergoing change. Adults in particular need support during this period of exploration.

1. Their life experiences and the broader perspective of their life history can be an asset in helping adults identify and explore alternatives. They may have narrowed down many choices since they are more familiar with their strengths and limitations and what is of interest to them.
2. Adults often present a sense of urgency to make a decision since

they feel the need to make up "lost" time. While this can be motivating, it may also work against them, since they may become discouraged in projecting the time it takes to complete an education. Being undecided may be perceived by them (though this is not necessarily true) as a time extender.

3. Adults need to see the relevance of what they are learning and need to be able to apply what they learn immediately. Helping undecided adults access the resources for gathering information and process the information in a personal frame of reference is the type of assistance they need to make a realistic, satisfying educational decision.
4. Older adults feel hesitant to ask for advising help since they feel they are "off time." They need assurances that what they are experiencing is a natural part of personal and intellectual development. They need to know that such anxieties are felt by many other older students experiencing the same type of change. The support of a counselor or advisor at this juncture can be critical.

Accurate knowledge of nontraditional students' concerns about family, school, and work can enable advisors and counselors to serve nontraditional students more effectively, especially as they pertain to educational and career decisions.

Underprepared Undecided Students

Perhaps the most challenging group of undecided students is those who have poor academic backgrounds. Students who underachieve or who lack the skills to perform a certain level of academic work place great limitations on the areas they may realistically explore. Early research by Ashby, Wall, and Osipow (1966) found that academically poor students were actually more decided than their more capable peers. Being decided may offer a certain sense of security as underprepared students enter college.

Some students may have learning difficulties that make choosing a major more complicated. Layton and Lock (2003) indicate that students with learning disabilities often have difficulty choosing a major since many are less mature in their decision-making ability and often are unable to make an academic or career choice. They may have difficulties, for example, in examining the advantages and disadvantages of alternative major choices or matching their personal strengths with these alternatives. The authors suggest that advisors need to focus on the reasoning problems these students may be having (i.e., making generalizations, problem-solving, executive functioning, understanding consequences) as they relate to college major selection.

Ender and Wilkie (2000) emphasize that it is critical for underprepared students to assess their academic competence and formulate a detailed plan to address their areas of academic need. They recommend that advisors be "direct, emphatic, and prescriptive when designing the plan to overcome deficiencies" (p. 135). Advisors need to help students develop an internal locus of control and provide frequent feedback that is positive and encouraging.

When working with academically underprepared students, the following considerations are offered:

1. Advisors must be careful not to discourage students prematurely in eliminating alternatives perceived by the advisor to be unrealistic. An underprepared freshman must be given the time and opportunity to overcome certain academic deficiencies.
2. Advisors must help students deal with academic deficits before emphasizing major exploration. Students must be able to set their priorities in order. Learning how to be a successful student is where initial energies must be concentrated.
3. Advisors should be aware that some students may have undiagnosed learning disabilities that may impede their decision-making abilities.
4. Upperclassmen who are in academic difficulty sometimes need help in reassessing their original goals and identifying alternatives in which they are more apt to succeed. Advisors must be well trained in alternative counseling, since many academically poor students need to change their major. Often, changing from an unrealistic major helps a student out of academic difficulty (as in the case of a premed major who receives excellent grades in social sciences but fails chemistry, math, or physics).
5. As a last resort, decided and undecided academically deficient students may need to be counseled out of college or into a different level or type of educational program. Before that happens, these students deserve educational and career advising that helps them realistically set goals that reflect their potential.

UNDECIDED COMMUNITY COLLEGE STUDENTS

While many undecided community college students display the same characteristics as baccalaureate degree students, there are some important differences that make them unique. Many students enter two-year programs with the intent of transferring to four-year degree programs. Transfer concerns, therefore, are a critical issue in the decision to enter college "undecided," since some programs do not have the flexibility of course work that some baccalaureate programs do. This means "undecided" students need careful scheduling and an awareness of the transfer criteria they face.

Many of the "special category" students mentioned earlier make up a large segment of the community college population. Undecided students within these student populations present a challenge that must encompass an understanding and sensitivity to their special needs. King and Raushi (1994) identify certain themes that may be related to undecided community college students. Many community college students are first in their family to attend college. Unrealistic expectations, either too high or too low, may act as a detriment. The demands of a college coursework and degree requirements may not be familiar to them, so some students may schedule unrealistic course loads or take courses for which they do not have appropriate preparation.

In addition to school work, employment may create stress because of family and time commitments. They may be limited in their choice of programs because of lack of openness and may not want to spend the time to explore realistic alternatives. Some community college students need remedial work due to inadequate preparation or a long hiatus from formal education. This may delay the student's progress toward a degree program and thus delay a decision about an educational or occupational direction.

Adult students make up a large segment of the community college population. While some admit to being unclear about their academic and occupational choices, they often feel pressured to make decisions because of family or job responsibilities. Spending time exploring is just as important for some older adults as it is for traditional age students.

Many community colleges enroll large numbers of commuter, multicultural, and first generation students. Some students may feel pressured to make decisions based on family pressures, financial concerns, multiple responsibilities, or local work-force conditions. Commuter students living at home, for example, may not want to explore new options or opportunities that may uproot them. Advisors may need to encourage these special students to spend some time in exploration when a narrow perspective or resistance to change interferes with the need to examine more realistic and exciting alternatives.

King and Raushi (1994) suggest a developmental approach to advising community college students. Choosing to be "undecided" may be difficult for some two-year students, but spending time exploring might save them from making hasty, narrow decisions that they may need to change later. By using a developmental approach, advisors can help community college students make effective decisions, taking into consideration their unique personal qualities and the priorities they have established in other aspects of their lives.

King and Raushi (1994) indicate that advisement strategies that are especially helpful in advising undecided students in community colleges include

> identifying and providing services for exploration upon entry; creating programs to teach decision making as a process; helping students, especially adults, identify and use life patterns that have been successful in other situations; and embracing a developmental approach so that the student's "whole-life context" is incorporated into the decision-making process. (p. 99)

SUMMARY

Many campuses narrowly define *undecided students* as those who enter their institutions openly admitting to a lack of major choice. There are multiple subgroups within the undecided populations, each with special characteristics and needs. Undecided first-year students can be identified and provided services immediately, and orderly programs for helping them explore can be established.

A larger and often neglected group is the students who enter college ostensibly decided, but who become less certain of their choice over time. Students who change their major often need special opportunities for information-gathering, self-assessment, and counseling as they proceed through a sometimes difficult transition period. Undecided upperclassmen also comprise a unique group with special concerns about timing and institutional policies. Other special categories of undecided students, such as honors, adults, athletes, and underprepared students, have special needs that dictate different approaches to programming and advising.

Each institution, two- and four-year alike, needs to obtain a profile of the types and numbers of undecided students on its campus in order to identify the programs and services that are needed. Counselors and advisors working with undecided students must be sensitive to the uniqueness of each group and gear their advising approaches accordingly. At any given time, a majority of college students are in some state of doubt or indecision about their educational and career goals. Many students need a carefully organized plan in order to explore. Others need help in confirming a decision that they have already made. A very few may have debilitating psychological problems; their indecision is only a symptom of a more serious dysfunction. All students may be considered unique, developing individuals with very different needs and concerns but with a common need for exploration and help with academic and career decision-making.

REFERENCES

American Council on Education. (1993). *Minorities in higher education: 1992 eleventh annual status report.* Washington, D.C.: Author

Arce, E.M. (1996). The effects of social support and self-esteem on career indecision: A cross-cultural comparison between two groups of undergraduate students. Paper presented at the Annual Meeting of the American Educational Research Association (New York, NY, April 11, 1996).

Aries, E., McCarthy, D., Salovey, P., & Banaji, M. (2004). A comparison of athletes and nonathletes at high selective colleges: Academic performance and personal development. *Research in Higher Education, 45*(6), 577–602.

Ashby, J., Wall, H., & Osipow, S. (1966). Vocational uncertainty and indecision in college freshmen. *Personnel & Guidance Journal, 44,* 1037–1041.

Barefoot, B.O., & Searcy, D.N. (1994). Freshman seminars and other courses for undecided students. In V.N. Gordon (Ed.), *Issues in advising the undecided college student,* (pp. 59–66). Columbia, SC: National Resource Center for The Freshman Year Experience.

Beatty, J.D. (1994). Advising special groups with the undecided student population. In V. Gordon (Ed.), *Issues in advising the undecided college student,* (pp. 67–83). Columbia, SC: National Resource Center for The Freshman Year Experience.

Berrios-Allison, A.C. (2005). Family influences on college students' occupational identity. *Journal of Career Assessment, 13*(2), 233–247.

Bland, F.W. (1985). Intercollegiate athletic competition and students' educational and career plans. *Journal of College Student Personnel, 26,* 115–118.

Blustein, D.L. (1988). A canonical analysis of career choice crystallization and vocational maturity. *Journal of Counseling Psychology, 20,* 113–120.

Brown, D., Minor, C.W., & Jepsen, D.A. (1991). The opinions of minorities about preparing for work: Report of the second NCDA national survey. *Career Development Quarterly, 40,* 5–19.

Cahill, M., & Martland, S. (1995). *Counseling career drifters.* (ERIC Reproduction Service No. ED 401498)

Carlstrom, A.H. (2005). Preparing for multicultural advising relationships. Retrieved March 28, 2006 from NACADA Academic Advising Today website: http://www.nacada.ksu.edu/AAT/NW28_4htm

Champagne, D.E. & Petitpas. (1989). Planning developmental interventions for adult students. *NASPA Journal, 26,* 265–271.

Chao, R., & Good, G.E. (2004). Nontraditional students' perspective on college education: A qualitative study. *Journal of College Counseling, 7*(1), 5–12.

Chartrand, J.M., Martin, W., Robbins, S., McAuliffe, G. Pickering, J., & Calliotte, J. (1994). Testing a level versus an interactional view of career indecision. *Journal of Career Assessment, 2*(1), 55–69.

Chase, C., & Keene, J. (1981). Major declaration and academic motivation. *Journal of College Student Personnel, 22,* 496–501.

Chickering, A.W., & Reisser, L. (1993). *Education and identity* (2nd Ed.). San Francisco: Jossey-Bass.

Christensen, T.K., & Johnston, J.A. (2003). Incorporating the narrative in career planning. *Journal of Career Development, 29*(3), 149–160.

Chung, Y.B., & Sedlacek, W.E. (1999). Ethnic differences in career, academic, and social self-appraisals among incoming college freshmen. *Journal of College Counseling, 2*(1), 14–24.

Cohen, C.R., Chartrand, J.M., & Jowdy, D.P. (1995). Relationships between career indecision subtypes and ego-identity development. *Journal of Counseling Psychology, 42*(4), 440–447.

Crites, J.O. (1981). *Career counseling: Models, methods and materials.* New York: McGraw-Hill.

Cunningham, L. (2003). Multicultural awareness. Retrieved February 21, 2004 from the NACADA Clearinghouse of Academic Advising Resources website: http://www.nacada.ksu.edu/Clearinghouse/Advising_Issues/Multicultural.htm

Daubman, K., & Johnson, D.H. (1982). *Comparisons among continuing, withdrawing, and nonreturning students.* Academic Leave and Withdrawal Office Research Report #7, University of Maryland. (ERIC Document Reproduction Service ED 233628)

DeVaney, S.B., & Hughey, A.W. (2000). Career development of ethnic minority students. In D.A. Luzzo (Ed.), *Career counseling of college students,* (pp. 233–252). Washington, D.C.: American Psychological Association.

Elliot, E.S. (1984). Assisting high academic risk athletes: Recommendations for the academic advisor. *NACADA Journal, 4,* 39–45.

Ender, S.C. (1983). Assisting high academic risk athletes: Recommendations for the academic advisor. *NACADA Journal, 3,* 1–10.

Ender, S.C., & Wilke, C.J. (2000). Advising students with special needs. In V. Gordon & W. Habley (Eds.), *Academic advising; A comprehensive handbook,* (pp. 118–143).

Falconer, J.W., & Hays, K.A. (2006). Influential factors regarding the career development of African American college students. *Journal of Career Development, 32*(3), 219–233.

Feldman, K., & Newcomb, T. (1969). *The impact of college on students.* San Francisco: Jossey-Bass.

Fletcher, T.B., Benshoff, J. & Richburg, M. (2003). A systems approach to understanding and counseling college student-athletes. *Journal of College Counseling, 6,* 35–45.

Foote, B. (1980). Determined-and-undetermined major students: How different are they?

Journal of College Student Personnel, 21, 29–34.

Friedman, P.G., & Jenkins-Friedman, R.C. (1986). *Fostering academic excellence through honors programs. New Directions for Teaching and Learning, No. 25.* San Francisco: Jossey-Bass.

Fuqua, D.R., Blum, C.R., & Hartman, B.W. (1988). Empirical support for the differential diagnosis of career indecision. *Career Development Quarterly, 36,* 364–373.

Gaston-Gayles, J.L. (2003). Advising student athletes: An examination of academic support programs with high graduation rates. *NACADA Journal, 23*(1&2), 50–57.

Gerrity, D.A., Lawrence, J., & Sedlacek, W. (1993). Honors and nonhonors freshmen: Demographics, attitudes, interests, and behaviors. *NACADA Journal, 13*(1), 43–52.

Ginzberg, E. (1972). Toward a theory of occupational choice: A restatement. *Vocational Guidance Quarterly, 20,* 169–176.

Glennen, R.E., Martin, D., & Walden, H. (2000). Summer honors academy: A descriptive analysis and suggestions for advising academically talented students. *NACADA Journal, 20*(2), 38–45.

Goodson, W. (1981). Do career development needs exist for all students entering colleges or just the undecided major students? *Journal of College student Personnel, 22,* 413–417.

Goodstein, L. (1965). Behavior theoretical views of counseling. In B. Steffre (Ed.), *Theories of counseling,* (pp. 140–192). New York: McGraw-Hill.

Gordon, R. L. (1986). Issues in advising student athletes. *NACADA Journal, 6,* 81–86.

Gordon, V.N. (1981). The undecided student: A developmental perspective. *Personnel and Guidance Journal, 59,* 433–439.

Gordon, V.N. (1983). Meeting the career development needs of undecided honors students. *Journal of College Student Personnel, 24,* 82–83.

Gordon, V.N. (1998). Career decidedness types: A literature review. *Career Development Quarterly, 46*(4), 386–403.

Gordon, V.N., & Sears, S.J. (2004). *Selecting a college major–Exploration and decision-making.* Upper Saddle River, NJ: Prentice Hall.

Gordon, V.N., & Steele, G.E. (1992). Advising major changers: A longitudinal study. *NACADA Journal, 12,* 22–27.

Gordon, V.N., & Steele, G.E. (2003). Undecided first-year students: A 25-year longitudinal study. *Journal of the First-Year Experience, 15*(1), 19–38.

Gruber, C.A. (2003). What every academic advisor should know about advising student athletes. *NACADA Journal, 23*(1&2), 44–49.

Hagstrom, S.J., Skovholt, T.M., & Rivers, D. A. (1997). The advanced undecided college student: A qualitative study. *NACADA Journal, 17*(2), 23–30.

Hanna, F.J., Bemak, F., & Chung, R.C. (1999). Toward a new paradigm for multicultural counseling. *Journal of Counseling & Development, 77*(2), 125–135.

Holland, J. L., & Holland, J.E. (1977). Vocational indecision: More evidence and speculation. *Journal of Counseling Psychology, 24,* 404–414.

Hoyt, K.B., & Hebeler, J.R. (1974). *Career education for gifted and talented students.* Salt Lake City: Olympus.

Jones, L., & Chenery, M.F. (1980). Multiple subtypes among vocationally undecided college students. A model and assessment instrument. *Journal of Counseling Psychology, 27,* 469–477.

Kelly, K.R., & Pulver, C.S. (2003). Refining measurement of career indecision types: A validity study. *Journal of Counseling and Development, 81*(4), 445–455.

King, M.C., & Raushi, T.M. (1994). Undecided students in community colleges. In V. Gordon, (Ed.), *Issues in advising the undecided college student.* Columbia, SC: National Resource Center for The Freshman Year Experience.

Kramer, G.L., Higley, B.H., & Olsen, D. (1994). Changes in academic major among undergraduate students. *College and University, 69,* 88–98.

Laff, N.S. (1994). Developmental advising for undecided students: Rethinking the relationships. In V. Gordon (Ed.), *Issues in advising the undecided college student,* (pp. 25–36). Columbia, SC: National Resource Center for The Freshman Year Experience.

Larson, L.M., Heppner, P., Ham, T., & Dugan, K. (1988). Investigating multiple subtypes of career indecision thorough cluster analysis. *Journal of Counseling Psychology, 35,* 439–446.

Larson, L.M., & Majors, M.S. (1998). Applications of the coping with career indecision instrument with adolescents. *Journal of Career Assessment, 6*(2), 163–179.

Layton, C.A., & Lock, R.H. (2003). The impact of reasoning weaknesses on the ability of postsecondary students with learning disabilities to select a college major. *NACADA Journal, 23*(1&2), 21–29.

Lee, C.C., & Richardson, B.L. (1991). *Multicultural issues in counseling: New approaches to diversity.* Alexandria, VA: American Counseling Association.

Leong, T.L., & Chervinko, S. (1996). Construct validity of career indecision: Negative personality traits as predictors of career indecision. *Journal of Career Assessment, 4*(3), 315–329.

Lewallen, W.C. (1993). The impact of being "undecided" on college student persistence. *Journal of College Student Development, 34,* 103–112.

Lucas, M.S., & Epperson, D.L. (1988). Personality types in vocationally undecided students.. *Journal of College Student Development, 29,* 460–466.

Lucas, M.S., & Epperson, D. (1990). Types of vocational undecideDness: A replication and refinement. *Journal of Counseling Psychology, 37,* 382–388.

Luzzo, D.A. (1993). Career decision-making between traditional and nontraditional college students. *Journal of Career Development, 20,* 113–120.

Luzzo, D.A. (1999). Identifying the career decision-making needs of nontraditional college students. *Journal of Counseling & Development, 77,* 135–140.

Luzzo, D.A. (2000). Career development of returning-adult and graduate students. In D.A. Luzzo (Ed.), *Career counseling of college students.* Washington, D.C.: American Psychological Association.

Martinelli, E.A., Jr. (2000). Career decision-making and student-athletes. In D.A. Luzzo (Ed.), *Career counseling of college students,* (pp. 201–215). Washington, D.C.: American Psychological Association.

Mau, W. (2000). Cultural differences in career decision-making styles and self-efficacy. *Journal of Vocational Behavior, 57,* 368–378.

McDonald, M.L. (2003). Advising high-ability business students. *NACADA Journal, 23*(1&2), 58–65.

Micceri, T. (2002). Will changing your major double your graduation chances? Retrieved June 16, 2004 from the Policy Center for the First Year of College, Brevard College: http://www.brevard.edu/fyc/listserv/remarks/mcceri.htm

Murphy, M. (2000). *Predicting graduation: Are test scoreS and high school performance adequate?* Paper presented at the AIR Annual Forum, Cincinnati, OH, May 21–24, 2000.

Multon, K., Heppner, M.J., & Lapan, R. (1995). An empirical derivation of career decision subtypes in a high school sample. *Journal Vocational Behavior, 47,* 76–92.

National Collegiate Athletic Association (2005). *2005-2006 NCAA Division I Manual.* Overland Park, KS: Author.

Okocha, A.A. (2002). *Working with undecided college students.* ERIC Reproduction Service No. 465914).

Orndorf, R.M., & Herr, E.L. (1996). A comparative study of declared and undeclared college students on career uncertainty and involvement in career development activities. *Journal of Counseling and Development, 74,* 632–639.

Osipow, S.H., Carney, C., Winer, J., Yanico, B., & Koschier, M. (1976). *Career Decision Scale* (3rd revision). Columbus, OH: Marathon Consulting and Press.

Parham, W.D. (1993). The intercollegiate athlete: A 1990s profile. *The Counseling Psychologist, 21,* 411–429.

Pearson, C., & Dellman-Jenkins, M. (1997). Parental influence on a student's selection of a college major. *College Student Journal, 31*(3), 301–313.

Perrone, P., Malex, R., & Karshner, W. (1977). Career development needs of talented students: A perspective for counselors. *The School Counselor, 27,* 16–23.

Pierce, R.A. (1970). Roommate satisfaction as a function of need similarity. *Journal of College Student Personnel, 11,* 355–359.

Plaud, J.P., Baker, R.W., & Groccia, J.E. (1990). Freshman decidedness regarding academic major and anticipated and actual adjustment to an engineering college. *NACADA Journal, 10,* 20–26.

Robinson, N.M. (1997). The role of universities and colleges in educating gifted undergraduates. *Peabody Journal of Education, 72*(3&4), 217–236.

Rojewski, J.W. (1994). Career indecision types for rural adolescents from disadvantaged and nondisadvantaged backgrounds. *Journal of Counseling Psychology, 41*(3), 365–363.

Rose, H., & Elton, C. (1971). Attrition and the vocationally undecided student. *Journal of Vocational Behavior, 1,* 99–103.

Savickas, M.L., & Jarjoura, D. (1991). The career decision scale as a type indicator. *Journal of Counseling Psychology, 38*(1), 85–90.

Shaffer, L.S. (1998). Maximizing human capital by developing multicultural competence. *NACADA Journal, 18*(2), 21–27.

Steele, G.E. (1994). Major changers: A special type of undecided student. In V. Gordon, (Ed.), *Issues in advising the undecided college student,* (pp. 85–92). Columbia, SC: National Resource Center for The Freshman Year Experience.

Steele, G.E. (2003). A research-based approach to working with undecided students: A case study illustration. *NACADA Journal, 23* (1&2), 10–20.

Steele, G.E., Kennedy, G., & Gordon, V.N. (1993). The retention of major changers: A longitudinal study. *Journal of College Student Development, 34,* 58–62.

Stroup, K., & Jasnosk, M. (1977). *Do talented women fear math?* Washington, D.C.: American Association of University Women (ERIC Document Reproduction Service No. ED 174395)

Super, D. Starishevsky, R., Matlin, N., & Jordaan, J. (1963). *Career development self-concept theory.* New York: College Entrance Examination Board.

Theophilides, C., Terezini, P.T., & Lorang, W. (1984). Freshman and sophomore experiences and changes in major field. *Review of Higher Education, 7,* 261–278.

Tiedeman, D., & O'Hara, R. (1963). *Career development: Choice and adjustment.* New York: College Entrance Examination Board.

Tinto, V. (1999). Taking retention seriously: Rethinking the first year of college. *NACADA Journal, 19*(2), 5–9.

Titley, R.M., & Titley, B.S. (1980). Initial choice of college major and attrition: The"decided" and "undecided" after 6 years. *Journal of College Student Personnel, 26,* 465–466.

Titley, R.M., Titley, B.S., & Wolf, W. (1976). The major changers: Continuity and discontinuity in the career process. *Journal of Vocational Behavior, 8,* 105–111.

Tutko, T.A. (1971). Anxiety. *Encyclopedia of Sport Science and Medicine.* New York: Macmillan.

U.S. Census Bureau (2001). *Age distribution of college students 14 years old and over by sex.* October 1947 to 2000. Washington, D.C. Author.

Valentine, J.J., & Taub, D.J. (1999). Responding to the developmental needs of student ath-

letes. *Journal of College Counseling, 2*(2), 164–179.
Vondracek, F.W., Hostetler, M., Schulenburg, J.E., & Shimizu, K. (1990). Dimensions of career indecision. *Journal of Counseling Psychology, 37,* 98–106.
Wanberg, C.R., & Muchinsky, P.M. (1992). A typology of career decision status: Validity extension of the vocational decision status model. *Journal of Counseling Psychology, 39,* 71–80.
Wyckoff, S.C. (1999). The academic advising process in higher education: History, research, and improvement. *Recruitment & Retention in Higher Education, 13*(1), 1–3.
Zaffrann, R., & Colengelo, N. (1977). Counseling the gifted and talented student. *Gifted Child Quarterly, 21,* 305–325.

Chapter 4

ADMINISTRATIVE MODELS AND SCOPE OF SERVICES

There are many administrative vehicles, program approaches, and advising services needed to help undecided students make realistic, satisfying, and stable educational and vocational decisions. The following questionnaire, "Assessing Your Advising Program for Undecided Students," will help to determine the comprehensives and scope of the services provided to the undecided students on a particular campus. The item(s) that describe the program should be checked. Scoring instructions are at the end of the questionnaire.

ASSESSING YOUR ADVISING PROGRAM FOR UNDECIDED STUDENTS

1. What delivery system do you use to advise undecided students? (Check all that apply.)
   _____ a. Randomly assigned faculty advisors
   _____ b. Faculty advisors who volunteer to work with undecided students
   _____ c. Designated advisors for undecided students in an advising center
   _____ d. Advisors in a unit specifically created for undecided students
   _____ e. We do not officially recognize students as undecided

2. As part of your orientation program for new students, what activities do you provide for undecided students? (Check all that apply.)
   _____ a. Special group scheduling sessions
   _____ b. Information sessions for parents of undecided students
   _____ c. Introduction to the special services offered undecided students
   _____ d. Individual advising
   _____ e. We do not offer special sessions for undecided students

3. Do you have a written policy or set of objectives for advising undecided students? (Select one.)
   _____ a. Yes
   _____ b. No

4. Is one person assigned either part-time or full-time to coordinate the advising services for your undecided students? (Select one.)
   _____ a. Yes
   _____ b. No

5. How do you provide *academic* information to your undecided students? (Check all that apply.)
   _____ a. Special website for exploring majors at your institution
   _____ b. Regularly scheduled group sessions with faculty in many academic areas
   _____ c. As part of a first-year orientation or career-planning course
   _____ d. Referral to individual faculty or departmental advisors in many academic areas
   _____ e. Work individually with advisor
   _____ f. We don't have any organized program for exploring academic options

6. How do you provide *career* exploration and planning for your undecided students? (Check all that apply.)
   _____ a. Special workshops with assessment tools to help them explore career fields
   _____ b. Special website for academic major and career information for your undecided students
   _____ c. Career planning course for credit
   _____ d. A list of websites with career information links
   _____ e. Program involving contact with alumni or workers in a variety of occupations in the community
   _____ f. Career library
   _____ g. Computerized career-guidance information system (e.g., DISCOVER, SIGI-PLUS)
   _____ h. Field experience courses for exploring occupational fields first-hand
   _____ i. Access to the same career services as regular students
   _____ j. No special programs

7. Do you conduct a specific training program for advisors of your undecided students? (Select one.)
   _____ a. Yes
   _____ b. No

8. What topics do you typically cover in your training sessions? (Check all that apply.)

_____ a. General academic information including scheduling priorities and organized information about many academic major areas
_____ b. Campus referral sources
_____ c. E-mail advising policies and techniques
_____ d. Student development concepts
_____ e. Career development concepts
_____ f. Special advising skills and techniques for undecided students
_____ g. Job and employment outlook information
_____ h. Decision-making models

9. How frequent are your training sessions for advisors of undecided students? (Check one.)
_____ a. Once a year
_____ b. Twice a year
_____ c. Once a month
_____ d. Weekly

10. What type of support materials do you provide the advisors of your undecided students? (Check all that apply.)
_____ a. Special advising manual for undecided students
_____ b. Special website with academic and career information
_____ c. List of Internet resources and how to use them
_____ d. Academic planning sheets for all majors online and in printed form
_____ e. Campus resource lists
_____ f. Community resource list
_____ g. No special materials

11. When do advisors have contact with undecided students? (Check all that apply.)
_____ a. Pre-scheduling for registration
_____ b. Registration time
_____ c. When they drop or add a course
_____ d. When they declare a major
_____ e. When they withdraw
_____ f. Regularly in a first-year orientation or survey course
_____ g. At least two times *per term* for discussing progress

12. What is your estimate of the frequency of contact between advisors and undecided students on your campus? (Select one.)
_____ a. Once a year
_____ b. Twice a year
_____ c. Five to seven times a year
_____ d. Eight or more times a year

13. How do you monitor the academic and career exploration progress of an undecided student? (Check all that apply.)

_____ a. Through regularly scheduled advisor conferences
_____ b. By checking their courses when they schedule
_____ c. By checking their grades at the end of a term
_____ d. When they declare a major

14. How do you evaluate your program for undecided students? (Check all that apply)
_____ a. Advisee evaluations (e.g., after appointments or other times)
_____ b. Research studies on advisee's progress as stated in your program mission and objectives
_____ c. Advisor self-evaluations and review
_____ d. Administrative review of your program objectives and service
_____ e. We don't evaluate our program

SCORING

Question	Points	Question	Points	Question	Points
1. a.	1	6. a.	3	10. a.	2
b.	2	b.	3	b.	2
c.	2	c.	3	c.	2
d.	3	d.	1	d.	2
e.	0	e.	2	e.	1
		f.	1	f.	1
2. a.	1	g.	2	g.	0
b.	2	h.	3		
c.	2	i.	0	11. a.	2
d.	3	j.	0	b.	1
e.	0			c.	1
		7. a.	3	d.	1
		b.	0	e.	1
3. a.	3			f.	3
b.	0	8. a.	1	g.	2
		b.	1		
4. a.	3	c.	2		
b.	0	d.	2	12. a.	0
		e.	2	b.	0
5. a.	3	f.	2	c.	1
b.	2	g.	2	d.	3
c.	3	h.	2		
d.	1			13. a.	3
e.	3	9. a.	0	b.	1
f.	0	b.	1	c.	1
		c.	2	d.	1
		d.	3		

14.	a.	2
	b.	3
	c.	1
	d.	2
	e.	0

Sum the total number of points you scored.

If you scored between 80 and 100 points, you probably need this book only to refine the excellent practices you already employ. Lower scores indicate this book may provide ideas and suggestions for creating an environment in which your undecided students can successfully explore and make academic and career-related decisions.

80–100	Outstanding program
70–79	Good
69–50	Fair
49–0	Poor

ORGANIZATIONAL MODELS

Habley (1994) adapts his seven basic models for advising (faculty-only, supplementary, split, dual, total intake, satellite, and self-contained models) to the needs of undecided students. He asserts that it is not possible to identify an organizational model for advising undecided students until a developmentally sequenced set of tasks are identified. He also states that there is no single best way to deliver and organize services for undecided students but whatever approach is used, services from both academic and support services must be integrated.

When undecided students are advised by "faculty only," they can be assigned randomly or used to "level" the advising loads of faculty in departments with fewer majors. Others may be assigned to Arts and Sciences faculty on the "premise that much of the general freshman curriculum resides in those departments" (p. 19).

The "supplementary" model, which in addition to faculty advising provides general information through an advising unit, is not generally know to be used to provide specialized services for undecided students. The "split" model, on the other hand, is designed to focus on the needs of specific groups of students, such as the undecided group. Sixty-eight percent of institutions reporting in an ACT survey (Habley,

2004) indicated that they had advising offices for undecided students. This is down from 85 percent in 1983.

The "dual" model, according to Habley, provides students with two advisors: a faculty advisor and an advisor in an advising unit. In this model, undecided students are the sole responsibility of the advisors in the advising unit until a decision about a major is made, at which time they are assigned to instructional faculty advisors.

The "total intake" model is the portal entry for all students who are advised until they fulfill specific requirements set by the degree units. In some total intake units, specially trained advisors may be responsible for undecided students, while in others, all advisors may be responsible. As Habley points out, however, there is great variation in advising undecided students in the total intake model.

In the "satellite" model of advising, each academic college (or school, division, etc.) assumes responsibility for advising its own students. Either a specific satellite office is established for advising undecided students or students are expected to identify a college and are advised there. The "self-contained" unit, which is often the model used in two-year colleges, features a centralized advising unit which advises students from point of entry to graduation. In this model, undecided students are often advised by counselors who are trained in a full range of services, including academic, career, and personal counseling.

Although Habley reiterates that "there is no one best way to organize services for undecided students," he does emphasize that there is a methodology for building a model that can best serve a particular institution's way of organizing advising services. These services must not only be effectively integrated but must be organized to meet the developmental needs of this special population.

Although Pardee (2000, 2004) doesn't apply her organizational structures specifically to advising undecided students, her constructs offer helpful suggestions for implementing and maintaining a program for them. Pardee outlines three models for delivery advising services: centralized, decentralized, and shared structures. In the centralized model, all advising occurs in an advising center or a counseling center. This is a common organizational structure that is adapted by many two-year community colleges (King, 1993).

The most common decentralized model is used where faculty perform all the academic advising. According to ACT's Sixth National Survey on the status of academic advising (Habley, 2004), the use of the faculty-only organizational model has witnessed a gradual decline (from 33 percent in 1987 to 25 percent in 2003). When the faculty-only model is used with undecided students, faculty may be randomly assigned to them or some institutions ask for volunteers to advise this special group.

The most common shared structure uses faculty as well as an advising center staff to advise. This is the split-model and is considered one of the most common delivery systems (27 percent for all institutions in the ACT survey, but 46 percent at four-year public colleges and universities) and the most common for advising undecided students. When students have declared a major or have fulfilled certain criteria, they are reassigned to faculty or other advisors in the major's school or department. As Pardee (2004) contends, "the determining factor in the success of any model is whether there is a good fit between the model and the institution, faculty, students and other variables" (p. 3).

General Advising Center

Advisement centers have been established in recent years to provide advising continuity and stability for all students (Habley, 2004; Pardee, 2000, 2004). These centers are usually staffed by full-time professional advisors, but faculty, peer, and paraprofessional advisors often augment advising center staff (Crockett, 1982; Habley, 2000). Sixty-eight percent of undecided students are advised in advising centers according to the survey.

In addition to general advising, advising centers often offer services to special groups of students such as the undecided population. These fall under the structure Pardee (2000) calls "shared" and the split or supplemental models described by Habley (2004). The number of advising centers according to the ACT survey increased dramatically from 30 percent in 1983 to 73 percent in 2003. The advantages of this system for these students are many. Information is easily accessible and current. The continuity of contact with well-trained professional advisors who are knowledgeable about many academic areas is especially advantageous to undecided students. Advising centers are often able to provide the integration of academic and career information that is vital to an exploring student.

Advising centers provide an easily recognized, central location for services for all students. Some students hesitate to identify themselves as undecided; an advising center provides the type of anonymity that these students prefer. There are many levels of decision among freshmen; the advising center can offer a wide range of services while providing the specialized information that many students require. This system is especially helpful to the student who changes majors and needs special help during this transition period.

Disadvantages of an advising center only model is the lack of faculty contact that students need (Pascarella & Terenzini, 2005; Reinarz & White, 1995). This can be overcome, however, through careful programming and referral. Another disadvantage is the direct cost of maintaining such a center (Crockett, 1982). When student retention is an issue, however, advisement centers have proved to be an extremely effective method for providing comprehensive services to all types of students (Crockett, 1985; King, 1993). The advantages of a centralized system thus far outweigh the disadvantages.

Faculty Advising

The oldest system for providing academic advising services is faculty advising. The sixth annual ACT survey found that 80 percent of instructional faculty serve as advisors in academic departments. Faculty members are considered the most knowledgeable and appropriate individuals for providing academic information, scheduling help, and long-range program planning. Since many faculty advisors are subject matter oriented, this creates a distinct disadvantage to the undecided student who may wish to explore several unrelated academic areas.

While many faculty advisors are student centered and provide a very personalized approach to program and course selection, they often lack the background knowledge and skills needed to advise undecided students. Advising these students requires a great deal of concentrated time and effort. Unfortunately, faculty are infrequently rewarded for the time spent in advising. This creates a certain amount of pressure on conscientious faculty who are already involved in teaching, research, and committee assignments.

When faculty are used to advise undecided students, they must be selected on the basis of their willingness to work with this special group, must be aware of the time and effort involved, and must be willing to attend frequent training and in-service programs to develop their expertise in advising this group. Faculty advisors to undecided students need to become generalists in academic information, become knowledgeable about student development theory and practice, and understand career development as well as career and academic relationships. They need to maintain up-to-date and accurate information about the academic programs at their institution. These faculty need to be rewarded for the additional time and energy this system requires (for example, a decreased course load or monetary rewards).

The advantage of a faculty advising system is the opportunity for student-faculty contact and a climate for establishing a relationship that is an important part of the college experience. When faculty advising is carefully integrated into other delivery systems such as an advising center, the best of all possible programs can be realized.

Advising Centers for Undecided Students

As reported by Habley (2004) in the most recent ACT's national survey, 68 percent of institutions using a "split" model indicated they offered special advising centers for undecided students. Compared to the 85 percent who reported such centers in 1981, recognition of the special needs of undecided students is decreasing.

Advising centers specifically designed to meet the needs of undecided students provide certain advantages. Early identification of students means that they may become involved in special programs and services immediately. A special center provides:

1. An identifiable location, so that exploratory students know where services are available and can become familiar with the programs that are offered on their behalf;
2. Specially trained professional advisors who are sensitive to the needs of this population;
3. An organized approach to exploration, which can be initiated by advisor and student immediately;
4. Continuity of contact with an advisor who knows the individual student's unique interests, abilities, needs, and values;
5. Special program elements, which may be designed to offer a comprehensive service;
6. Career exploration, which may be provided through special individual and group sessions or through career-planning courses for

credit;

7. A career library service, which can help students access current and accurate occupational and job market information. Internet, websites, and computerized career information systems are usually available as well;
8. A means for initiating needs assessments as well as monitoring individual students' progress;
9. An evaluation of services, which can provide information about the program's effect on student satisfaction and retention.

Many of the above functions may also be provided by a general advising center. A general center that assigns advisors exclusively to the undecided population is frequently used for providing services for these students. The advantages of the special center, however, are that all efforts are concentrated on the undecided group and that specialists can be developed to work with a smaller population. Advisors in a special center are usually not from specific disciplines, and therefore can advise from a student-centered perspective rather than being concerned about loyalty to a certain discipline. Full-time professional advisors are more apt to be trained in career as well as academic advising.

One disadvantage of a special center is that a few students do not wish to be identified as undecided, and so do not use the services even though they need them. This can be overcome by creating a climate that encourages all students to explore during their freshman year and providing an atmosphere that supports students who are initially decided but who need to change majors later. Further, a special center, like the general advising center, requires a direct cost that many small institutions, in particular, find difficult to justify for a small number of students. A combination of delivery systems including a special center for undecided students may be cost-effective, however, when the retention of students is considered.

Residence Hall Centers

Another vehicle for delivering coordinated services to undecided students is a residence hall program created especially for students who wish more concentrated help with academic and career planning (Abel, 1981; Schein & Bowers, 1992). An advantage of such an approach is that entering freshmen can identify themselves immediately and participate on a voluntary basis. Small groups within the dorm may be formed early, and help with adjustment concerns as well as academic and career planning may be provided in a very personalized environment.

A freshmen orientation or career-planning course for credit can be taught in the residence hall. Classes can be held on the premises, and many career-related activities can be incorporated into the residence hall programming. A career resource library may be established in the center, so that students have easy access to many printed materials, Internet, and other computer resources.

A residence hall program for undecided students can provide an ongoing, coordinated program effort that can meet the developmental needs of students during the freshman year. Upperclass students who need a structured approach to career exploration could also be included as a separate component of the overall program.

A disadvantage of this delivery system is that many students who need this type of help do not wish to be identified in this way. It obviously eliminates the many commuter students who need this type of intensive advising service, as well.

University Colleges or Divisions

Some larger institutions have developed advising systems through a special college of enrollment, such as a "university college" or "university division" (Gordon & Steele, 1992; Strommer, 1993). Not only are most entering freshmen provided advising services especially designed for their needs, but undecided students may be easily identified and served. Students wishing to commit themselves tentatively to a general academic area such as business, engineering, education, or the health professions may do so while taking general education requirements. Students may confirm their choice or change major with few bureaucratic limitations. A university college system offers all entering freshmen, whether decided or undecided, the same opportunity and time to identify, study, and confirm a major decision in a supportive, carefully supervised environment.

A university college system may provide the best delivery method for academic and career advising for undecided students, since many of the resources for exploring can be provided within one physical location. Referral for academic information may be made within the college, since most academic areas are represented by advisors trained to advise in specific major fields. Freshman orientation courses can also be taught within the context of a university college (Minnick, 2003; Strommer, 1993), and career counseling and career information resources may also be provided. Many university colleges are also responsible for the orientation of new students, so the undecided group can be easily identified and assigned as they enter advising services designed especially for them.

The university college system recognizes that many freshmen need the time to explore and confirm educational and vocational decisions. Advisors within a university college system are trained to work with freshmen students and become specialists in advising this population. Undecided students are able to explore in a well-coordinated program while not feeling separated from their classmates.

Other Delivery Systems

Other areas that advise undecided students, identified in the ACT's national survey, include individual colleges or departments and academic and student affairs offices. Undecided students who must choose a specific degree college or academic department while exploring may find limited help in gathering information about a wide variety of unrelated majors. Advisors in colleges or departments are rarely generalists and can only refer a student with interests outside their expertise to other departments or faculty. This creates a fragmented approach to the search process and may discourage the student from looking beyond the confines of the enrollment unit. While this system is better than none, it severely limits and complicates the exploration process.

Student affairs offices are also less desirable, since their information about majors is generally limited. Student affairs professionals will be able to provide the personalized, student developmental perspective that is essential to the advising process, but they may not have access to the complex academic information that undecided students need.

The delivery system selected by an institution to advise undecided students will depend on the importance it attaches to these special students; its philosophy regarding the right of, and the need for, individuals to explore; and the resources, both human and financial, that it is willing to allocate to this function. Special or general advising centers that target programs for the undecided are increasingly recognized as effective vehicles for providing the type and extent of academic and career advising that undecided students require. Once the delivery method is established, there are certain administrative considerations to take into account. Setting program objectives, selecting, training, and evaluating staff, creating and refining program elements, and evaluating the effectiveness of the overall effort are a few of the areas to consider. The need for one individual to coordinate this overall program quickly becomes apparent.

ADMINISTRATIVE CONSIDERATIONS

Regardless of the delivery system that is used, there are certain administrative factors that need to be considered for effective operation of an academic advising program.

1. *A program philosophy and a set of objectives based on this philosophy need to be established.* Such a philosophical statement for a program might include the following:

a. Not declaring a major or career field when entering college is acceptable and, for some students, encouraged;
b. Exploring students may spend time and will receive organized help in assessing their personal strengths and limitations as they relate to major and occupational choice;
c. Exploring students may spend time and receive help in researching information about a variety of academic majors and career areas;
d. Exploring students will make an academic decision within a time frame that is developmentally theirs.

Objectives must be developed to put this philosophy into action. Possible objectives include:

- By the beginning of their sophomore year, entering exploratory students will:

a. understand the career development process as it relates to different stages of their lives, especially the college years;

b. have gained insights and knowledge about their own decision-making styles and strategies;

c. have learned and practiced information-seeking behaviors;

d. have considerable information about majors gathered and have discussed these majors with faculty or college counselors in at least three areas;

e. have chosen a major or narrowed their choice to several realistic alternatives;

f. express satisfaction with the advising help they have received during the exploration process.

Another set of objectives would need to be developed for each group of students, such as those who change majors or are undecided upperclassmen. It is difficult to evaluate the effectiveness of an advising program without a written policy or objectives statement. While these objectives may change periodically, they serve as a framework within which the various services and activities may be developed.

2. *The staff needed to initiate and maintain a program for undecided students may be composed of full-time professional advisors, faculty, graduate students, peer advisors, or a combination of these.* One professional staff member must be designated to coordinate the program. No matter how large or small the institution or the effort, a program without this coordination cannot function effectively or be accountable.

Administrators or coordinators of an advising program for undecided students may be trained in academic advising philosophy and functions or career development and counseling, have knowledge and experience in testing and administration, and be able to bring together in one concerted effort all areas on campus engaged in working with this population. On smaller campuses this may be a part-time position, while in a setting with larger numbers of undecided students, a full-time professional administrator may be required.

The staff working with undecided students should be professionally trained advisors or counselors. Undecided students not only need generalists in academic information but also need advisors with a solid foundation in student and career development concepts, as well as knowledge for securing and interpreting career and job market information. In addition to excellent communication skills, counseling techniques are often required in certain situations. If faculty members are working with undecided students, they need to be trained in these areas as well. The number and type of staff vary greatly with the institution's resources and the number of students being served.

3. *Creating, developing, and refining program components are continuous processes.* On some campuses, certain programs and services are already in existence. Some campuses offer academic information sessions, decision-making workshops, or career-planning courses to all students, for example, and undecided students may become involved in these or in special adaptations designed for them. Other program components need to be initiated where these services do not already exist. Internet testing resources, small group advising sessions, a website dedicated to academic and career exploration, small-group advising sessions, or special sections of a freshmen orientation course might be created just for undecided students. These components need to be carefully coordinated to present a comprehensive, unified program.

A team approach is necessary to advising undecided students, since their needs cut across many academic departments and student services. Every academic department on campus needs to become involved as a resource for undecided students, through websites or printed information about their majors and requirements, and as a referral source, as students require in-depth information about their alternatives. Advisors, faculty, admissions, and orientation personnel, counseling and testing resources, administrators, and career librarians all interact with undecided students throughout the academic year. Collaboration among academic and student services is essential if students are to be served in a "seamless" way (Bohlman & Deal, 1997).

An important component of a program is its technology resources and how they are geared to the needs of undecided students. Some campuses have created special websites for this population, which may include self-assessment activities and information about the institution's academic majors and related career fields. Links to many academically-related career areas can be included so that information resources are expanded and students' perspectives broadened.

Community resources are also important in the overall advising of undecided students. Field experience sites as well as exposure to workers in a variety of careers may be used as components of a career exploration program. Health and social agencies, counseling resources, and other educational institutions are other community resources that may be integrated into student services.

Coordination of these services is critical if they are to function as a unified effort. Duplication or overlap of services is not as likely with careful supervision of the overall program.

4. *Program and staff evaluation must be carried out on a regular basis.* Evaluation of each program component, as well as periodic assessment of the total program, provides information on which to decide to retain certain successful elements and to make future changes (Creamer, 1994). Soliciting student and staff evaluations of the program provides different perspectives in measuring the effectiveness of the overall effort. Periodic evaluation of advisors' effectiveness also needs to be initiated. (Chapter 5 describes evaluation techniques in more detail.)

Once the delivery method is established, and objectives, staff, and program components are identified, services need to be organized and implemented. The scope of services begins with the first admissions contact and ends with the implementation of a decision by the student. Follow-up services may be necessary for certain students as well.

SCOPE OF SERVICES

There are many contact points for identifying and intercepting undecided students. Since some students enter college undecided and others become undecided after an initial choice is rejected or thwarted, services need to be available at many junctures.

Pre-entry Considerations

The first contact many students have with an institution is through the institution's website and the literature published to attract and provide information to prospective students. A clearly defined statement of the institution's philosophy toward exploration on the website and in catalogs and other printed materials alerts students and parents to the option of not declaring a major initially. Actively recruiting undecided students may also be a positive activity. However, admission contacts encouraging exploration must be backed by services and programs that will help students accomplish this task. A description of the counseling services available to all students is usually incorporated into the admission's website and institutional literature. Special descriptions of programs for the exploring student may also be included. the extent to which and emphasis with which this information is provided may affect the number and type of students willing to enter a specific institution undecided (Gordon & Steele, 2003).

Parents are often an integral part of the admissions process. Some students feel a great deal of pressure to choose a major from parental and other sources. Educating parents to the role of self- and academic information in the decision-making process and describing the type of help students can receive during the exploration period helps to alleviate some of their concerns (Smith & Gordon, 2003). Parents are often fearful of a student losing time or "wasting courses" if he or she does not decide upon a major immediately upon entering college. While this may be true in isolated cases, parents need to be assured that the time taken for exploration may lead to a more stable and satisfying result. Admissions contacts can be an important time to help parents understand the tentativeness of many initial decisions and the possibility for future changes.

Most recruiting efforts include high school visitations, the institution's website, and bringing prospective students on campus for informational programs. Many informational preadmissions contacts are made as well. The institution's philosophy on being uncertain about major or career decisions and the advising and counseling services offered can be described during these activities. Knowing these services are available may positively influence a student's decision to attend an institution.

Orientation

New student orientation is another critical point which parents and students make major decisions. It is estimated that over 20 percent of all students change majors between admissions and the start of classes (Steele, 2000). Orientation can be an important time to assure students that not being sure of their major at this point is a natural state and that specific help is available over a period of time to help them make choices in an orderly way.

Some institutions offer preorientation workshops at which academic and career information is provided. Some workshops incorporate self-assessment activities as well. While this offers a very superficial exposure to majors and requirements, it helps to take the mystery out of what appears to be a complicated and confusing body of information. Special sections on the institution's website can also offer orientation information.

Special orientation sessions are especially enlightening to parents of undecided students, since many are concerned about their child's lack of commitment and view undecidedness from a perspective rooted in another generation. Once they realize that their student will not wander aimlessly but will participate in an organized program for exploring, these fears are usually alleviated.

Academic Advising

Advising services involve many offices on campus. A unified effort is essential if the advice students receive is to be consistent, current, and appropriate. Areas that may become involved in advising the undecided student include academic departmental offices, individual faculty, counseling centers, residence halls, office of records, and libraries. Each office or resource contributes to the advising function. Departmental offices and faculty can act as sources of information about programs, majors, and courses. Student affairs involvement may provide special programs in residence halls, while counseling centers may offer individual counseling and testing as well as workshops on such topics as self-assessment and decision-making. The computer technologies that now support advisors in their work with students have increased efficiency and facilitated the access and management of information. On large campuses, the variety and scope of services are undoubtedly broader, and the services more decentralized, than on smaller campuses.

Career Advising

The scope of career advising extends from helping students access career information from the Internet to the teaching of a career-planning course for academic credit. Several areas on campus may be involved in providing a comprehensive career-counseling and information service to students. These include counseling services, the career-planning and placement centers on campus, and the library system, which can provide career information in a variety of formats.

Integrating academic and career information is an important part of the advisement process (Bogenschutz, 1994). This requires the cooperation of both academic and career advising services (McCalla-Wriggins, 2000). Many campuses provide programs that are jointly sponsored by academic and career services. These include academic and career information through "career days," career decision-making courses, and academic major exploration courses (Gordon & Sears, 2004). Internet resources for career exploration have revolutionized the amount and variety of career information that is available. The advantage of accessing information in this form is the immediacy and scope that it offers. For example, The U.S. Department of Labor's O*Net website (http://online.onetcenter.org) offers occupational information from many perspectives, including self-information inventories, occupation summaries, and links to many other online information resources.

Some obstacles to cooperation include staff, turf-related problems such as reporting to different supervisors, no overall coordination, and a lack of priority on the part of the institution. Communication between academic and career services personnel is cited as important to the effective coordination or academic and career services. Personal contacts, written information, professional compatibility, proximity of offices, and administrative support are noted as conducive to encouraging this communication and coordination process.

Career Planning and Placement Services

The placement function on many campuses is combined with career-planning services. Undecided students benefit from current information about the job opportunities implicit with certain majors. Placement offices can provide current information that reflects the placement of recent graduates. Most career planning and placement offices encourage first-year students to become familiar with their services. Placement directors are an excellent resource for undecided students, since they can offer not only occupational information but also information about employers' requirements and preferences. Many have access to Internet programs that can help students see the relation between major fields and the type of jobs their graduates are obtaining. They often provide seminars in job-hunting skills that can be helpful to students searching for summer jobs. Work experiences can provide students with firsthand knowledge about the career areas they are considering.

An organizational structure to advise undecided students must reflect the mission statement of the institution and the stated mission and goals of the advising program itself. Melander (2005) outlines some basic principles for organizing and managing advising systems. He stresses that educative-advising provides "intentional learning opportunities so that students plan, acquire, and assess their own educations" (p. 88).

As Pardee (2000) states, the best organizational models are well integrated into the structure of the institution, yet are so clearly defined that advisors and students know how to operate within them. Advising programs are pervasive across many institutional boundaries, and this is especially important when advising undecided students, since they need to access many institutional resources as they explore. Whatever organizational model is implemented, the focus must always be on the student.

SUMMARY

There are many possible administrative models for delivering advising and counseling services to undecided students. Some campuses use existing faculty advising systems, while others create a special administrative unit for this purpose. A combination of systems is also used, such as faculty advisors and full-time professional counselors in an advising center. Regardless of the delivery system, certain administrative considerations must be recognized as important to an effective program.

Program objectives must be established before advising services can be identified and created. A person designated to coordinate and monitor a program for undecided students is critical if a unified approach is to be achieved. Staff associated with the program must be carefully selected and trained. A team approach is required, since so many offices and departments on campus are involved in working with undecided students.

The scope of services involved in working with undecided students begins with the first recruitment and admissions contact, includes the orientation of new students, and incorporates academic advising, career counseling, career planning, and placement services. Since undecided students comprise a heterogeneous population, and since their needs are so diverse, an efficient administrative system, the identification and implementation of a wide range of services, and the coordination and collaboration of many campus offices are essential if an effective program is to be initiated and maintained.

REFERENCES

Abel, J. (1981). Residence hall coordinators: Academic advising for undecided students. *NACADA Journal, 1,* 44–46.

Bogenschutz, M. (1994). Career advising for the undecided student. In V. Gordon (Ed.), *Issues in advising the undecided college student,* (pp. 49–58). Columbia, SC: National Resource Center for the Freshman Year Experience.

Bolman, L.G., & Deal, T.E. (1997). *Reframing organizations: Artistry, character and leadership.* San Francisco: Jossey-Bass.

Creamer, E.G. (1994). Evaluating advising programs for undecided students. In V. Gordon (Ed), *Issues in advising the undecided college student,* (pp. 109–121). Columbia, SC: National Resource Center for the Freshman Year Experience.

Crockett, D.S. (1982). Academic advising delivery systems. In R. Winston, S. Ender, & T. Miller (Eds.), *Developmental approaches to academic advising.* San Francisco: Jossey-Bass.

Crockett, D.S. (1985). Academic advising. In L. Noel, R. Levitz, & D. Saluri (Eds.), *Increasing student retention.* San Francisco: Jossey-Bass.

Gordon, V.N., & Sears, S.J. (2004). *Selecting a college major–Exploration and decision-making* (5th Ed.). Upper Saddle River, NJ: Prentice-Hall.

Gordon, V.N., & Steele, G.E. (1992). Advising major changers: Students in transition. *NACADA Journal, 12,* 22–27.

Gordon, V.N., & Steele, G.E. (2003). Undecided first-year students: A 25 year longitudinal study. *Journal of the First-Year Experience, 15,* 19–38.

Habley, W.R. (1994). Administrative approaches to advising undecided students. In V. Gordon (Ed.), *Issues in advising the undecided college student,* (pp. 17–23). Columbia, SC: National Resource Center for the Freshman Year Experience.

Habley, W.R. (2000). Current practices in academic advising. In V. Gordon, W. Habley & Associates (Eds.), *Academic advising–A comprehensive handbook,* (pp. 35–43). San Francisco: Jossey-Bass.

Habley, W.R. (Ed.) (2004). *The status of academic advising–Findings from the ACT sixth national survey.* NACADA Monograph Series, No. 10. Manhattan, KS: National Academic Advising Association.

Habley, W.R. & McClanahan, R. (2004). *What works in student retention?* Iowa City: ACT, Inc.

King, M.C. (1993). Advising models and delivery systems. In M.C. King (Ed.), *Academic advising: Organizing and delivery services for student success. New Directions for Community Colleges, No. 82.* San Francisco: Jossey-Bass.

McCalla-Wriggins, B. (2000). Integrating academic advising and career and life planning. In V. Gordon, W. Habley, & Associates (Eds.), *Academic advising–A comprehensive handbook,* (pp. 162–176). San Francisco: Jossey-Bass.

Melander, E.R. (2005). Advising as educating: A framework for organizing academic advising. *NACADA Journal, 25*(2), 84–91.

Minnick, T.M. (2003). *University survey: A guidebook for new students.* Columbus, OH: The Ohio State University.

Pardee, C.F. (2000). Organizational models for academic advising. In V. Gordon and W. Habley, & Associates (Eds.), *Academic advising–A comprehensive handbook,* (pp. 162–176.) San Francisco: Jossey-Bass.

Pardee, C.F. (2004). Organizational structures for advising. Retrieved March 28, 2006 from NACADA Academic Advising Today website: http://www.nacada.ksu.edu/ATT/NW28_4htm

Pascarella, E.T., & Terenzini, P.T. (2005). *How college affects students,* Vol. 2. San Francisco: Jossey-Bass.

Reinarz, A. & White, E. (Eds.) (1995). *Teaching through academic advising: A faculty perspective. (New Directions for Teaching and Learning).* San Francisco: Jossey-Bass.

Schein, H.K., & Bowers, P.M. (1992). Using living/learning centers to provide integrated campus services for freshmen. *Journal of Freshman Year Experience, 4,* 59–77.

Smith, D.C., & Gordon, V.N. (2003). *A family guide to academic advising.* Columbia, SC: National Academic Advising Association and National Resource Center for the Freshman Year Experience and Students in Transition.

Steele, G.E. (2000). A researched-based approach to working with undecided students: A case study illustration. *NACADA Journal, 23*(1 & 2), 10–20.

Strommer, D.W. (Ed.) (1993). *Portals of entry: University colleges and undergraduate divisions.* Columbia, SC: National Resource Center for The Freshman Year Experience.

Chapter 5

PROGRAM COMPONENTS: METHODS AND TECHNIQUES

The comprehensive academic and career advising services required by undecided students suggests a variety of program elements and resources. Zarvell and Rigby (1994) describe three categories of resources needed by undecided students: academic, career, and personal. They contend that advisors need to enhance undecided students' intellectual state, so they can accept and process new information that can lead to the fulfillment of their academic goals. Perceived student barriers can be identified through student interviews, surveys, or group discussion. In this way, program components and resources will be current and targeted to undecided students' very special needs.

While some of these services already exist on many campuses, programmatic emphasis or expansion may be needed to adapt them to the special needs of the undecided population. Program components fall into several categories: (1) those pertaining to individual advising and counseling, (2) those created for group involvement, and (3) those initiated to improve the expertise and techniques of advisors or others working with undecided students.

INDIVIDUAL STUDENT APPROACHES

Although many program components and materials may be applied to both individuals and groups of students, some are especially effective for working on a one-to-one basis. Since each student has a unique set of personal characteristics and decision-making style, some of these approaches are more applicable to one type of student than to another. For example, one student may find a workshop or course more conducive to exploration than does a student who prefers to gather information in a search of the Internet. Advisors must be able to recognize and implement different methods and approaches that reflect the needs of individual students.

Although many services may be offered, one-to-one advising is still the core of most advising efforts. Advisor and student need to establish the roles and responsibilities of their relationship from the outset. One example of how this can be done is to draw up a contract so that these responsibilities are discussed and clearly stated. Students need to understand the time and energy involved in exploration. They need to acknowledge that the responsibility for exploration is theirs, as well as the responsibility for a decision, once it is made.

Advisor's responsibilities include helping students define their goals, helping them assess their personal strengths and limitations, and acting as a resource for information and referral, as well as helping them generate viable alternatives. Advisors can offer the support that students need during the exploration process.

Both advisor and advisee need to determine the outcomes of the exploration process. Too often advisor and student exchange information as though this were the goal of the advising relationship. Students not only need help in gathering information, but need help in processing it as well. Self-, academic, and career information needs to be integrated in a personal framework. Only then can tentative decisions be reached and action taken to implement them.

Advisors can teach students decision-making by modeling the process during the advising exchange. This means that an orderly progression of tasks need to be accomplished. These tasks are outlined below.

Task 1: Help the student determine why he or she is undecided.

As noted in Chapter 1, there are as many reasons for being undecided as there are students. Any academic or career advisor working with undecided students quickly discerns the complexity and number of reasons for indecision in individual students. The list below summarizes a few of these causes. An individual student may be involved in more than one of them simultaneously.

- *Lack of independence in decision-making*–Some students have had decisions made for them for many years by parents, teachers, and external circumstances. They have never had the opportunity to make decisions for themselves or taken responsibility for decisions once they were made. Some students entering college expect the same patterns to continue. They anticipate that faculty, counselors, or academic advisors will make academic and career decisions for them. They believe that all decisions will come from some force outside themselves.
- *Lack of knowledge of the decision-making process*–Many entering college students are unaware that there is an orderly process for exploring and selecting an academic major or career field. They have made decisions in the past but have rarely stopped to analyze all the factors involved in the process itself. They tend to approach important decisions such as career and life planning in the same way as insignificant ones. Thus, they have no experience upon which to draw when they are confronted with academic and vocational decisions in college.
- *Lack of information*–Very often students have no concrete, realistic information on which to base an educational decision, even if they know how to make it. Informational deficits are one of the most common problems among undecided students (and among some decided ones as well). Often students do not know how, where, what, or from whom to collect the information that is so vital to informed educational decisions.
- *Multiplicity of interests*–Some students have so many areas of interest they cannot decide between them. In some cases, it takes more detailed information to help them sort out the real differences in their alternatives. For some, it is a matter of "giving up" some closely held alternatives. For others, it may mean combining several areas of interest into one new alternative.
- *Lack of interests*–On the other end of the continuum are the students who claim they have absolutely no interests at all. Many students have difficulty verbalizing interests even though they have them. This situation is more difficult to overcome than that of students with many interests. Students unable to express their interests may have had very few experiences on which to base an opinion. They may be fearful of uttering an idea aloud, since they feel that it may be construed as a commitment. Some may have

difficulty expressing themselves about other areas of life as well.

- *Lack of ability*–Some students' interests are in areas in which they have doubts about their abilities to succeed. Some college freshmen do not know their abilities, since they have never really tested them. If they exerted a minimum amount of effort in high school, they may doubt their capabilities in some areas. They may not be motivated to take risks, or may not be willing to invest the energy required to find out what their abilities are. Others may not know *how* to determine what they are capable of.
- *Lack of knowledge about educational and occupational relationships*–Many students are concerned about the types of occupations to which a particular major leads. Others have career goals but do not know the majors that will help them attain these goals. These educational and occupational links are perceived as mutually inclusive by some students. Some will not choose an academic major unless it has an obvious relationship with an occupational field. Whether to choose a major or an occupation first is the "chicken and egg" question with which many students struggle. Many decided students make initial choices because this relationship is obvious. This is a particularly difficult issue with students who are inclined toward the liberal arts.
- *Lack of desire to attend college*–Some students are undecided because they do not want to be in college. They enrolled because of outside pressures, but their interests and goals do not include a college degree. They may not feel "ready" to tackle the college environment. They are therefore not motivated even to explore some of the options a particular campus offers.

Studies on indecision types have spawned many new diagnostic tools to help identify the important reasons why students do not make academic and career decisions (Chartrand et al., 1990; Swanson, Daniels, & Tokar, 1996; Luzzo, 1996). These can be very useful in an initial contact, since they can pinpoint concerns in areas of self-identity, informational deficits, or external barriers very quickly. Helping the student identify and verbalize the issues that are involved in his or her situation can be an important first task in the exploration process.

Crites (1981) discusses three diagnostic approaches and the contributions that various counseling models make to the advisor or counselor of undecided students. *Differential diagnosis* tries to determine the student's career decision problems. For example, a student's choice of a major or occupation may require a level of aptitude that he or she does not possess. This makes the choice unrealistic. *Dynamic diagnosis* is concerned with *why* the student cannot decide. The student may be indecisive in most decision-making situations, and therefore have difficulty with this one. To determine the developmental context of the decision-maker, Crites suggests a *decisional diagnosis.* This takes into consideration the student's career maturity at a given point. The student, for example, may not be able to assess her or his personal strengths objectively.

Other issues to explore with the student during the initial contact are:

- *Determining the level of indecision*–If the student has a tentative idea in mind, he or she requires a more informational approach than a student who is totally undecided, for whom more self-assessment activities might be indicated.
- *Determining the level of commitment to exploring*–How motivated is the student to devote the time and energy necessary to the exploration process? Students who are feeling some discontinuity or anxiety for changing their undecided status need to become involved in the tasks necessary to reach a decision. Some students may not be ready to choose a major. They may be in Tiedeman and O'Hara's (1963) awareness stage and so are not prepared to explore or crystallize a choice. Career maturity may also be a factor here. A plan for gathering information will not be used by a student who feels no need to change the status quo.
- *Exploring personal concerns about being undecided*–An advisor can help a student articulate feelings associated with being undecided. Some students feel eager and ready to explore. Others feel anxious or pressured by parents, friends, or the institution to make a decision. The affective dimension must be acknowledged and dealt with before any serious exploration can take place.
- *Identifying the student's decision-making style*–Some students need to determine how past decision-making experiences affect their search for alternatives. Has their decision-making style been productive or nonproductive in the past? Do they rely on external forces to decide for them? Who has been involved in their academic and career planning in the past? Are they ready to take responsibility for the decisions they will eventually make?

During this initial phase of individual advising, the advisor needs to establish a supportive, caring climate so that the student feels comfortable in identifying the problem and feels confident that the exploration process will be a positive, productive experience.

Task 2: Help the student organize a plan for exploring.

This is the information-gathering part of the process. Some students need to assess their personal characteristics in depth. Many times this means referring them to a career counselor, a career-planning course for credit, or pointing out testing possibilities on the Internet. There are many aspects to self-appraisal, and the advisor and student need to determine the extent and depth that are needed. Personality instruments, interest and value inventories, aptitude and ability measures, and decision-making instruments are a a few resources that may be used. Many of these are now available on the Internet or on computer-assisted career guidance systems. There is always a danger, however, that students will use these results in a literal translation of what their choice should be. The real value of an interest inventory, for example, is as a starting place for helping the student focus on areas that are (often) being considered anyway. To subject an undecided student to a battery of tests indiscriminately without a rationale or plan may only serve to complicate the problem. Testing experiences, however, if properly controlled, can help a student integrate a great deal of personal information into a framework in which alternatives may be identified and studied.

Both test and nontest data might be needed to clarify the causes of indecision, which can then suggest solutions. Accumulating and integrating self-knowledge are critical components of decision making.

Another area of information that is vital to the exploration process pertains to college majors. Many students enter college with limited knowledge of majors, program options, course requirements, and electives. Most advisors are on comfortable ground in this area. Although much information is provided in college websites, catalogs, and bulletins, these sometimes do not have an easy format for exploration and frequently change. Many students need the personal, one-to-one contact that only direct personal interviewing provides.

When gathering information about academic programs, undecided students need:

1. *A general overview of all majors offered on a campus.* This introduces them to programs they may not know exist and places parameters on all possible options. Knowing the outside limits of possible choices is often revealing to a student who does not know where to start.
2. *A summary of the basic requirements for all majors.* This reveals all the common course requirements across the areas being considered. The summary also aids students in scheduling courses that overlap all the majors of interest to them. Scheduling in this way keeps options open while the exploration process is in progress.
3. *Help in generating a list of questions to ask faculty, college counselors, and other resource persons,* so that when informational contacts are made their questions will be organized and relevant. Teaching interviewing skills helps students become more confident in this important aspect of exploring.
4. *The opportunity to share information and reflect on it with a generalist advisor.* The advantages and disadvantages of each possibility can be weighed and discussed. This is a very important step in the information-gathering phase of exploration. An advisor can serve an important function here–to listen, question, and help students reflect on the information collected.

Another informational area concerns occupations and job market projections. This is a complex body of knowledge and one that changes rapidly. Since advisors cannot be expected to become experts in this area, other resources must provide students the opportunity to be exposed to this information. The Internet is an excellent source in this area. It is important, however, to carefully identify sources that are relevant to the individual student's interest. Other resources are faculty in specific fields, career planning and placement offices, and career libraries. Since this search can be overwhelming for students, a classification system needs to be available to help them translate their interests, abilities, academic major interests, and other personal data into occupational groups.

Gordon (2006) demonstrates the relationship between personal information (e.g., interests, abilities, values) and occupational fields by comparing the similarities between three classification systems: The U.S. Government's *Guide to Occupational Exploration* (GOE) codes, Holland codes, and ACT, Inc.'s *World of Work Map.* The GOE can help students explore career options based on their areas of interests. Holland pairs personality types with work environments (see Chapters 1 and 2 for detailed descriptions). The *World of Work Map* is based on the degree that occupations work with data, people, things, and ideas. Both occupations and college majors can be plotted using six occupational clusters. The three systems are similar in the way they organize work tasks and worker characteristics, and can be useful to students who are trying to make connections between their strengths and interests and academic majors.

Another important resource is the computer-assisted career guidance systems (CACGS), such as DISCOVER (http://www.act.org/discover), SIGI Plus (http://www.valprint.com), or Focus II (http://www.focuscareer.com). These systems can access vast, current occupational and job market information, and are updated frequently.

One danger in the information-gathering task is the possibility of overwhelming students with an overload in a short period of time. Information-gathering needs to take place with frequent breaks for reflection and thought. Too much information too quickly only confuses some students and makes them feel even more pressured and bewildered. Advisors need to help students pace themselves in keeping with their individual ability to gather and assimilate information in a productive way.

Task 3: Help the student integrate all the information that has been collected.

This is the step that many students find difficult. Gathering information can be a very positive experience, but pulling it all together into meaningful, manageable form can be overwhelming for some students. This is why each student's level of maturity and ability to assimilate information is important to ascertain. A dualistic student, for example, may still be looking for the right and only choice, and thus not be able to integrate or synthesize the information they have gathered.

Advisors can help students generate or confirm realistic alternatives from the data that have been collected. Students need to see relationships between their personal strengths and certain academic alternatives.

Occupational implications clearly influence many students' choices, since finding a career is a reason many of them give for being in college. Helping students determine these relationships may be the most important advising task

Certain resources on the Internet and the computerized career information systems mentioned above are extremely useful in helping students integrate information about self, majors, and occupations. Many students find these systems not only help them access information in an organized, readily understandable form but also help them integrate it in a very personal decision-making framework.

Task 4: Support the student while he or she makes decisions.

It is obvious that students alone must make final academic and career decisions, but they may need support, as they sometimes struggle with making a commitment to a choice. This is why understanding the individual student's decision-making background and style is important. Some students reach this point and find they need to return to the information-gathering task if no alternative emerges. Others are hesitant to make a decision because of lack of confidence in their ability to do so. Other students find external forces negate a specific alternative (for example, lack of financial support for entering a professional college such as medicine).

Advisors needs to encourage students to return for discussion if the need arises. Many students find the personal support of a caring adult reassuring at this stage.

Task 5: Help the student initiate an action plan.

Making a decision is only the beginning. A carefully considered plan for implementing the choice must also be initiated. Many students feel a great sense of relief after a decision is reached. Advisors can:

- help students outline an action plan that specifies the activities to be done and the time frame in which these need to be accomplished;
- point out short- and long-term action steps the perhaps need to be in sequence;
- help students realize that plans need to be periodically reevaluated and changed as new information or circumstances indicate.

Task 6: Encourage follow-up contact

Advisors need to make it clear to students that they are always available for future discussions. Making a major decision and implementing it are important accomplishments for many students. Knowing that an interested, caring adult is available can be reassuring as they live out the decisions they have made.

Not all students progress through this process in an orderly way. Some may not be ready to finalize a decision and may stop their search at any point. When advisor and student can formulate a plan for exploration that is clearly defined and personalized, however, the outcome is usually satisfying.

ACADEMIC AND CAREER RESOURCES

Testing

Many counseling and career centers offer testing opportunities that can help students become personally involved in self-assessment. A few examples of testing resources are listed below. A description of these instruments and their publishers may be found in a number of resources such as Buros' *Tests in Print IV* (Murphy et al., 2002) (http://www.unl.edu/buros).

Interest Inventories

Interest inventories are probably the best known and most widely used of all career self-assessment tools. Their main value is in helping students organize or focus on what they enjoy or like. Interest patterns have been researched extensively for thirty years, and certain patterns are known to be predictive of satisfaction with certain career fields (Campbell, Strong, & Hansen, 1994).

There are many familiar inventories such as the *Strong Interest Inventory* or *Kuder Career Search with Person Match* (Kuder & Zytowski, 1999). Some inventories help students compare their interests with those of workers in a certain career field who are satisfied with their occupations; others help students measure their interests in relationship to tasks performed in the occupation. Since interest inventories can help students relate their interests or what they like with specific groups of occupations, they help build that important bridge between the "Who am I?" question and the work world.

Aptitude Assessment

Many students use the terms *achievement, ability,* and *aptitude* interchangeably. *Achievement,* however, can be viewed as a measure of what has already been learned. The *American College Test* (ACT) and *Scholastic Achievement Test* (SAT) are measured in the present tense–what students know about their strengths and limitations at this point in time. *Aptitudes* are future oriented–what the student's potential is. The *Generalized Aptitude Test Battery* (GATB) (http://onetcenter.org) and the *Differential Aptitude Test* (DAT) (http://www.harcourtassessment.com) are examples of aptitude tests. The Department of Labor has identified aptitudes that are inherent in all occupations. Students can measure potential for certain careers by assessing their level of aptitude in such areas as verbal and abstract reasoning, numerical reasoning, and spatial or mechanical aptitude. Aptitudes are then related to specific occupational clusters.

Values Assessment

Some students have never questioned what is inherently important to them in a major or career. Work values such as prestige, money, power, creativity, and independence are implicit in certain occupations. When students can identify what is of value to them, they can relate these values to specific occupational fields.

Brown and Crace (1996) suggest that values with high priorities are the most important determinants of choices made, assuming the alternatives available to the decision-makers easily satisfy their values. When values are not satisfying, choices will be made that leave final decisions open. Choosing a liberal arts major, for example, might be easier than choosing a more circumscribed major. Brown and Crace (1996) have identified fourteen life values and created the *Life Values Inventory* (LVI) (http://www.life-values.com). Students rank their values and relate them to their primary life roles (e.g., career, relationships, leisure).

Another values inventory may be found in the *Guide for Occupational Exploration* (GOE) by the U.S. Department of Labor. The GOE provides a crosswalk from fourteen work groups to work values. Examples of values on the list are autonomy, authority, moral values, recognition, social status and working conditions. Other value-based approaches include qualitative methods such as checklists, games, guided fantasies, or card sorts. Colozzi and Colozzi (2000) have observed a relationship among clients' Holland-type scores and their implied value themes, and past research has confirmed this relationship (Holland, 1997). When tests incorporating Holland's personality types are interpreted, these implied values can be related to college majors as well as work environments.

Personality Inventories

Many important career theorists (Holland, 1997; Super, 1957) stress the importance of considering personality factors and characteristics in making educational and career decisions. Such personality variables as needs, temperament, anxiety, and extraversion/introversion can be related to occupational groups. The *Myers-Briggs Type Indicator* (MBTI) (Myers et al., 1998) (http://www.capt.org) is used to help students confirm ideas they may have about certain career fields or open up possibilities they had not yet considered (Gordon & Carberry, 1984; Keller, Piotrowski, & Rabold, 1990).

The Keirsey Character Sorter (http://www.keirsey.com) uncovers individuals' innate tendencies, preferences, and motivations that reveal an integrated view of their personalities.

While testing is helpful to students in broadening their perceptions of careers and themselves, it is not to be considered an end in itself. It is only one method for gathering information. Some students think the test will tell them what decision to make. Advisors and counselors must be ready to place testing into its proper perspective–as one information source among many.

Diagnostic Tools

New assessment tools have emerged from the research on indecision types. These diagnostic tools show great promise in helping advisors and counselors design interventions that can be tailored specifically to an individual undecided student's needs. By understanding the reasons for indecision, advisors can provide a more personalized approach. The advantage of being able to pinpoint causes of indecision is that modular or group approaches can be created and implemented for many diverse populations and settings. A few examples follow.

Chartrand, Robbins, Morrill, and Boggs (1990) developed the *Career Factors Inventory* (CFI) to measure both personal-emotional and informational needs. The scales include career choice anxiety, generalized indecisiveness, need for career information, and need for self-knowledge. The authors suggest that if administered before the start of a course or workshop, the group profile can be used to adjust the curriculum (Chartrand & Nutter, 1996; Cohen, Chartrand, & Jowdy, 1995; Lewis & Savickas, 1995). The CFI can be used in individual career counseling to help understand an undecided student's career decision-making difficulties and to teach or illustrate the elements of effective career decision-making. It has also been used for institutional planning (Chartrand & Nutter, 1996).

The *Career Decision-making Difficulties Questionnaire* (CDDQ) (Gati, Krausz, & Osipow, 1996) includes three major categories of difficulties that individuals face when making career decisions. The first is lack of readiness that includes lack of motivation, general indecisiveness, and dysfunctional beliefs. The second, lack of information, includes lack of knowledge about the process of career decision-making, lack of information about self, lack of information about occupations, and lack of information about the ways of obtaining additional information. The third major category is inconsistent information, which is the result of unreliable information about internal and external conflicts. The advantage of the CDDQ is that it permits a more detail evaluation of the specific type of difficulties (Osipow & Gati, 1998). Gati, Osipow, Krausz, and Saka (2000) sought counselor judgments to ascertain the compatibility of their perceptions of difficulties and their counselees' self-reported difficulties. They found that the CDDQ may be used to assess systematic categories of difficulties which share common features such as a similar cause, timing impact, or intervention required.

The *Career Barriers Inventory* (CBI) (Swanson, Daniels, & Tokar, 1996) consists of a wide range of barriers that college students might perceive. Examples of these barriers include sex discrimination, lack of confidence, multiple-role conflict, racial discrimination, inadequate preparation, decision-making difficulties, dissatisfaction with career, or difficulties with networking/socialization. The authors suggest that counselors assess whether students have an awareness of barriers that they are likely to encounter and how these might interfere with their academic and career plans. Help can then be given to assist them in responding to these barriers in appropriate ways.

These are a few examples of instruments that have been developed from studies to determine the causes of indecision. They can be used with individuals, in group settings, or in workshops to determine the best approaches for assisting students with career decision-making.

Internet

The Internet has revolutionized the ability to access academic and career information. The amount of information, however, is so vast that advisors and counselors need to help students narrow down and identify the information that is most relevant to their specific situation. Examples of websites for assessments and academic major and career information are given throughout this book. Government sources, for example, are especially useful since they are free and include many types of informational Web sites. One of the most thorough sites is O*Net (http://online.onetcenter.org) which has replaced the old *Dictionary of Occupational Titles.* This tool provides a "snapshot" of occupations that includes every facet of its requirements, characteristics, and details about personal qualifications needed to enter it. Links are provided to many other government career-related information sources.

Counseling

Some undecided students need the services of a psychological counselor. If a great deal of anxiety is experienced with the decision-making process, the student may need help alleviating the stress or learning to cope with it. Some identity concerns also require personal counseling. Some students feel controlled by another person or situation and are unable to negotiate the decision-making process because of these external constraints. Counseling can help students develop a more internal locus of control so they can make decisions independently. Some developmental concerns, such as social adjustment problems, also require individual counseling. Counseling may be needed to alleviate many kinds of temporary concerns that students experience.

As described in Chapter 1, another group of students who are unable to make decisions may have serious psychological dysfunctions. These students need longer-term psychological counseling. although there are few reliable diagnostic procedures for identifying these students at present, the number with serious psychological problems is probably small. Psychological services can help students with temporary developmental concerns or with more serious personality dysfunctions. On small campuses, this help may need to come from a community mental health center or private practitioners.

Career Centers

Many campuses have career centers or career library facilities organized to help students obtain information about academic major fields and careers. With the advent of the Internet, libraries have taken on a new role. Along with printed materials, computer software is now the source of information that is constantly changing and updated. Access to the Internet is an important resource in these centers or libraries.

Gordon (2006) points out the advantages of using established systems for organizing career information. She outlines the similarities across three systems: the *General Occupational Exploration* (GOE) codes used by O*Net, the Department of Labor's career information site; Holland's codes; and the *World of Work Map* (ACT, Inc., 2001). Although these systems are widely used on Internet sites, they are also appropriate for organizing career library materials.

Whichever organizing system is incorporated (including the simple alphabetical listing of occupations), students need to learn how to use it. This may be accomplished through individual contacts, group workshops, freshman orientation courses, or career-planning courses. Individual students can spend as much time as they wish and learn at their own pace on the Internet or in a career library.

Care must be exercised to maintain information sources that are not unrealistically slanted or biased. For example, sex biases may be hidden in certain information, or company brochures may make generalizations that do not apply to local situations. Career libraries need to be initiated and maintained by professionals who are trained in this area.

Computer-assisted Career Guidance Systems (CACGS)

Computer-assisted career guidance systems were created in the 1960s. One of the earliest to be developed was the *System for Interactive Guidance Information* (SIGI) by Katz for the Educational Testing Service in 1963. It was designed to teach work values and connect them to occupations. The current system, *SIGI-Plus,* integrates self-information with college major and occupations as part of a career planning process.

According to Niles and Harris-Bowlsbey (2002), choosing a CACGS should be based on some of the following factors: (1) theoretical base of the system, (2) online inventories, (3) quality and comprehensiveness of databases, (4) ease of searches, (5) content of system, (6) user friendliness, and (7) multimedia capabilities.

Some advantages for accessing personal, academic, and career information through CACGS are:

1. *Computer systems provide a personalized exploration of self.* If students wish to take an interest inventory or an ability measure, or to clarify work values, the computer program offers these opportunities in a clear, easy-to-access way.
2. *Voluminous, up-to-date occupational information is offered in an easy-to-understand format.* It is critical that occupational and job market information is current. Computer systems are updated at least annually based on many sources, including current government, business, and industry data.
3. *Computerized systems are excellent tools for helping students integrate personal and occupational information.* Computer programs can relate students' interests, values, and abilities to specific career fields. The students often can receive a detailed description of these alternatives in a printout. They should be encouraged to share their results with an advisor or counselor.
4. *Computer systems can teach students decision-making strategies.* Some systems have built-in programs for helping students experience the decision-making process itself. Students can simulate a variety of choices without taking the risks associated with real-world decisions. Computer systems are a safe place to practice different decision-making styles and strategies.
5. *Students are in control.* The computerized approach encourages stu-

dents to be intimately involved in their own career planning. They are not relying on other people's opinions or wishes. Through different combinations of personal factors they can experience different outcomes.

6. *Computer systems can help students plan for appropriate action.* Once certain decisions are made, students are presented with a list of action steps in some systems. Implementation of a decision becomes more structured and easier to accomplish. Some examples of these systems include DISCOVER, SIGI-Plus, and Focus II.

Advisor and counselor competencies to use CACGS, according to Niles and Harris-Bowlsbey (2002), include the ability to help students identify their needs in order to determine what approach is appropriate, the ability to help students process the information they are gathering so that it is personally meaningful, the ability to motivate students to use the system, and the ability to help students develop and implement an action plan. Without the encouragement and help of an advisor or counselor, many students may not complete the career planning process or integrate all the fragments of information they have gathered.

Computers will never replace advisors or counselors but they can enhance the quality of the one-to-one exchange. The routine part of advising–specific information-giving–can be accomplished effectively by computer systems. This allows the advisor and student to concentrate on personal impressions and applications of that information.

Career Modules

There are many programmed materials that provide students with a structured vehicle for assessing personal characteristics and relating them to occupational fields. The Self-Directed Search (Holland, 2001) and the Career Decision-Making System (CDMS) (Harrington-O'Shea, 1992) are examples of tools for helping students understand interests and abilities. These modules can also help students integrate self-information and occupational information when printed materials are most convenient. An advisor or counselor can use these materials as an initial effort in helping students identify and focus on certain alternatives (Miller & Woycheck, 2000). These comprehensive, self-contained units are excellent for individual advising or for use in small groups, since they are self-scored and results can be obtained immediately.

Community Resources

An invaluable source of information for undecided students is the worker in the field. Some campuses have established lists composed of graduates of the institution who have volunteered to discuss their occupational field with exploring students. This personal contact has several advantages. It provides students with the names of individuals who are willing to talk to them about a field in which they have an interest. Discussing accounting with two or three accountants working in different settings can broaden a student's perception of what the work really entails. The student may discuss this occupation with the alumni on the telephone or by actually visiting the work environment for a day or longer. This program also has the advantage of involving alumni in their alma mater's mission beyond the usual fund-giving activity.

Some students are able to receive course credit for actual work experiences on some campuses. Spending a school term in a school, a hospital, a social agency, or a business, for example, provides the type and depth of information students need in order to make informed choices. Experiencing programs may be organized with the help of the alumni office or with community leaders and business personnel. A list of volunteer work sites is another method for providing the experience opportunity to undecided students.

Some institutions have co-op or intern programs, in which students can get practical experience in a particular work environment, often for pay. Some campuses have federally funded programs for co-op experiences.

Printed Resources

Advisors need to have in their possession comprehensive printed resources that can be used directly with the student. Curriculum sheets listing all requirements for a major, for example, can be useful in helping undecided students understand exactly what courses and sequences are required in a major. When these sheets are in the form of checklists, the student and advisor can monitor progress as well. These sheets should reflect immediately any change in curriculum, so that information is always current. Although college websites, catalogs, and bulletins typically contain information about academic programs, disposable curriculum sheets are conducive to making notes and recording personal information. Providing this structure helps take the mystery out of curricular information and clarifies all the requirements for a degree.

Other printed information can be created to serve the unique needs of the institution and the individual student on that campus. Although sometimes on the institution's website, a printed version of the advisor's manual is a critical printed resource for both advisor and student, and booklets containing the location and purpose of student services can provide important information for the student and advisor.

PROGRAMS FOR GROUP ADVISING

While a great deal of advising is geared to individual contact, group activities have several advantages. Providing information to small groups of students is a more efficient use of time, since many students may be served with one effort. Groups also provide an opportunity for students to share common concerns.

The group format usually provides structured experiences and involves students in specific tasks and varies in duration and length of meeting. Group career advising or counseling experiences are enhanced when a cooperative and inclusive group environment is created where members focus on goals that are acceptable to all (Niles & Harris-Bowlsbey, 2002). When undecided students realize they are experiencing many of the same problems as their peers, they may not feel as isolated or different.

Malott and Magnuson (2004) use genograms in a five-session group experience to examine career choice in relation to influences from family experiences. The authors adapt traditional family genograms to analyze occupational patterns, themes and values. Genograms help students uncover a broad range of information about family work and economic expectations, family work values and students' perceptions of their family roles.

Dziuban, Tango, and Hynes (1994) give a career exploration assignment (an English course writing assignment) to career-decided students. The students are given interest and personality inventories, which they then discuss in class. The researchers expected that the interest inventory test scores would remain the same before and after the career exploration activity. The students' assignment was to deduce from the personality and interest inventories what they believed were the reasons for their particular profiles. The exercise did have an impact on the decided students. They became less certain when stimulated by the issues raised during discussions of the relationship between their personalities and their interests. The students' uncertainty after the treatment led the researchers to conclude that confronting one's personality core is the fundamental work of career decision-making. It is often useful to help decided students question their initial decisions.

Workshops

Small-group activities such as workshops can be provided on many topical areas. A workshop format may include, for example, test-taking and interpretation, which can be an effective beginning to self-assessment or discussion of an Internet assignment. Decision-making skills may be taught in a workshop. Other examples of workshop topics include values and careers, sex-role identity and careers, an overview of academic majors, academic major alternatives, the job outlook, and careers in business (or engineering, health fields, psychology, etc.). Workshop subject matter is unlimited when the need for information and academic counseling is considered.

Santos (2004) used a career dilemma (hypothetical or real) to initiate discussion in a workshop group setting. The purposes of this technique are to promote more complex thinking abut career choices and to enhance the interaction between group members. When the group participants analyzed the career dilemma that they experienced themselves, they were able to generate more than one approach or solution to the problem.

Programmed career modules also lend themselves to group activity, since students can work through the exploration process in a structured way and can immediately share results with peers and counselors. There are many commercial products available, but they may be developed locally as well.

Freshman Orientation Courses

The need for an extension of the normally brief precollege orientation is well known. The first freshman seminar course was taught in the late 1800s, and by 1925 over one hundred institutions offered such courses (Fitts & Swift, 1928). Today many institutions have implemented such courses. In the 2000 National Survey of First-Year Seminar Programming (Hunter & Linder, 2005), the types of first-year seminars most often used were the extended orientation seminar (62 percent); academic seminars (13 percent), and others that included discipline linked courses, basic study skills seminars, or writing seminars (7 percent). Hunter and Linder indicate that "first-year seminars facilitate learning: learning about a subject or combination of topics, learning about the institution, learning about the diversity within campus communities, but most important, learning about oneself and one's abilities" (p. 276).

Cuseo (2003) outlines the advantages of first-year seminars as promoting retention and academic performance, and offering support in the form of academic information, academic and career planning, connecting students to support services, identifying "at risk" students early, and peer bonding, to name a few. The purpose of most freshman orientation courses is to support and provide information to new students during their first weeks in college (Barefoot & Searcy, 1994). Designing a course format especially for undecided students has many advantages:

1. *Undecided students receive immediate individual attention.* They are provided with help in gathering information or adjusting to college when they need it most. The class provides a support group during their initial contact with the campus environment.
2. *The instructor may be the student's academic advisor.* If advisor assignments are made in this way, regular contact is established; advisor and student can begin to form a working relationship immediately.
3. *Immediate adjustment concerns are identified and resolved.* Students with poor study habits, for example, can learn how to improve them during the freshman orientation course.
4. *Self-assessment is provided in a structured way.* Self-information can be collected, organized, and processed immediately.

5. *Academic major information is provided in depth.* The student is offered breadth and depth of information that would otherwise take a great deal of time and motivation to gather individually.
6. *Educational and occupational relationships are identified and explored.* The "what can I do with a major in . . . ?" question can be answered directly.
7. *The decision-making process is learned in a safe environment.* Helping students become aware of their own approaches to selecting a major can be dealt with in class.

Shoemaker (1995) describes a two-quarter extended orientation course for new undecided students. When compared to undecided students who did not attend the course, enrolled students obtained significantly higher grade point averages (GPA) and completed more academic units by the end of the school year.

Schnell, Louis, and Doetkott (2003) report that students who enrolled in a first-year seminar were tracked to graduation to determine if their rates differed from a matched comparison group who were not enrolled in the course. They found that graduation rates for students who were enrolled in the first-year seminar were significantly higher than the match group. Schnell et al. suggest that students entering college at a disadvantage may statistically increase their odds of graduating by involvement in a first-year seminar.

The greatest advantage of a freshman orientation course or seminar is that students can experience personalized attention during the weeks that are identified as most conducive to attrition. Helping students negotiate the first months of college successfully facilitates their feeling more comfortable and self-confident about their new environment.

Career Courses

Career development courses have served college students for over seventy-five years (Maverick, 1926). Collins (1998) found in a survey by the National Associations of Colleges and Employers that more than half of the institutions reported they offered a career course. Devlin (1974) surveyed career offices and found that courses in the 1970s covered three major areas: (1) career choice factors, (2) career information, and (3) job-seeking techniques. Many comprehensive career courses include these three topics today. The course approach is popular with students, since the academic credit provides incentives to complete the intervention.

Reese and Miller (2006) found that students who completed a career course showed increased career decision-making self-efficacy in obtaining career information, setting career goals, and career planning. The course also seemed to lower perceived career decision difficulties. The *Cognitive Information Processing Model* (CIP) (Sampson, Peterson, Lenz & Reardon, 1992) was used as a framework for the course content. They urge that the use of established career theory can insure significant gains in accomplishing the objectives set for the course.

When career courses are compared to individual counseling, the results are mixed. Oliver and Spokane (1988) found that group or class interventions were more effective than individual career counseling. Whiston, Sexton, and Lasoff (1998) reported, however, that after examining 47 studies conducted between 1983 and 1995, individual and group counseling interventions were more effective than career classes.

Some of the advantages of career planning courses are that at one level they can provide efficient career services to large numbers of students. More importantly, however, is the way they benefit students. Folsom and Reardon (2003) found forty-six studies in the literature that reported outcomes for career planning courses. Examples of outcomes are job satisfaction, selecting a major, course satisfaction, time to graduation from college, cumulative grade point average (GPA) and retention. They suggest that career courses may be especially beneficial to undecided students, especially those who are at risk for dropping-out of college.

To test the effectiveness of a career course over time, Vernick, Reardon, and Sampson (2004) compared student ratings of their career course over a five-year period. They found that students' perceptions of the course are consistent over time and more positive when classes meet multiple times a week.

Folsom and Reardon (2003) found that career courses are quite different in design, scope and function. When Folsom and Reardon checked Amazon.com for names of texts for college-level career courses, more than fifty books were revealed. They also cite the growing interest in career development courses that are international in scope. Career courses can help students concentrate on the career-planning process and help them focus on specific areas of interest. Many career courses lead students through a series of decision-making steps. Gathering self-, academic, and career information is an integral activity in most career courses. The small-group atmosphere also supports students while they are involved in this process.

ADVISING AND COUNSELING APPROACHES

Effective advisors use many techniques and methods for helping undecided students. These include interviewing techniques that reflect proficient communication skills. Referral techniques are extremely important, since no one campus resource is adequate for providing undecided students with the wide breadth of information they need. Printed materials are another important advising tool. These techniques and skills need to become a part of all effective advising, regardless of the type of student being helped. They are particularly important, however, in working with students who need to be guided and encouraged to negotiate the decision-making process in an expeditious way.

Interviewing Techniques

Many undecided students have been helped to make a decision by discussing their situation over time with a caring advisor or counselor. Communication techniques such a reflecting and clarifying can be used to help students focus their thinking. Some suggestions for improving communication in the advising interview are:

1. *Opening*–Greet student by name. Be relaxed, warm. Open with a question, e.g., "How are things going?" or "How can I help?"
2. *Phrasing questions*–Conversational flow will be cut off if questions are asked so that a yes or no reply is all that is required. A good question might be, "What have you thought about taking next term?" or "What are some things that have made you think about business as a career?"
3. *Out-talking the student*–Good advising is effective listening, and listening is more than the absence of talking. Identify the fine shades of feelings behind the words.

4. *Accepting the student's attitudes and feelings*–Students may fear that advisors do not approve of what they say. Advisors must convey their acceptance of these feelings and attitudes in a nonjudgmental way. Cardinal principle: If the student thinks it is a problem, the advisor does, too.
5. *Cross-examining*–Do not fire questions at the student so that they feel they are under pressure to answer too quickly.
6. *Allowing silence in the interview*–Most people are embarrassed if no conversation is going on. Remember, the student may be groping for words or ideas.
7. *Reflecting the student's feelings*–Try to understand what the student is saying. For example, it is better to say, "You feel that your father expects you to major in premed" rather than, "Everyone has trouble getting along with his father sometimes."
8. *Admitting your ignorance*–If a student asks a question regarding facts and you do not have them, admit it. Go to your resources for the information immediately, or call the student back.
9. *Setting limits on the interview*–It is better if the advisor and the student realize from the beginning that the interview lasts for a fixed length of time.
10. *Ending the interview*–Once limits have been set, it is best to end the interview at the agreed time. A comfortable phrase might be, "Do you think we have done all we can for today?" or "Let's make another appointment so that we can go into this further."

Probing Questions

The following probing questions are examples of what an advisor might use to help students articulate why they are undecided and help them become aware of certain aspects of the choice process they have not considered. Many undecided students simply need help in analyzing their needs before they can move forward in the exploration process. The questions are divided into three categories since information gathering sometimes falls into these three important areas.

Self-exploration

- As far back as you can remember, what general occupational fields have you thought of?

- What subjects did you enjoy in high school? In what subjects did you receive your best grades?
- Do you consider your strengths to lie in the math/science areas or in the social sciences? In the arts?
- In what type of extracurricular activities did you take part in high school? What were the most enjoyable? What did you learn about yourself from them?
- What are your best personal qualities? What do your friends like most about you?
- What do you see as your limitations?
- Name the highest point in your life so far (your greatest accomplishment). What about the experience made it special?
- In what kind of work environment do you picture yourself five years out of college?
- If you have a spare hour to use, what do you do?
- Why are you in college?
- What does a college degree mean to you?

Academic Major/Occupational Information

- What academic areas are you currently considering? What do you like about these areas?
- What occupations are you considering? What about these occupations attracts you?
- How do your abilities and skills fit the tasks necessary to succeed in these areas?
- Will these occupations provide the rewards and satisfactions you want for your life? Why?
- What are the differences between the two majors (occupations) you are tentatively considering? The similarities?
- Who has influenced your ideas about these alternatives?

Decision-Making

- Do you ever have trouble making decisions? Little ones? Important ones?
- How do you generally go about making a decision? Describe the process.
- What specific strategies do you use?

- Do you use the same method for all types of decisions?
- Would you describe yourself as a spontaneous or systematic decision-maker?
- Do you make decisions by yourself or do you need other people's opinions first?
- Are you feeling anxious about deciding on a major? Pressured? Why?
- How long do you think it will take you to make a decision? How long do you *want* it to take?

Rugsaken (2006) emphasizes the importance of "body language" in communicating. According to Argyle (1978, as cited by Rugsaken), humans have more than seven hundred thousand forms of body language. Rugsaken describes different forms of body language and how they differ in various cultures. She uses facial expressions as an example of how different cultures use body language to reflect emotions, feelings, and attitudes. In the West, "true" feelings and emotions are valued; in the East, self-control is valued. Direct eye contact in the East, for example, is considered disrespectful, while in other cultures such as Asian or African, it is seen as a challenging gesture. Rugsaken recommends that advisors can communicate more effectively if they understand the clues that body language provides.

Jordan (2000) emphasizes listening as a communication tool that is applicable to advising undecided students. When a new perspective is needed, taking a negative situation and reframing it in a positive way can sometimes offer a new or different perspective. Jordan also describes a narrative technique that requires careful listening so that the advisor hears students' stories or their point of view. Listening for times when comfort and support are needed is important as well. Listening for hidden messages when students are talking about nonadvising issues might reveal concerns that advisors may want to address.

As discussed before, indecisive students with personal blocks to making a decision may require psychological counseling by a trained expert. Students with severe psychological problems often do not benefit from the types of interviewing or communication techniques outlined above. Advisors need to be sensitive in identifying these students and to make appropriate referrals as soon as the difficulty is discerned.

Referral Techniques

Learning when and how to refer a student to a selected resource is an important advising skill. Referring too quickly or too broadly can create a situation that adds to the student's confusion. Students should have an understanding of what areas of study they are considering before a referral is made. They need to have analyzed how their past academic record fits these areas, and they need some knowledge of the major requirements involved. The referral resource can then refine the student's understanding of this particular area. Students often need help in formulating questions before they make contact with the referral source, and advisors can help them frame questions that will ensure the most efficient use of the time.

Setting up an organized network of resources is another important aspect of referral. All resource persons on campus associated with academic information, for example, need to be aware of their responsibility to the referred student. Providing information in a clear and organized way can help students analyze and integrate it later. The network should include all academic and student service resources on campus. The advisor referring and the recipient of referrals need to work together so that the purpose and content of these contacts are clearly defined. A list of names, locations, e-mail addresses, and phone numbers as well as areas of expertise should be widely disseminated among advisors, faculty, and student affairs personnel.

Career Counseling Approaches

Many specific career advising and counseling approaches have been researched and reported in the literature. In a survey by Lynch and Stucky (2001) the majority of academic advisors report the average length of time spent in an advising meeting is fifteen to thirty minutes. Twenty-five percent indicated they spent less than fifteen minutes. Career counselors at many institutions also experience the pressure of time constraints and too many needy students. This lack of time and staff emphasizes that the methods used with students must be efficient and based on sound theoretical principles and techniques that are achievable and produce real outcomes.

Theoretically-based Approaches

Solution-focused Advising/Counseling: The solution-focused approach is a model based on constructivist theory that emphasizes strengths and goal achievement. It is particularly suited to advising because it can be used in single sessions as well as longer contacts or group settings. Mayhill and Burg (2002) advocate solution-focused advising for undecided students because it can move them forward "in small steps from a perceived problem toward a goal" (p. 76). Advisors can use solution-focused advising to help undecided students identify barriers that are preventing them from making a decision and help them set specific academic and career goals (p. 78).

Mayhill and Burg offer five solution-focused techniques that may be used in advising undecided students: (1) scaling questions–defining beliefs about how students enjoy a current activity, (2) the miracle question–focusing on a future where the problem no longer exists, (3) presuppositional questions–asking leading questions where part of the answer is assumed in the question, (4) cheerleading–offering support for the positive aspects of the student's efforts in choosing a major, and (5) the task or homework–engaging the student in activities that will lead to a decision.

Mayhill and Burg stress that solution-focused advising helps undecided students overcome self-doubts and perceived barriers, encouraging them to move forward in small steps rather than looking for the whole solution at once.

Constructivist Career Theory: The constructivist theory described in Chapter 2 suggests some practical applications for advising undecided students. Constructivist career counseling is a general method for life planning. Several practical considerations are offered by Peavy (1995). Informal relationships with family and peers and those generated by the media are seen as "patterns of influence" since they influence students' thinking and acting. "Mindfulness" is a technique where the creation of new constructs helps interpret new experiences, helps expand openness and receptivity to new information, and helps generate an awareness of more than one perspective on educational and career choices. Involvement in career-related activities such as work and volunteer experiences, job shadowing, or work-site visits can provide "creative meaning through activity." Peavy emphasizes that such activity is enhanced through reflection on the activity and in discussions with a counselor.

Brott (2004) also provides practical applications from constructivist theory. She uses the narrative approach through the life line, card sort, life role circles, and the goal map strategies. These activity-oriented techniques offer a holistic and integrative picture of the student through personal narratives. Brott endorses these strategies as a way to obtain the students' personal story that is grounded in life themes and meanings.

Savickas (1995) applies constructivist counseling to career indecision. He suggests that after learning the details of the student's current indecision, the counselor proceeds to elicit stories that reveal the student's life themes. "life stories deal with the interaction between linear incidents (life events) that make the plot (i.e., the plan of action) and the timeless, motionless, underlying themes that make a life" (p. 367). As described in Chapter 2, the counselor narrates the life theme back to the student who collaborates on editing it. The theme is then used to understand and resolve the career indecision. Once the indecision is clarified, the student is prepared to "extend imaginative plot lines into the future" (p. 368). Savickas indicates that narratives that put career indecision in the context of a life theme, can clarify choices and enhance the ability to decide.

Cognitive Career Information Processing (CIP): The cognitive information-processing theory of Sampson, Peterson, Lenz, & Reardon (1992) was also described in Chapter 2. One useful application of the CIP theory is to teach the career decision-making process. The CASVE cycle represents a generic model of information-processing skills related to career decision making. The CASVE cycle involves communication, analysis, synthesis, valuing, and execution skills. The communication part of the cycle involves awareness on the part of the student that a gap or career problem exists. The problem must then be analyzed to determine how it will be resolved (for example, what type of information will be needed to solve the problem?). The next part of the cycle, synthesis, involves identifying as many potential solutions to the problem as possible. In this phase, a manageable list of alternatives is identified. The valuing phase involves examining each of the generated alternatives and then prioritizing them according to their implicit values and outcomes that each can provide. Students then create and commit to a plan of action in the execution phase, as the plan is implemented for the decision chosen in the valuing phase.

Sampson and Peterson (2000) suggest applications of CIP theory for career problem solving and decision-making. CIP theory specifies that effective career decision-making requires effective information processing, including self-knowledge, occupational knowledge, decision-making skills, and executive processing. They suggest self-help career services should involve self-guided use of self-assessment, career information, and instructional resources that can be housed a library, career center, or in an Internet-based site. Sampson and Peterson apply their theory to the career problem and decision-making taxonomy of decided, undecided, and indecisive individuals. Decided and undecided students are most cost-effectively served by self-help and brief staff-assisted interventions. Indecisive students, however, are most cost-effectively served by individual counseling interventions.

Strengths-based Advising: Strengths-based advising emphasizes helping students fulfill their potential. It uses students' talents as the basis for educational and career planning. Smith (2006) declares that strength-based counseling represents a paradigm shift from the deficit medical model to one that stresses an individual's strengths.

Schreiner and Anderson (2005) indicate that strengths-based advising "enables advisors to see diverse groups of students fulfill their potential and achieve excellence" (p. 20). By focusing on their natural talents, students build confidence and motivation to achieve and persist in college.

Schreiner and Anderson encourage advisors to ask questions of students that will reveal the student's talents. Talents can often be identified from past accomplishments and exploring the elements that led to their success. Advisors also need to help students recall "flow experiences" where excellence was achieved unconsciously. Once identified, advisors can help students analyze their strengths, so they can be incorporated in their plans and can be further developed during their college experience. In addition to interests, students can match their strengths and talents to general fields of study or majors as well as establishing educational and career goals.

Decision-Making Approaches

When vocational counseling was first recognized as a need after the Civil War, decision-making was seen as a simple task. Later the trait-factor approach, as espoused by Frank Parsons, viewed vocational decision-making as matching a person's "qualities" with different "lines of work" (Parsons, 1909). As described in Chapter 2, during the period between 1950 and 1970, many theories were developed to explain how career decisions are made in general. In the next two decades, a great deal of research about indecision was generated, including its application to undecided students.

Tinsley, Tinsley, and Rushing (2002), for example, provided a structured career intervention for undecided women that identified barriers of career decision-making. The participants explored their career interests and formulated provisional college major and occupational choices. They were then followed up three weeks later. Reactions to the interventions seemed to cluster into three groups. Those that preferred a rational approach to decision-making reported little need for additional career information; those that preferred a greater use of intuitive decision-making style did need more career information. Participants who used an external information-processing style and a dependent decision-making style were associated with lower levels of vocational self-concept crystallization, and a stronger need for additional career information at the follow-up. The researchers concluded that structured career interventions may be less effective with individuals who prefer a dependent decision-making style or with those who prefer an external information processing approach. Not all career undecided women respond in the same manner to well-designed interventions that emphasize a rational approach to career decision-making.

After drawing on qualitative interviews of one thousand youth, Mortimer, Zimmer-Gembeck, Holmes, and Shanahan (2002) identified multiple themes from a longitudinal study of work through adolescence and early adulthood. The themes included unfulfilled expectations, the postponement of decisions, turning points that crystallized decisions, and resources and obstacles including family, work, school counseling, and teachers. The authors suggest that recent social changes in the United States may be affecting vocational decision-making and that social policies need to be modified to facilitate young people's quest for vocational identity and work.

Educational and career indecision is viewed today as a complex construct. The career decision-making process encompasses personal variables, social and economic factors, cultural influences, the decision-maker's past experiences and personal decision-making style, and desired outcomes, to name a few. This section offers a small sampling of the diverse factors involved in the educational and career decision-making process.

Deciding on a Major: The first important academic decision that students presume they are required to make at most colleges and universities is choice of major. In the 2000 National Survey of First-Year Curricular Practices (Barefoot, 2005), 8 percent of institutions reported they required first-year students to declare a major at point of entry. Thirty-six percent of liberal arts colleges do not permit entering first-year students to select an official major. At community colleges, 45 percent of the institutions do not require students to declare a major upon entering but it is "strongly encouraged." Fifty-four percent of four-year institutions permit a major choice at entry, but students are not forced or strongly encouraged to do so. Many students who are admittedly undecided have mixed feelings about their situation. As noted earlier, some undecided students are very comfortable with not making an initial choice, while others experience doubt and anxiety about their inability to make a decision.

Schein, Laff, and Allen (2004) indicate that students often think of "major" in terms of prescribed coursework in a catalogue, course scheduling, and fulfilling course requirements. They suggest that instead, advisors encourage students to consider fields of study. In this way, students can think in terms of areas of interest and ways of studying them thematically.

Schein and Laff (1997) describe a hands-on, time-limited strategy that uses undecided students' self-descriptions, rather than the curricula, as a starting point. They contend that administrative structures put arbitrary boundaries on disciplines, and discourage use of more creative ways of major exploration. Their method relies on the academic inquiry process. Rather than center the student's exploration around the traditional or program availability model, Schein and Laff recommend a student-centered choice mode. This strategy entails the students asking themselves what they want from college, how to get it, and then finding the major that fits them best. The method includes generating a personal profile; examining, with advisor's input, courses that fit the profile; and listing all the majors that are compatible with their personal list. The third step is finding the major that incorporates the courses listed in Step 2. This method, according to the authors, is more personally conceptualized, and better understood by students than choosing a major from a catalog.

Galotti (1999) surveyed students in two colleges their first year and again one year later. The purpose of the study was to describe how students structure the important educational decision about choosing a major. Another objective was to examine predictors of student satisfaction and comfort with decision-making using a linear or rational model. Students were asked to list the criteria they were using in making a decision about a major, and to weigh its importance by their criteria. They were also asked to list all the majors they were currently considering and rate how good they thought the choice was for them. Students also rated their attitudes and affective reactions toward the decision-making process.

Galotti found that in the first year students were using about seven criteria to make a decision about a major. Although the number of criteria remained stable over the year, about half of the criteria had changed a year later. The number of alternative majors students considered at the beginning of the first year dropped significantly by the end of the year. Galotti suggests that students who consider more options might see themselves as less decisive and less effective decision-makers because they consider effective decision-making as being fast and having unambiguous outcomes. She speculates that the early focus on a small number of criteria and the small number of alternative majors students considered is a strategy that they adopt to manage the cognitive demands of the task.

When surveyed one year later, Galotti found that the participants recalled about half the criteria they had originally listed. Recalled criteria were more related to ideal and current criteria than to their original criteria. This suggests that one's recall is filtered through a cognitive framework that is current, not retroactive. Galotti recommends that educators help students become comfortable with cognitive processes that involve ambiguity and doubt, as well as those that require an investment of time and cognitive effort (p. 386).

Smart, Feldman, and Ethington (2000) examined the fluidity in student's choices of academic major during their freshman year and their actual majors four years later. They used Holland codes for academic environments, so a broad range of academic major areas were considered. Over 67 percent of the students sampled were in the Investigative, Social, and Enterprising academic environments. Fourteen percent of the participants were undecided.

Four years later the proportion of the students in the Enterprising environment remained rather constant. The greatest increase was in the Social environment, where the proportion grew from 22 percent to 34 percent. The proportion of students in the Investigative environment increased 5 percent, while the proportion in the Artistic environment almost doubled to 15 percent. Students whose initial choices were in the Investigative, Artistic, and Enterprising environments changed to the Social academic environment. Ultimately, not quite 50 percent of the students who eventually majored in the Investigative, Enterprising, and Social environments started there. Nearly half of the students who ultimately majored in an Artistic academic environment started there or were undecided. Smart et al. conclude that these results illustrate "the overall fluidity in students' initial selection of academic majors and the heterogeneous composition of students (in terms of their initial selection) within each of the four academic environments after a lapse of four years" (p. 109).

Decision-Making Style and the Undecided Student: Although making decisions is implicit in any research on undecided students, some authors have used it as a central focus. Bertram (1996) observes that today, advisors work with "many dualistic students in an information flooded culture that is based on the rationalistic western tradition" (p. 22). He advocates moving away from the traditional rational model of decision-making. He offers five suggestions for using a nonrational model for advising them: (1) focus more on the process of choosing a major and less on outcomes, (2) try to find the question within the question by asking why they are really asking, (3) consider the context by answering a factual question within the context of the circumstances it is being asked, (4) raise questions that help students think critically about their decision, and (5) foster relationships based on informal student contact (pp. 22-23). Bertram points out that while most undecided students want specific solutions to their uncertainty, advisors can help them realize that uncertainty does not end when they declare a major. The act of choosing a major opens the door to a whole new set of questions and challenges.

Unlike Bertram, Mau (1995) endorses rational decision-making as a positive style. He defines a rational style as making decisions deliberately, systematically, and logically. A rational style has also been found to be associated with career maturity, planning, and information-gathering, ego-identity, career decisiveness, problem-solving efficacy, and occupational certainty (p. 89).

In a study using a two-phase computer-assisted program by Mau, an intuitive strategy was used first (i.e., students fantasized and brainstormed their career options, and then narrowed them down by considering the career aspects that were important to them). This phase was to encourage students to accept uncertainty and promote positive attitudes toward their temporary undecidedness. The program continued with the rational strategy of making educated guesses about the likelihood of each chosen action leading to an anticipated outcome.

Mau found that a rational decision-making style is positively related to career certainty; a negative relationship existed with the exploration stage of decision-making. He also suggests that a rational decision-making style might be situational since it was not significantly related to career indecisiveness, decision anxiety, and reason complexity. As suggested in other studies, both rational and intuitive strategies in career intervention are necessary to accommodate the idiosyncratic way people make career decisions.

Singh and Greenhaus (2004) also found that a combination of rational and intuitive styles in a study of job changers and their newly accepted jobs was most effective. The use of a rational career strategy was associated with the selection of a job. They found that individuals who used extensive rational *and* intuitive strategies made more effective career choices, because they achieved high levels of self- and environment awareness.

Another technique that involves a decision-making format is one suggested by Bloom and Martin (2002). *Appreciative Inquiry* (AI) can be a powerful tool for advisors when used to intentionally reframe their interactions with students. There are four phases that are typically used in AI: Discovery, Dream, Design, and Destiny. When applied to advising, Bloom and Archer indicate advisors should (1) use positive open-ended questions (Discovery), (2) assist students with formulating life and career goals (Dream), (3) help students devise concrete, incremental, and achievable goals to make their dreams come true (Design), and (4) give students support and help them update and refine their goals as they progress (Destiny). The authors suggest that by using the principles of AI, the impact on students can be greater and more rewarding.

Decision-making Assessment: When the search term "career decision-making" is entered into the *Tests In Print* database (http://www.

buros.unl.edu), fifty-five instruments can be examined. Many of these are more recent versions of older tests, while some are newer instruments based on more recent research.

The question then becomes why and when should advisors and counselors use instruments as they work with undecided students? Obviously, the roles of academic advisor and career counselor are different and the use of career assessments will vary with each situation. *Computer-assisted career guidance systems* (CACGS) are good resources for both advising and counseling offices, since they provide the student with a broad view of their personal characteristics, as well as a repository for educational and career information. The advantage of many of these systems is that they also provide a vehicle for students to make connections between self- and career information. These systems will never replace the personal contact of a professional, so great care must be taken to organize a way for the student to receive an interpretation of the information gathered by the student and a discussion on its meaning. Many instruments are also available online and the use of these or printed versions may be up to the advisor's or counselor's expertise and method of offering them (for example, use in a one-to-one contact, classroom, or workshop).

Care must also be taken to view any computer or test result as one piece of data in the overall decision-making process. Every student comes with a unique set of educational and career-related experiences, self-knowledge, aspirations, and a different place in the decision-making process. Selecting the right form of assessment should be a decision made by both student and counselor. Students need to understand the purpose of the test, and be motivated to follow-up with an interpretive session with a professional.

Some career decision-making tests are more useful for student contacts, some for research purposes, while many serve both purposes. The approaches cited above are an extremely small sample of those proffered in the literature. As Osipow (1999) points out, prior to the 1960s, even though one of the most frequent problems college students presented to advisors and counselors was that of educational and career indecision, there was no standardized method to assess either its degree or nature. In addition, there were few theoretical contexts available to guide counseling or assessment measures. In the last thirty years, counseling and measurement approaches have become more plentiful and sophisticated. There is no reason to neglect or ignore undecided students who are in need of professional academic and career advising or counseling. The number of advising and counseling techniques, methods, programs, assessments, and resources now available make offering very personal academic and counseling assistance to undecided students possible.

Brown et al. (2003) offer some insights into the ingredients of career decision-making interventions. They summarized the meta-analysis of the career choice intervention literature and identified five ingredients that are individually associated with career choice outcomes. They define each of the critical ingredients and suggest how they might be implemented to maximize their effectiveness. The most critical components are: workbooks and written exercises, individualized interpretations and feedback, world of work information, modeling (i.e., exposure to models of career exploration, decision-making, career implementations, etc.) and attention to building support. These five ingredients not only seem to be individually important to at least one career choice outcome, but a combination of them yielded larger effect sizes than any one individually.

The brief descriptions of the advising and counseling approaches for undecided students offered in this chapter provide examples of the wide variety of methods, techniques, and resources that need to be available to them. Some institutional programs incorporate a few of these resources, while others offer more comprehensive programs. The danger in offering such a wide variety of individual and group interventions is the lack of organization or integration that makes them most effective. On most four-year large campuses, the advising and counseling functions are separate. At two-year campuses, they are often offered by the same office. Regardless of the organizational structure, advising and career services must be easy to find and coordinated so that fragments of activities, resources, and services aren't strewn around campus. Undecided students need to experience a unified approach so the exploratory process is smooth and consistent. Perhaps the outcome that is most important is that students feel they are involved in a highly personal approach to academic and career decision-making, while learning skills that can be used the rest of their lives.

PROGRAM EVALUATION

Creamer (1994) suggests four foci for evaluating programs for undecided students. They include (a) the overall program, (b) a specific program intervention, (c) advisors, or (d) student outcomes. She outlines specific evaluation methods for each of the four foci. Examples are the *ACT Academic Advising Audit,* the *Council for the Advancement of Standards in Higher Education* (CAS Standards), the *ACT Survey of Academic Advising,* the *Academic Advising Inventory,* and other methods such as focus group interviews and needs assessments (p. 115). Creamer (1994) points out that the quality of program evaluation "is ultimately judged by the utility and timeliness of the information gathered, and whether this information contributes to decision-making that leads to enhancement of program, specific program interventions, and/or of the skills and effectiveness of individual advisors" (p. 120).

Campbell (2005) calls assessment a "systematic, systemic, relational process" (p. 16). She summarizes the steps required for an effective process: (1) determine reasons for assessment, (2) identify key stakeholders, (3) address values, vision, mission, and goals, (4) develop program, student, and advisor learning outcomes, (5) map opportunities to learn, (6) identify multiple measures and set benchmarks for performance, and (7) design a report and dissemination plan for the results.

Banta et al. (2002) concentrate on methods to assess student success through advising. They reiterate that effective assessment must be based on the purposes and goals of the program, and theory should shape the process. They outline three phases of assessment: planning, implementing, and improving and sustaining the process. In the planning phase, careful considerations should be paid to the involvement of stakeholders or those who are involved in determining purposes and outcomes, implementing assessment activities and those who will be responsible for interpreting results and following up on improvements. Banta et al. describe the implementation phase as involving leadership, learning-centeredness, professional development, the number and type of measurements needed, and communication to stakeholders and others who are involved in some way. The last phase, improving the process, requires effective use of evidence. Sustaining the process requires continuity, continuous use of the findings, and adjustment to the program where indicated. Banta et al. point out that in this way the assessment process itself is ongoing and responsive to changing needs and circumstances of the institution and the students.

When evaluating a program, for undecided students, several factors must be considered. The first is *why* evaluation is needed. Greater accountability is often required during times of fiscal uncertainty or restrictions. For example, being able to show positive outcomes of a program can often ensure its continuance. If the mission of higher education is to foster academic and personal growth of its students, then evaluation must become a critical function of any program. There are rarely perfect programs, so evaluation can help pinpoint where changes need to be made or which new program components have met their objectives. Understanding the effect of services on the personal and intellectual growth of undecided students is perhaps the major impetus toward establishing a comprehensive evaluation program.

The next consideration is *what* needs to be evaluated. This is why the objectives set for programs and services (discussed in Chapter 4) are important. What needs to be evaluated depends on the desired outcomes already established. For example, is one of the program's objectives that undecided students acquire knowledge? If so, what kind of knowledge? Occupational knowledge? Academic knowledge? Self-knowledge?

Does the program attempt to change student attitudes toward work? Toward certain academic possibilities? Toward themselves? Does it attempt to change students' behavior? How does it foster information-seeking behavior, is this is a goal of the program? Does it attempt to make students aware of their personal growth over a period of time? The advisor may observe this change, but does the student? If a student makes a decision as a result of the program, is that decision stable over time? There are many variables that can be measured within an evaluation system based on set objectives.

Some campuses are concerned about student attrition, and, since undecided students are considered a high-risk group in this regard, evaluation can include projections of or actual figures on the retention of undecided students. Questioning students as they withdraw is a valuable source of information about the effectiveness and accessibility of services for students, for example.

What is evaluated comes from the well-thought-out objectives of the total program and also its parts. Both the students' and the advisors' perceptions of how well these objectives are being met must be included.

The last consideration of an evaluation program is *how* to evaluate. The methods used depend on what is being measured. A standardized instrument such as those described earlier, or a simple, locally developed questionnaire can help determine the progress students are making in identifying and implementing academic and career choices.

As to *when* to evaluate, there are many points at which evaluation may be accomplished. When undecided students finally declare a major is an excellent time to ask simple questions about their reactions to and satisfaction with the help they have received. Alternatively, each program element, such as workshops or classes, may be formatively evaluated as it is completed. Interviewing random samples of undecided students also may provide insights into how students perceive, participate in, and react to specific program elements.

Evaluating a total program is also important (Creamer, 1994; Gordon, 1992). Summative evaluations may be performed at the end of each school term or at the end of a year. While there are commercial products available to conduct an evaluation, it is sometimes more efficient to create one that reflects local program objectives. In any case, data describing the effectiveness of a program are imperative for administrators making budget decisions.

Evaluating advisors' contributions to the program is equally important. There are several approaches to overall advisor evaluation. Evaluation of an advisor's performance from students' perspectives may be accomplished by a simple questionnaire during the scheduling period, for example. If advisor evaluation procedures are already in place, a few additional questions on the form regarding undecided students, may provide more detailed information about the special services created for them. Advisors may also be asked to evaluate their own performance, including their reactions to the materials provided them, their suggestions for administrative changes, or the need for new or different program directions. Advisors' immediate supervisors may also evaluate their performance. Many advisors appreciate positive suggestions for improving their skills. They also need to hear praise when they have performed a task well.

As with any assessment effort, one person must be responsible for coordinating the whole. One individual needs to be responsible for gathering the information, analyzing it, and disseminating it to the persons involved. If changes are to be made, they must be based on current, accurate information from both students' and advisors' perspectives. In this way, a program will continue to reflect the ongoing, changing needs of the students for whom it exists.

Research

Evaluation efforts often provide information that would be helpful to other campuses involved in the same or similar programs. Many campuses have gathered data about their undecided students but do not consider it important enough to write up for broader dissemination. If data is carefully gathered and statistically evaluated, evaluation results may be written up for submission to professional journals. this is why well-formed objectives and outcome statements are critical. New programs can more realistically shape their efforts when established programs share experiences that have been successful and carefully evaluated.

ADVISOR TRAINING

A critical aspect of any advising program for undecided students is the development of the special individuals who are responsible for advising and counseling them, whether faculty members, professional advisors, or counselors. While many of the same kinds and levels of expertise are required for advising and counseling students in general, greater emphasis on certain content areas is required.

Nutt (2003) emphasizes how important advisor training-development programs are for effective academic advisors. He describes three important elements in advisor training programs: the participants, the content, and the instructional or delivery mode of the program. The type of advisor for whom the program is being designed (e.g., faculty or nonfaculty advisors or counselors) must always be considered, since this will influence the frequency, content, format, and delivery mode of training activities.

Nutt also discusses the conceptual, relational, and informational components of an advisor training program. Although emphasis is often on informational content, the conceptual elements that present the constructs and theories that undergird the content are important, especially for those who do not have this background. The relational elements that include interpersonal and communication skills are also as important as information. All three of these areas are equally important when designing training programs for undecided student advisors.

Advisors working with undecided students have special needs. There are certain kinds and levels of expertise required to work effectively with students who are in the process of making educational and career decisions. The following outlines some of the elements that might be included as part of a new advisor training program and as inservice content for an established program. The background and experience of an advisor must be taken into consideration; faculty advisors working with undecided students may need a greater emphasis on student and career development concerns, while full-time professional advisors may, on the other hand, need more training in academic information. There are certain content areas that all training programs need to emphasize, however.

Advisor Training Content

Student Development

As stated previously, many undecided students go through a normal transition period as they enter college and are in need of certain kinds of advising as these changes occur. Advisors working with undecided students need to be aware of student development theory and concepts so they are prepared to recognize and acknowledge individual differences among students. Advisors need to be aware of students' struggles to develop competencies, their need to establish interpersonal relationships, and their need to become autonomous (Chickering & Reisser, 1993). Helping students identify, clarify, and prioritize their personal values and goals is an important task that takes place within the advising relationship.

Training advisors in student development concepts enhances their perceptions of students as unique, developing individuals. This framework for advising undecided students answers many questions regarding the reasons for indecision and provides advising techniques that can reflect student needs.

Career Development

Like student development theory, career development concepts help explain many of the so-called problems of undecided students. Many advisors from an academic background are not aware of these theories. A review of the theoretical frameworks of Holland (1997), Super (1967), and Tiedeman and O'Hara (1963), for example, can provide a working knowledge of how students explore, crystallize, and clarify decisions relating to career. Advisors with this background knowledge can begin to recognize different stages of the decision-making process as students identify and explore alternatives. Many of these theoretical concepts can help advisors individualize their advising approach to suit each student's needs.

Jordan (2000) reviews many of these theories within the context of advising college students in this new century. She suggests that prescriptive advising, developmental advising, and counseling may be viewed as a continuum to meet the changing needs of today's students. Jordan indicates that while many institutions use technology to offer career and advising information on the World Wide Web, the closer the needed services fall toward the counseling end of the continuum, the less likely electronic formats will be useful to students.

Advisors also need a working knowledge of how the student's interests, values, and abilities form a unique set of personal characteristics. They need to be able to recognize when a student may need referral for this type of self-assessment.

Gordon (2006) emphasizes the importance of career advising and describes many competencies that advisors must master in order to be effective. Some that are closely related to career advising are competencies for decision-making, teaching, career assessment, technology, and research. Gordon provides specific activities that can be used in training programs to develop each competency.

A seven-step model for the career-decision process and how it can be used by advisors to help students make academic and career choices is described by Dollarhide (1999). In the first stage, understanding self, she suggests advisors need to discuss two life philosophies with students: "work to live" or "live to work." Students who choose the "live to work" philosophy are basing their primary life activities around this viewpoint and need to find those activities within the work context that give them the greatest personal satisfaction.

In stage two or understanding the world of work, advisors should tap students' own way of learning so they can help them become aware of the potential challenges and satisfactions inherent in each option. In stage three, students should be challenged to experience first-hand the reality of the options they are considering. Students who can't commit to a choice (stage four) might need to be referred for additional help. Stage five involves discovering and accessing appropriate training for their choice. When students are ready to access the workplace, advisors should help them develop the professional skills they will need. The last stage, evaluation, involves asking students if their career choice matches the person they are now. If the answer is yes, the advisor can help students access lifelong learning opportunities; if the answer is no, advisors can help students catalog the skills they are carrying over in the next career and begin again at Stage 1.

General Academic Information

Undecided students' interests and abilities cover such a wide range of programs that becoming a generalist advisor is absolutely essential. Advisors need to be able to discuss all the possible options that a student may present in an advising exchange. This means that their training must familiarize them with academic requirements that are both special and general. Possible career opportunities for each major must also be known, since it is often impossible for students to separate them. Being a generalist advisor does not require an in depth knowledge of each major, but it does mean that one advisor must have ideas that cut across many different academic areas or degree programs.

When advisors are knowledgeable about exploratory courses in many disciplines, they can suggest courses that will help students experience different areas. Generalist advisors know enough about the academic offerings at their institutions to provide an initial introduction to any option the student may be considering. This knowledge may be too extensive or complex to assimilate during one training program. This implies that extended training is needed, and a series of workshops or inservice programs must be initiated to provide additional information.

Much of this information should be presented to the advisor in the form of an advisement manual. The training program can then provide more refined approaches. Perhaps no training topic is more important than academic program and requirement information. Methods for providing undecided students with this information in an organized way are also important.

Referral Agents

Advisors need to be trained in how, when, and where to refer. Once students have identified options, advisors need to have an organized referral system in place. Introducing advisors to the other people in the academic information network helps to make the referral more personal and accurate.

Referrals may also be made to other campus resources such as study skills or tutoring centers, career planning and placement offices, and counseling or health services. Training programs can familiarize advisors with all these resources by making actual site visits or by asking representatives of these services to explain their mission and function during the training program. Although it is often assumed that referral skills are automatically acquired, very often they need to be taught. Referring too quickly (before the student is ready) or broadly may be detrimental rather than helpful.

Other possible training content areas include campus policies and procedures, communication techniques, and course content and teaching skills, if the advisor is responsible for small-group advising or a freshman seminar section. After an extended period of time, advisors may have suggestions for topics for other inservice programs. Their expressed needs should be the basis for future training efforts. These needs may be assessed by listening to verbal suggestions or solicited through written questionnaires or checklists.

Steele (2003) describes a technique for training advisors who work with undecided students. The case study approach using a research base offers a way to focus on undecided student issues. Steele provides many examples of how case studies may be used, including an indecisive student versus an undecided one, a decision-making model, and case study examples of subtypes of decided and undecided students. The integrated approach that combines both research component and case studies can provide a unique training opportunity for advisors of undecided students.

Nelson (2006) contends that advisors who have been trained in traditional advising approaches, may become proficient in career advising with additional reading and preparation. She suggests that advisors need to shift from an information focus in career advising to a student focus, from thinking in terms of the present to connections in the future, and from curriculum completion to career salience. Nelson offers a lengthy list of resources for career advising that could frame a training program's content. Some examples are career development theories (e.g., Holland, Super, Roe), computer software for occupation exploration, student profiles, Tinto's *Student Integration* model, student development theory, publications about career choice and decision-making, and career assessment materials. She also recommends networking with advisors for sharing new ideas and resource.

Spight and Baldridge (D. Spight, personal communication, May 15, 2006) created a training game for advisors who work with undecided students. Their *Maximizing Academic Advising Outcomes* (MACAO) game uses fictional or real students' records. The object of the game is to gamble on your students.

In a training version, advisors would:

1. Review the undecided student's academic record and other information
2. Roll the MACAO Advising Die
3. Write down as many questions as possible to ask the student. The questions must begin with the question word shown on the top face of the die when rolled: Who, What, Where, Why, and When?
4. Play can continue until the number of questions is exhausted. Winners are those students whose advisor roll the dice and gamble on them.

Following are examples of questions generated by advisors of undecided students who have played the MACAO game

Who Questions:

Who has been an influence in your life?
Who has motivated you?
Who have you asked for assistance?
Who in your family has a job you admire?
Who are your role models?

What Questions:

What advice have you received from other people? What do you think of their advice?
What do you want to know on graduation day?
What resources have you used?
What are you interested in? What are you not interested in?
What do you like to do in your free time (other than gaming or TV)?

Where Questions:

Where shall we start? . . . Tell me about yourself.
Where have you experienced success?
Where do you feel empowered or motivated?
Where is your passion?
Where have you gone to look at majors or career options?

Why Questions:

Why are you in college?
Why is choosing a major so important?
Why do you enjoy this class?
Why do you dislike this class?
Why are you interested in that career?
Why do you feel concerned about indecision?

When Questions:

When do you feel positively challenged?
When do you find you are most productive?
When have you had an enjoyable classroom experience? Why?
When have you experienced a difficult decision? Describe it.
When do you feel you need to make a decision?

Spight and Baldridge believe that advising undecided students is not just about helping them choose a major or a career. They contend it is also about teaching life skills such as critical thinking, decision-making, and communication skills.

Other than the knowledge and skills provided by a relevant, well-planned training program, there are other advantages. When advisors hear other colleagues' ideas and concerns, it helps them recognize problems or challenges they have experienced. It is also useful to hear how others have solved problems or reacted to student concerns. Sharing ideas and developing new perspectives can be an important outcome of an advisor development program.

Evaluating Advisor Training Programs

Evaluating advisor development or training programs can be done at many levels and at many time periods. As stated in the preceding description of program evaluation, setting objectives or goals is the first important step. The objectives or purposes established for the program will determine the method and timing of the evaluative process. Lynch (2000) recommends that evaluation address both process and outcomes. In evaluating development programs for advisors of undecided students, process can be defined as the effectiveness of the continuing activities and their content. Outcomes can be defined as what and how objectives have been met.

King (2000) points out that although faculty and nonfaculty advisors may approach the advising process from varied perspectives, the advising information and skills they need are the same. The program elements described previously may suggest advising topics or content for a one-time training activity or for the entire training program. The outcomes for each part of the development program must be stated clearly so the evaluation method used yields the information that will help to improve future efforts. The outcomes must also align with the overall program goals. For example, if a goal of the advising program for undecided students is to make students aware of the Internet resources for academic and occupational exploration, training sessions for advisors might include learning about related and relevant Web sites. An assignment such as a case study could help to determine if advisors were able to use this information in a practical, effective way.

Miller and Alberts (2003) suggest that "Purposeful and appropriate training makes the learning experience more effective and learned skills more sustainable" (p. 113). Training activities for advisors of undecided students should contain and emphasize those elements that make their advisees unique in the advice they require. Understanding why students are undecided, their special characteristics, and the type of help they benefit from will dictate the advising topics and activities that need to be included.

An effective method now used for advisor development is Web-based training modules. Clow (2003) outlines the steps necessary to develop an electronic advisor training site. While the steps are similar to those needed to develop any advisor training activity, technological expertise is obviously needed for designing Wed-based segments. Clow recommends that assistance of an institutional Web trainer may be useful. Looking at existing sites can not only offer ideas, but the site developers can provide information about its effectiveness and usage. Online advisor training programs have great potential for solving the problems of time and space that are often impediments in offering current information, content, and skill-building activities.

SUMMARY

Many program elements may be created to help undecided students make educational and career decisions. Individual students may be served through testing programs, which can foster knowledge about interests, abilities, values, and other personal characteristics. The Internet, career centers, and computerized career information guidance systems can also provide resources for self-assessment, as well as academic and occupational information. Programmed modules containing self-assessment activities leading into an occupational classification system can also be used in advising an individual student.

Group advising can take place through workshops on many topics, such as decision-making, goal-setting, exploring academic alternatives, and relating personality measures to careers. Freshman orientation seminars and career planning courses for credit provide a structured format in which undecided students can explore within a given time frame.

Advisor techniques and methods are important aspects of a successful program. Advisors need to be proficient in communication skills, so that they can relate to students in a personal way. Advisors need good referral techniques to help students make informative and productive contacts. Internet and printed materials are also critical to good advising. Making sure materials are current and accurate is an advisor's responsibility.

When training advisors who work with undecided students, certain topics are especially relevant. Knowledge of student and career development and academic information can be provided in a training program. Teaching advisors when, how, and where to refer students is also important.

Evaluation of a program for undecided students must be geared to the objectives that are initially set. Both formative and summative evaluation methods may be used, to ensure that both the individual components and the overall program are responsive to student needs. The overall program may be measured against the philosophy and mission statements that were established at the outset. Evaluation efforts must always reflect the unique needs and approaches that individual campuses use to serve their undecided students.

REFERENCES

ACT, Inc. (2000). DISCOVER [Online]. Available: www.act.org/discover

Banta, T.W., Hansen, M.J., Black, K.E. & Jackson, J.E. (2002). Assessing advising outcomes. *NACADA Journal 22*(1), 5–14.

Barefoot, B.O. (2005). Current institutional practices in the first college year. In M.L. Upcraft, J.N. Gardner, B.O. Barefoot & Associates (Eds.), *Challenging and supporting the first-year student,* (pp. 47–63). San Francisco: Jossey-Bass.

Barefoot, B.O., & Searcy, D.N. (1994). Freshman seminars and other courses for undecided students. In V. Gordon (Ed.), *Issues in advising the undecided student,* (pp. 59–66). Columbia, SC: National Resource Center for The Freshman Year Experience.

Bertram, R.M. (1996). The irrational nature of choice. A new model for advising undecided students? *NACADA Journal, 16*(2), 19–24.

Betz, N.E., & Luzzo, D.A. (1996). Career assessment and the career decision-making self-efficacy scale. *Journal of Career Assessment, 4*(4), 413–428.

Bloom, J.L., & Martin, N.A. (2002). Incorporating appreciative inquiry into academic advising. Retrieved January 31, 2006 from *The Mentor: An Academic Advising Journal* website: http://www.psy.edu/dus/mentor/020829jb.htm

Brott, P.E. (2004). Constructivist assessment in career counseling. *Journal of Career Development, 30*(3), 189–200.

Brown, D, & Crace, R.K. (1996). Values in life role choices and outcomes: A conceptual model. *Career Development Quarterly, 44*(2). 211–224.

Brown, S., Ryan Krane, N., Brecheisen, J., Castelino, P., Budisin, I., Miller, M., & Edens, L. (2003). Critical ingredients of career choice interventions: More analyses and new hypotheses. *Journal of Vocational Behavior, 62*(3), 411–428.

Campbell, D., Strong, E., & Hanson, J.C. (1994). *Strong Interest Inventory.* Palo Alto, CA: Consulting Psychologist Press.

Campbell, S. (2005). Why do assessment of academic advising? Retrieved April 15, 2006 from http://www.nacada.ksu.edu/AAT/NW28 4htm

Chartrand, J.M., Robbins, S.B., Morrill, W., & Boggs, K. (1990). Development and validation of the Career Factors Inventory. *Journal of Counseling Psychology, 37,* 491–501.

Chartrand, J.M., & Nutter, K.J. (1996). The career factors inventory: Theory and applications. *Journal of Career Assessment, 4*(2), 205–218.

Chickering, A.W., & Reisser, L. (1993). *Education and identity* (2nd Ed.). San Francisco: Jossey-Bass.

Clow, E. (2003). Ten steps to online advisor training. *Advisor Training: Exemplary practices in the development of advisor skills.* NACADA Monograph Series No. 9. Manhattan, KS: National Academic Advising Association.

Cohen, C.R., Chartrand, J.M., & Jowdy, D.P. (1995). Relationships between career indecision subtypes and ego-identity development. *Journal of Counseling Psychology, 42*(4), 440–447.

Collins, M. (1998). Snapshot of the profession. *Journal of Career Planning & Employment, 41*(2), 32–36.

Colozzi, E.A., & Colozzi, L.C. (2000). College students' callings and careers: An integrated values-oriented perspective. In D.A. Luzzo (Ed.), *Career counseling of college students,* pp. (63–91). Washington, D.C.: American Psychological Association.

Crace, R.K., & Brown, D. (1992). *Life-Values Inventory.* Minneapolis, MN: National Computer Systems.

Creamer, E.G. (1994). Evaluating advising programs for the undecided student. In V. Gordon (Ed.), *Issues in advising the undecided college student,* (pp. 109–121). Columbia, SC: National Resource Center for The Freshman Year Experience.

Crites, J.O. (1981). *Career counseling models, methods, and materials.* New York: McGraw Hill.

Cuseo, J.B. (2003). Comprehensive academic support for students during the first year of college. In G. Kramer (Ed.), *Student Academic Services,* (pp. 287–294). San Francisco: Jossey-Bass.

Dollarhide, C.T. (1999). Career process and advising: Tools for the advisor. *NACADA Journal, 19*(2), 34–36.

Devlin, T. (1974). Career development courses: An important part of the counselor's repertoire. *Journal of College Placement, 34*(4), 62–68.

Dziuban, C.D., Tango, R.A., & Hynes, M. (1994). An assessment of the effect of vocational exploration on career decision-making. *Journal of Employment Counseling, 31*(3), 127–136.

Educational Testing Service. (1999). Focus II. [Online]. Available: www.ets.org/sigi

Fitts, C.T., & Swift, F.H. (1928). *The construction of orientation courses for college freshmen.* University of California publications, Vol. 2, No. 3, 45–250.

Folsom, B., & Reardon, R. (2003). College career courses: Design and accountability. *Journal of Career Assessment, 11*(4), 421–450.

Galotti, K.M. (1999). Making a "major" real-life decision: college students choosing an academic major. *Journal of Educational Psychology, 91*(2). 379–387.

Gati, I., Krausz, M., & Osipow, S.H. (1996). A taxonomy of difficulties in career decision-making. *Journal of Counseling Psychology, 43*(4), 510–526.

Gati, I., Osipow, S., Krausz, M., & Saka, N. (2000). Validity of the career decision-making difficulties questionnaire: Counselee versus career counselor perceptions. *Journal of Vocational Behavior, 56,* 99–113.

Gordon, V.N. (1992). *Handbook of academic advising.* Westport, CT: Greenwood Press.

Gordon, V.N. (2006). *Career advising: An academic advisor's guide.* San Francisco: Jossey-Bass.

Gordon, V.N. & Carberry, J. (1984). The Myers-Briggs Type Indicator: A resource for developmental advising. *NACADA Journal, 4,* 75–81.

Harrington, T.F., & O'Shea, A.J. (2005). *Harrington-O'Shea Career Decision-Making System–Revised.* Circle Pines, MN: American Guidance Service.

Holland, J.L. (1997). *Making vocational choices: A theory of vocational personalities and work environments.* Odessa, FL: Psychological Assessment Resources.

Holland, J.L. (2001). *Self-Directed Search.* Lutz, FL: Psychological Assessment Resources.

Hunter, M.S., & Linder, C.W. (2005). First-year seminars. In M.L. Upcraft, J.N. Gardner, & B.O. Barefoot (Eds.), *Challenging and supporting the first-year student,* (pp. 275–291). San Francisco: Jossey-Bass.

Jordan, P. (2000). Academic advising in the 21st century. *NACADA Journal, 20*(2), 21–30.

Jurgens, J.C. (2000). The undecided student: Effects of combining levels of treatment parameters on career certainty, career indecision, and client satisfaction. *Career Development Quarterly, 48,* 237–250.

Katz, M. (1963). *Decisions and values.* New York: College Entrance Examination Board.

Keirsey, D.M. (2000). *Keirsey temperament sorter.* [Online]. Available: http://www.keirsey.com

Keller, J.W., Piotrowski, C., & Rabold, F.L. (1990). Determinants of career selection in undergraduates. *Journal of College Student Development, 31,* 276–277.

King, M. (2000). Designing effective training for academic advisors. In V.N. Gordon, W.R. Habley, & Associates (Eds.), *Academic advising: A comprehensive handbook* (pp. 289–287). San Francisco: Josey-Bass.

Kuder, F., & Zytowski, D. (1999). *The Kuder Career Search with Person Match.* Adel, IA: National Career Assessment Services, Inc.

Larson, L.M. & Majors, M.S. (1998). Applications of the coping with career indecision instrument with adolescents. *Journal of Career Assessment, 6*(2), 163–179.

Lewis, D.M., & Savickas, M.L. (1995). Validity of the career factors inventory. *Journal of Career Assessment, 3,* 44–56

Lynch, M.L. (2000), Assessing the effectiveness of the advising program. In V.N. Gordon, W.R. Habley, & Associates (Eds.), *Academic advising: A comprehensive handbook,* (pp. 324–338). San Francisco: Jossey-Bass.

Lynch, M.L., & Stucky, K. (2001). Advising at the millennium: Advisor roles and responsibilities. *NACADA Journal, 21*(1&2), 15–31.

Malott, K.M., & Magnuson, S. (2004). Using genograms to facilitate undergraduate students' career development: A group model. *Career Development Quarterly, 53,*

178–186.

Mau, W. (1995). Decision-making style as a predictor of career decision-making status and treatment gains. *Journal of Career Assessment, 3*(1), 89–99.

Maverick, L.A. (1926). *The vocational guidance of college students.* Cambridge, MA: Harvard University Press.

Mayhill, J., & Burg, J.E. (2002). Solution-focused advising with the undecided student. *NACADA Journal, 22*(1), 76–82.

Miller, M.A., & Alberts, B.M. (2003). Assessing and evaluating the impact of your advisor training and development program. *Advisor training: Exemplary practices in the development of advisor skills,* (pp. 109–113). NACADA Monograph Series, No. 9. Manhattan, KS: National Academic Advising Association.

Miller, B., & Woycheck, S. (2000). The academic advising implications of the self-directed search and Holland's theory: A study of Kent State University exploratory students. *NACADA Journal, 23*(1&2), 37–43.

Mortimer, J.T., Zimmer-Gembeck, M., Holmes, M., & Shanahan, M. (2002). The process of occupational decision making: Patterns during the transition to adulthood. *Journal of Vocational Behavior, 61*(3), 439–465.

Multon, K.D., Heppner, M.J., Gysbers, N.C., Zook, C., & Ellis-Kalton, C. (2001). Client psychological distress: An important factor in career counseling. *Career Development Quarterly, 49,* 324–335.

Murphy, L., Plake, B., Impara, J., & Spies, R. (Eds.). (2002). *Tests In Print.* Lincoln, NE: University of Nebraska.

Myers, I.B., McCaulley, M.H., Quenk, N.L., & Hamer, A.L. (1998). *MBTI manual: A guide to the development and use of the Myers-Briggs Type Indicator.* Palo Alto, CA: Consulting Psychologists Press.

Nelson, D.B. (2006). Integrating career and academic advising. Retrieved March 28, 2006 from the *NACADA Clearinghouse of Academic Advising Resources* website: http://www.nacada.ksu.edu/Clearinghouse/AdvisingIssues/Advising-FYE.htm

Niles, S.G., & Harris-Bowlsbey, J. (2002). *Career development interventions in the 21st century.* Upper Saddle River, NJ: Merrill Prentice Hall.

Nutt, C.L. (2003). Creating advisor-training and development programs. In *Advisor training: Exemplary practices in the development of advisor skills.* NACADA Monograph Series, No. 9. Manhattan, KS: National Academic Advising Association.

Oliver, L.W., & Spokane, A.R. (1988). Career-intervention outcome: What contributes to client gain. *Journal of Counseling Psychology, 35,* 447–462.

Osipow, S.H. (1983). *Theories of career development* (3rd Ed.). Englewood Cliffs, NJ: Prentice-Hall.

Osipow, S.H. (1999). Assessing career indecision. *Journal of Vocational Behavior, 55,* 147–154.

Osipow, S.H., & Gati, I. (1998). Construct and concurrent validity of the career decision-making difficulties questionnaire. *Journal of Career Assessment, 6*(3), 347–364.

Parsons, F. (1909). *Choosing a vocation.* Boston: Houghton Mifflin.

Peavy, R.V. (1995). A constructive framework for career counseling. In T.L. Sexton & G.L. Griffin (Eds.), *Constructivist thinking in counseling practice, research, and train-*

ing (pp. 122–140). New York: Teachers College Press.

Reese, R.J., & Miller, C.D. (2006). Effects of a university career development course on career decision-making self-efficacy. *Journal of Career Assessment, 14*(2), 252–266.

Rugsaken, K. (2006). Body speaks: Body language around the world. Retrieved March 1, 2006 from the *NACADA Clearinghouse of Academic Advising Resources* website: http://www.nacada.ksu.edu/Clearinghouse/AdvisingIssues/Advising-FYE.htm

Sampson, J.P., Jr., & Peterson, G.W. (2000). *Career Development Quarterly, 49*(2), 146–174.

Sampson, J.P., Jr., Peterson, G.W., Lenz, J.G., & Reardon, R.C. (1992). A cognitive approach to career services: Translating concepts into practice. *Career Development Quarterly, 31,* 67–74.

Santos, P.J. (2004). Career dilemmas in career counseling groups: Theoretical and practical issues. *Journal of Career Development, 31*(1), 31–44.

Savickas, M.L. (1995). Constructivist counseling for career indecision. *Career Development Quarterly, 43,* 363–373.

Schein, H.K., & Laff, N.S. (1997). Working with undecided students: A hands-on strategy. *NACADA Journal, 17*(1), 42–48.

Schein, H.K., Laff, N.S., & Allen, D.R. (2004). Giving advice to students: A road map for college professionals. In *Monograph Series, No. 11,* National Academic Advising Association, Manhattan, KS.

Schnell, C.A, Louis, K.S. & Doetkott, C. (2003). The first-year seminar as a means of improving college graduation rates. *The First-Year Experience & Students in Transition, 15*(1), 53–75.

Schreiner, L.A., & Anderson, C. (2005). Strengths-based advising: A new lens for higher education. *NACADA Journal, 25*(2), 20–29.

Shaffer, L.S. (1998). Maximizing human capital by developing multicultural competence. *NACADA Journal, 18*(2), 21–27.

Shoemaker, J.S. (1995). *Evaluating the effectiveness of extended orientation for new undecided freshmen.* (ERIC Document Reproduction Service No. ED 384303)

Singh, R., & Greenhaus, J.H. (2004). The relation between career decision-making strategies and person-job fit: A study of job changers. *Journal of Vocational Behavior, 64,* 198–221.

Smart, J.C., Feldman, K.A., & Ethington, C.A. (2000). *Academic disciplines: Holland's theory and the study of college students and faculty.* Nashville, TN: Vanderbilt University Press.

Smith, E.J. (2006). The strength-based counseling model: A paradigm shift in psychology. *The Counseling Psychologist, 34*(1), 134–144.

Steele, G.E. (2003). A research-based approach to working with undecided students: A case study illustration. *NACADA Journal, 23*(1&2), 10–20.

Super, D.E. (1957). *The psychology of careers.* New York: Harper & Row.

Swanson, J.L., Daniels, K.K., & Tokar, D.M. (1996). Assessing perceptions of career-related barriers: The Career Barriers Inventory. *Journal of Career Assessment, 4*(2), 219–244.

Tiedeman, D. & O'Hara, R. (1963). *Career development: Choice and adjustment.* New York: College Entrance Examination Board.

Tinsley, H.E., Tinsley, D.J., & Rushing, J. (2002). Psychological type, decision-making style, and reactions to structured career interventions. *Journal of Career Assessment, 10*(2), 258–280.

Vernick, S.H., Reardon, R.C., & Sampson, J.P. (2004). Process evaluation of a career course: A replication and extension. *Journal of Career Development, 30*(3), 201–213.

Whiston, S.C., Sexton, T.L., & Lasoff, D. (1998). Career-intervention outcome: A replication and extension of Oliver and Spokane (1988). *Journal of Counseling Psychology, 45,* 150–165.

Zarvell, R.K., & Rigby, D. (1994). Essential resources for advising undecided students. In V. Gordon (Ed.), *Issues in advising the undecided college student,* (pp. 37–47). Columbia, SC: National Resource Center for The Freshman Year Experience.

Chapter 6

EXEMPLARY PRACTICES FOR UNDECIDED STUDENTS

When initiating or refining a program for undecided students, it is often helpful to know what organizational structures other institutions have used and how certain programmatic components or activities have been implemented. Each campus is unique, and the final form of any program reflects the academic and career advising structures and delivery systems that are already in place. For example, what type of general advising system does the institution have? Is there a career center? What type of web-based programs are available? Is there a career library or computerized system already in place? A program for undecided students must be integrated into many existing resources.

Habley (1994) discusses different advising model systems and describes how an institution's organizational structure influences the type of advising program a campus develops. Effective programs have assessed student needs, have established efficient communication and information flow patterns, and have in place a system for coordination and supervision. The delivery system used to provide services for undecided students depends on the organizational structure in which the program resides.

As noted in Chapter 3, undecided students comprise a heterogeneous population and since their needs are so diverse, the administrative system, mission and goals, and the scope of services offered to them require different academic and career advising approaches than students who are truly decided. The exemplary practices for undecided students described below are only a sample of the outstanding programs and services offered by many colleges and universities across the country. The following program descriptions are provided by institutional contacts who are actively engaged in working with the undecided students on their campuses. Program descriptions include: (1) how undecided students are identified, (2) the type of delivery system used to academically and vocationally advise undecided students, (3) examples of program components, and (4) evaluation approaches employed.

IDENTIFYING UNDECIDED STUDENTS

A large national survey of institutions conducted over twenty-five years ago (Crockett, Silberhorn, & Kaufman, 1981), found that the majority of institutions identified undecided students through admission data or through registrars' and advising offices. This is still true today. The representatives of institutions describing the following programs report that their undecided students for the most part are self-identified through these sources. Others note that during freshman orientation many students choose to be undeclared about a major.

In a survey of institutions by NACADA's Commission for Undecided/Exploratory Students the terms most often used to identify this population are Undecided and Undeclared. The third most often used is Exploratory. These names have not changed much over the last twenty-five years. A few other names cited were General Studies, Pre-Majors, Deciding, General Curriculum, Open Enrolled, Open Option, Academic Exploration Program, or No Preference. The term "undecided," however, is still used by researchers and other writers about this student population.

DELIVERY SYSTEMS

Many approaches for delivering academic and career advising services to undecided students are described by the following institutions. Most programs were established as the result of a perceived need to identify and advise this special population. For example, *Pennsylvania State University* established the Division of Undergraduate Studies, and the Undergraduate Studies Program was initiated as a separate unit at *Purdue University* to serve their undecided students.

The Division of Undergraduate Studies at *Penn State University* is one of the oldest and most comprehensive programs of its kind in American higher education. The earliest predecessor of DUS, the Division of Intermediate Registration (DIR), was created in 1948 to meet the academic needs of World War II veterans. In 1965, DIR was replaced with the Division of Counseling (DOC). As part of its work, DOC helped students better understand their personal characteristics and how these characteristics related to a new educational environment.

In 1973, after a three-year study, the University Faculty Senate recommended the creation of DUS to improve enrollment and advising for undecided students as they developed their academic plans. DUS is now the largest unit of enrollment for entering baccalaureate students. The mission of the Division is to provide these exploratory students, both new and in transition, with an academic home and high-quality advising. Each student enrolled in the Division is assigned a primary advisor. These advisors are responsible for providing academic advising to the students on their rosters. The work of advisors in the Division is guided by the following beliefs and values:

- Academic advising is integral to the educational mission of the University.
- There is a synergism between classroom teaching and advising.
- Students should have the opportunity to assess their abilities and interests before making a curricular choice.
- Academic advising should be responsive to the intellectual development of the individual student.
- Academic advising is the primary way students learn about the full range of academic opportunities at the University.

Students are officially enrolled in the Division. They can enter as first-year students (part of the admission process) or transfer to the Division after enrollment, if their educational plans change and they are not eligible to transfer to a degree-granting college of the University or cannot decide on a new college of enrollment.

Students cannot graduate from the Division, but rather, in a specified amount of time, must declare a major in one of the University's degree-granting colleges. Thus students either self-identify themselves as part of the admissions process or request enrollment after initially being a student in one of the colleges of the University (E. White and M. Leonard, personal communication, May 18, 2006).

The Undergraduate Studies Program (USP) at *Purdue University* began as a pilot program in 1996. It was established to serve as a gateway into the University through which undeclared incoming freshmen and continuing upper-class students would be provided the guidance and have the freedom to explore and identify their best academic and career opportunities. In 2000, when it became a bona fide program, the stated mission of the program was:

- To provide a smooth and academically sound transition to the student's chosen degree-granting program;
- To help students develop information seeking and decision-making skills;
- To increase student retention;
- To reduce the current Change of Degree Objective (or major-changing) activity at the University.

The Undergraduate Studies Program staff is comprised of eight full-time and one part-time academic advisor along with a Program Director (who carries a half-time advising load), and a full-time clerical staff member. Each full-time advisor carries an average advising load of 150 advisees. We ascribe to individualized academic and career counseling sessions tailored to meet the individual needs of each of our advisees. In addition to mandatory registration meetings, other topics included in the one-to-one advising sessions involve discussions about possible majors, careers, internships, and/or personal issues.

Prospective Purdue University students can select USP as their point of entry to the University. Approximately 10 percent of the incoming freshmen class selects USP as their school choice. These students are called Explorers. They are required to enroll in a three credit hour graded course entitled "Academic and Career Planning" (EDPS 105) their first semester. This course is taught either by the advisee's academic advisor or by a graduate student in Educational Psychology. Exploring students can remain in USP for a maximum of 4 semesters.

A second set of USP students are those who decided to enter the University in a declared school/college, only to discover it was the wrong choice for them. They move into USP by performing a Change of Degree Objective (CODO). These students are strongly encouraged to take a similar academic and career planning course their first semester in USP. These students can remain in USP for sixty credit hours or until they have completed ninety-five total college credits, whichever comes first. (S. Aufderheid, personal communication, May 24, 2006)

Another delivery approach is that of incorporating a program for undecided students into another unit (e.g., college, division, or department). The Exploratory Student Resources at *Indiana University* is a program designed to complement and support academic advising for exploratory and major changing students in the University Division at Indiana University. With only a few exceptions, all first-year students, whether they are declared or exploratory, matriculate and continue in the University Division until they meet admission requirements for a declared major and degree-granting school. Exploratory Student Resources provides training, resources, and tools to all freshmen and major changing students, and provides resources and exploratory counseling directly to these students. In addition, the program collaborates with all academic and student affairs units on campus.

The mission of Exploratory Student Resources is to motivate undecided/exploratory students and major changing students at Indiana University to take a positive, proactive, and timely approach to their college major exploration and decision-making, and to provide resources and guidance to help these students make a successful and rewarding choice of major. The program goals established to meet this mission are to: (1) support a seamless transition for academic exploration from pre-admission through matriculation the freshmen year, continuing status in the University Division, and until each student enters the degree-granting school for their major; (2) provide services and resources targeted for each of these phases; (3) honor individual readiness by offering support when indicated; (4) encourage students to explore all of the academic options available to them–majors, second majors, interdepartmental majors, minors, certificates; (5) guide students in utilizing all of the appropriate academic and career resources available to them, while placing an equal emphasis on the academic and career aspects of the decision; and (6) create a campus-wide atmosphere of encouragement and support for academic exploration (T. Kenyon, personal communication, May 11, 2006).

The *University of Mississippi* established the Academic Support Center (ASC) within the College of Liberal Arts to support and guide their undecided student population. The Center's mission is to offer professional, quality advising and support to the University of Mississippi community through efficient service, communication of university policy, and open collaboration with University departments and support services in an effort to facilitate the educational experience. Students entering the University without a declared major are listed as 'Liberal Arts Undecided.' The College of Liberal Arts uses a split model for academic advising. Undecided students are advised in the Academic Support Center, while students with a declared major are advised by faculty in their department. The ASC advisors use a developmental approach when counseling undecided students, as well as students considering changing their major. The ASC advisors work individually with students with major exploration, future goals, and University policies and procedures (K. Ellis, personal communication, May 11, 2006).

The Transitional Advising Center (TrAC) at the *University of Texas at Austin* provides comprehensive advising services for students in transition who are enrolled in the College of Natural Sciences, including first-year Biology, Human Ecology, Pre-Computer Sciences students, and all undeclared students. Two offices assist students with major and career advising: one advises all first-year students in the college, while the other assists major changers, and undeclared sophomores, juniors, and seniors. Both offices function to assist students with major and career exploration and choice (D. Spight, personal communication, May 25, 2006).

Another delivery model is to incorporate academic and career advising services for undecided students into a special advising unit. *Kent State University's* program recognizes the need to advise undecided students in a special way. One response to an early 1990s institutional initiative to place more emphasis on undergraduate students was the creation of a new unit to house a wide range of then-independent programs operating under several vice-presidencies: adult services, career services, academic assessment, minority student services, University Orientation (course), transfer student services, student disability services, Upward Bound, Student Support Services, freshmen registration and advising, and advising for undeclared students. One expectation of this new unit was that it would curtail the high attrition of undeclared students.

The Exploratory Major was created for students who were not declared in a degree-granting major and were presumed to be undecided; however, it was clear that many of these students lacked the GPA to enter their preferred majors, while others were deciding between two equally attractive choices. This intersection between declaring and deciding about a major was conceptualized as a declaration/decision 2 x 2 contingency table.

A Student Advising Center (SAC) was created to serve approximately one thousand eight hundred Exploratory (EXPL) majors, about six hundred of whom are new freshmen each year. The SAC is analogous to a college office for students with an EXPL major code. These students are assigned to one of the seven full-time academic advisors, who help them explore academic and career options. Students are required to meet with their advisor once each semester until they declare a degree-granting program as their major. Students having academic difficulty are expected to schedule additional appointments. Students from throughout the University who are considering other areas of study also seek advice and receive assistance from the Exploratory advisors. These students are declared in a degree-granting major, but may still be questioning their choice of major (T. Kuhn & G. Padak, personal communication, May 10, 2006).

At the *University of Southern Maine,* students without a declared major are advised through the Advising Services Center. The Center's mission is to assist current and prospective students in identifying and

THE DECLARATION/DECISION CONTINGENCY TABLE

		Personal Decision about Major	
		Undecided	**Decided**
Formal Declaration of Major	**Undecided**	Exploratory student needs developmental advising	Student must get to appropriate office to declare major
	Declared	Student might need to change majors*	On path to graduation

*Students who are undecided and declared in a degree-granting major may have been computer-assigned the major they checked on the ACT test taken in high school but may change later.

achieving their educational goals and following a path toward intellectual discovery. Advisors work with students individually to facilitate:

- Exploration and navigation of opportunities both inside and outside of the classroom;
- Recognition of themselves as independent learners;
- Realistic assessment of their academic progress;
- Meaningful connections among their various experiences and discovery of ways in which these connections contribute to their educational and career goals.

Advisor assignments are made prior to a student's first semester, with assignments made based upon the student's area(s) of potential interest. "Through the 'Liaison Program,' individual advisors work with particular departments and students. Students benefit from this program that creates a partnership of expertise between the advisor and academic departments" (E.M. Higgins, personal communication, May 10, 2006).

According to *Johnson County Community College's* (JCCC) Office of Institutional Research, 40 percent of the students enrolled at JCCC indicate "undecided" as their choice of major on their admissions application. This percentage does not include the majority of students who indicate that they plan to transfer to a four year school. Although technically transfer students are not considered undecided by the Institutional Research Office, many of them are truly undecided.

The mission of Counseling and Advising Services at Johnson County Community College is to take an active role within each student's learning environment by facilitating the process of educational, career, and personal decision-making in a professional and caring manner.

Counseling and Advising Services is staffed by full-time and part-time professional counselors. Counselors use a developmental advising model that enables students to realize their maximum educational potential. Responsibility for this ongoing, multifaceted process is shared by the student and the counselor. The counselors at JCCC provide advising, career counseling, and personal counseling to the students they serve (J. Anderson, personal communication, May 24, 2006).

At *Valencia Community College* undecided students are advised in the

Career Development Services office which is a resource for exploring, developing, and implementing career options that result in personal and career satisfaction. Career Development Services programs are designed to help students learn more about their personality, interests, skills and values; career fields; connecting majors to careers; and making the transition to a four-year college or university or to employment. Career development is an ongoing, overlapping process of seeking the answers to three critical questions: (1) Who Am I? [Career Assessments], (2) Where am I going? [Research and Goal Setting], and (3) How do I get there? [Career and Educational Plan]. Undecided students are identified and participate through self-identification, referrals from faculty, academic advisors, staff, and other students, curriculum of specific classes, and the college's website.

The entire college is involved with advising undecided students through the LifeMap concept. Faculty and staff serve as "partners" with students on their journey. Early in the student's experience at Valencia, the student will have interactions with Advising Center staff through New Student Orientation. The career and educational planning and implementation process is described as:

A → As → AS → aS → S

"A" stands for "Advisor or Faculty" member;
"S" stands for "Student."

LifeMap is based on Valencia's developmental advising model. Developmental advising is a student-centered approach that fosters advising alliances among students, faculty, and other college professionals. This alliance develops through mutual trust, shared responsibilities, and commitment to helping students identify, clarify, and realize their personal, academic, career, and life goals. Developmental advising is an ongoing growth process that assists students in the exploration, clarification, communication, and implementation of realistic choices based on self-awareness of abilities, interests, and values. The results for students are social and academic integration, educational and career plans, and acquisition of study and life skills (C. Russo & C. Espenscheid, personal communication, May 11, 2006).

PROGRAM COMPONENTS

The program elements for undecided students described by the following institutions demonstrate a wide variety and type. At *Pennsylvania State University,* first-year students enrolled in the Division participate in exploratory activities through the DUS Navigator, a comprehensive program designed to enhance the quality and efficiency of DUS advising. Using a series of Web-based guides and worksheets that are distributed at critical times throughout the first year, exploratory students gain an understanding of the objectives of the educational planning process, learn how and when to initiate important steps in this process, and acquire information that is important for academic success. The Navigator enables students to take an active role in their educational planning and to work more productively with advisors to make informed decisions. (The DUS Navigator is on the Web at http://www.psu.edu/dus/navigate/.)

Penn State's eLion, a Web-based academic advising system, co-developed by DUS, also provides assistance to students who are exploring majors. Through interest surveys and other interactive eLion modules, students learn about curricular "themes" related to their general interests, see the impact that choice of courses can have on choice of major, design an "ideal" science/math-related major, and find the majors that most closely match their ideal, and more.

Many special programs and workshops are available for Exploratory majors at Kent State University. These include study skills, time management, decision-making, exploration of specific majors, and other relevant topics. The Exploratory Community Engaged in Learning (EXCEL) program is a living/learning experience offered to eighty of the approximately six hundred new freshmen exploratory students. The Academic Transfer Office coordinates academic advising and career counseling for exploratory transfer students, works with appropriate offices in determining applicability of transfer coursework, offers a transfer orientation class, analyzes current transfer procedures and assists transfer students in connecting with university staff and campus resources.

The Exploratory Student Resources at *Indiana University* has found that choosing a major is most effectively accomplished by breaking the student's major exploration and decision-making down into a step-by-step process. Further, by setting a goal for when each step will be completed, declaring a major on time can also be assured. The length of this process and the date set for the completion of each step is based on when each student begins their exploration and when they need to have their decision made. In order to make a good decision, which is defined by Exploratory Student Resources as "well-informed and well-thought-out," all of the steps in the process need to be completed by each student. However, by assessing which steps (or partial steps) may have already been accomplished, as well as the student's time frames, an individualized exploration plan is designed for each student in the Exploratory Student Resources model, so that they will complete all of the steps, make a good decision about their choice of major, and make it on time.

Exploratory Student Resources accomplishes the objectives by providing specialized exploratory advisor training, tools and resources (print and web-based) for advisors and students, group workshops and individual exploratory counseling, guest speaking in courses, involvement with the admissions and orientation processes, as well as with academic advising, and collaboration with all university units (admissions, orientation, academic schools and departments, career centers, residential programs, academic support centers, culture centers, and university marketing).

The *University of Mississippi's* program for undecided students works closely with its Career Center. Various assessments and career counseling help students explore possible majors and careers. After a session with a career counselor, students meet with an ASC advisor to determine the best course of action in order to successfully reach their desired goal. The two departments cooperate in teaching the Educational Leadership 201, Career-Decision Making class. Undecided students with between 25–45 hours take the course for three hours credit. The course utilizes three different personal assessments, major/career research, academic counseling, and various other methods needed to assist the students in selecting a major.

The program for undecided students in the Transitional Advising Center (TrAC) at the *University of Texas at Austin's* College of Natural Sciences uses several assessment activities to increase the students' self and educational knowledge. Students also work closely with the Career Exploration Center and the College of Natural Sciences career services office as well as other campus and community resources. Students have access to "How to Choose a Major" workshops, as well as a first-year interest small group seminar that focuses on major and career exploration. A "Major Exploration Assignment Sheet" is used to assign exploration tasks based upon each student's developmental level.

A game was developed (described in Chapter 5) to assist academic advisors and undeclared students with the process of major exploration. The game, known as MACAO (Maximizing Academic Advising Outcomes) "is played using a six-sided die labeled with the question words: Who, What, When, Where, Why, and How. The purpose of the game is to generate more purposeful and productive advising sessions by emphasizing basic relational skills. MACAO can be played many different ways, allowing for applicability in various advising situations. In all of the versions of the game, the die is rolled and, based upon the question word that is revealed, participants generate questions to ask based on the student's progress in the exploration process. Within the Transitional Advising Center and on the campus, advisors have used MACAO as a training tool, a way to prepare for advising appointments and workshops, during advising sessions with undeclared students, and as a tool for helping students generate questions to ask other campus resources. In addition, each advisor keeps a MACAO die on their desk as it also serves as a constant reminder that advisors need to take the time to ask more questions and engage in more dialogue with each student" (D. Spight, personal communication, May 5, 2006).

At *Johnson County Community College,* the counseling staff offers workshops for undecided students. The college also offers a three credit hour Career/Life Planning class. Through the cooperation of counselors and the Career Center, a Majors Fair is offered every year.

At *Valencia Community College,* career advisors and counselors meet with students individually for more in-depth counseling. A Career Exploration & Planning packet is given to each student participating in the Career Assessment Program. This packet is given to the student incrementally so that it can be used throughout the counseling process. Additionally, students use My Career Planner, a Valencia intranet LifeMap tool in which they take career assessments, do career research, and develop a career and educational plan. Group interaction and class presentations are also offered to reach greater numbers of undecided students.

The State of Florida provides two additional tools through

www.facts.org. One career tool is Florida CHOICES Planner and the other is SIGI 3. These career planning tools can be used by the student independently, but they are more effective when used with career counseling appointments. Student Success classes are instrumental in guiding students to Career Development Services, and the curriculum implements a career exploration paper that each student must write.

Student success classes are instrumental in guiding students to Career Development Services and the curriculum implements a career exploration paper that each student must write. Other Valencia programs include Bridges (The Bridges to Success program is available to disadvantaged high school grades from surrounding counties) and Skillshops.

At *Purdue University,* special programs and resources available to Undergraduate Studies Program students include their assigned USP advisor, the mandatory EDPS 105 class, the USP website www.purdue.edu/usp, an Explorers Learning Community, three one thousand dollar nonrenewable scholarships which make USP more competitive with other Purdue University colleges/schools for the high ability nondeclared student, and our Student Ambassador and Student Council programs. In addition, these students have access to standard Purdue University resources available to all students on campus such as the Center for Career Opportunities, the Academic Success Center, the Writing Lab, Supplemental Instruction, academic resource rooms, and college/school advisors across campus.

A special program, the Individualized Second-year Advising Program (ISAP), for second-year students has been initiated at the *University of Washington at Seattle.* A review of advising services revealed that second-year students receive less institutional support than other groups. ISAP targets students starting their second year of study, who are not yet in a major. The ISAP model is an outreach program whose efforts are three-pronged, consisting of phone calls, e-mail and postcards. The purpose of the outreach is to create a partnership between a student and a specific advisor to collaborate on a plan for the student's academic future. Plans include referrals to academic departments and recommendations for academic and nonacademic campus events. ISAP has five primary expected outcomes. Students will:

- identify academic, extracurricular, and professional areas of interest;
- become more knowledgeable about University resources;
- become more knowledgeable about majors;
- experience the intervention as helpful and useful; and
- declare majors earlier in their academic careers.

After each appointment, students complete feedback forms that generate responses directly related to program outcomes. Additionally, in focus groups, students explained the impact of ISAP on their second-year experience.

PROGRAM EVALUATION

Evaluation of the programs for undecided students is performed in at least two areas: evaluation of advisors involved in contact with students and evaluation of the program elements. Through eLion at *Penn State University,* advisors can use the Academic Review module to evaluate the progress of each advisee, taking into consideration the student's academic goals (even if tentative), amount of time remaining in DUS, semester and cumulative grade-point averages, grades in critical courses, and the courses the student has scheduled for the upcoming semester. Advisors then use the Academic Review to email individualized reports to their advisees informing them of their academic progress and making recommendations for the upcoming semester. This activity supplements, rather than replaces, regular appointments that students have with their assigned advisors, and is particularly critical for students who are exploring multiple majors and/or limited-enrollment majors. (eLion is on the Web at http://eLion.psu.edu.)

In addition to an annual assessment of each advisor, DUS also follows each entering cohort of students to graduation or to the point that they leave the University. Assessments are based upon how many students graduate, how many students leave the University, and the number of times a student might change majors after transferring from the Division.

Individual advisors and programs in Undergraduate Studies at *Kent State University,* are evaluated annually. The dean attends annual meetings with each program staff to assess short-and long-term goals.

Annual performance evaluations of academic advisors are conducted annually by the dean and the dean participates in a similar annual evaluation by the provost.

At the *University of Mississippi,* evaluations are one form of measurement used to determine the effectiveness of the Academic Support Center. Each year the department director meets with each ASC staff member to discuss the previous year and the year ahead. The ASC program is evaluated every other year. Students are given an anonymous survey, which they complete after their advising session. Once the results are collected, needed modifications are addressed. At the *University of Texas at Austin,* the services provided by the Transitional Advising Center are evaluated on a daily basis. As every student checks in for an appointment, an electronic survey is generated and then sent to them by e-mail. In addition, advisors are evaluated on an annual basis.

The assessment plan at the *University of Southern Maine* has been instrumental in ensuring a departmental focus on advising as a learning and developmental process. The process of thinking about what and how students learn through the academic advising process has been critical to making improvements to the program. The continuous nature of assessment makes it both a strength and challenge for the department. As a strength, assessment enables us to constantly work towards excellence. Its challenge is making sure that time is identified to step back and reflect on our program and practices.

At *Valencia Community College,* an Individual Learning Plan is created by each person annually and there are monthly/quarterly reviews of progression to an annual review. Career Development Services collects data through a computer sign-in procedure and a monthly report is generated to document which services are being used by students. Evaluations are also completed by the students that attend each workshop. The Classroom Performance System (CPS) is used with various presentations to develop evidence of learning through a pre-test and post-test. When a student spends at least twenty minutes with an advisor at *Johnson County Community College,* an evaluation is mailed asking for feedback for the counselor. The evaluations are collected and are part of the annual review counselors have with the Director of Counseling.

To assess the program and staff at *Purdue University,* each staff member is asked in September to prepare goals and objectives tied to their strategic plan. Discussion of department and career course goals and objectives are discussed weekly at staff meetings and more formally on an individual basis at the year-end review. During the review, the director and staff member discuss that staff member's individual major accomplishments and areas for continued improvement. Students are involved in the assessment process as well, by completing periodic evaluations during the career course regarding the course. All USP students complete a "change of degree objective" survey as they leave USP to move into their degree granting major. This survey allows them to share their thoughts about USP and ways our services could be improved.

SUMMARY

Although each program described above is unique in the way it serves students and the institution, some common elements can be seen. Some universities have created separate advising units for undecided students, some have established advising centers, while others have incorporated services for these students in smaller units such as colleges or departments. Community colleges tend to offer academic and career advising for undecided students within their counseling services. A few institutions have initiated special services for upperclass students who are still undecided or in the process of changing majors. Although most use some type of Web-based program, some have integrated more sophisticated Web-based academic and career information into their advising practices. Close working relationships with the career services offices on campus are emphasized by some. Almost all offer some type of career course, self-assessment tools, and workshops specifically developed for undecided students.

When asked to list some of the weaknesses and strengths of their programs, there were many in common. What some institutions indicated as a weakness, however, others listed as a strength (i.e., advisor to student ratios). Some weaknesses were more institution specific, such as minimally acceptable office space or low budgets. One institution raised a concern about the increase in restrictive courses and programs that affected the ability of undecided students to schedule or access them. This problem is true for many undecided students in large universities with selective and restricted majors. The lack of time for reflection and detailed program evaluation was mentioned by several institutions.

On the strength side, all mentioned their experienced advisors and counselors, who were committed and dedicated to working with undecided students. The central location of their office and their collaboration with career services were seen as real assets. Several indicated their administration's philosophy and support for serving students who are not ready to choose a major as extremely important to their success. Opportunities for professional development as a high priority were also listed as a strength. The University of Washington at Seattle described the greatest strength of its program for undecided students as its role in "creating a paradigm shift in how undergraduate advising serves students. Characteristics of this shift include a move to an intrusive model that is targeted, individualized, and relational." But perhaps *Pennsylvania State University's* statement sums up the philosophy of all these exemplary programs best:

> The existence of the Division of Undergraduate Studies at Penn State assures that any student, no matter how undecided, either at the point of entry to the University or anytime thereafter, has an academic home, access to a primary advisor, and the availability of the most technologically advanced advising resources.

The author would like to acknowledge the contributions of the following people who generously shared their programs for undecided students:

Thomas Kenyon, Indiana University
Jeff Anderson, Johnson County Community College
Terry Kuhn and **Gary Padak**, Kent State University
Eric White and **Michael Leonard**, Pennsylvania State University
Susan Aufderheide, Purdue University
Kyle Ellis, University of Mississippi
Elizabeth Higgins, University of Southern Maine
David Spight, University of Texas at Austin
Laura Avila and **Deborah Wiegand**, University of Washington at Seattle
Corinne Russo and **Catherine Espenscheid**, Valencia Community College

REFERENCES

Crockett, D.S., Silberhorn, C., & Kaufman, J. (Eds.) (1981). *Campus practices for students with undecided majors.* Iowa City: American College Testing Program.

Habley, W.R. (1994). Administrative approaches to advising undecided students. In V. Gordon (Ed.), *Issues in advising the undecided college student.* Columbia, SC: National Resource Center for the Freshman Year Experience.

NAME INDEX

Page numbers followed by "f" indicate figures.

SUBJECT INDEX

Page numbers followed by "f" indicate figures.

D

F

N

Q